The Naked Politician

Katie Hannon

Gill & Macmillan

Gill & Macmillan Ltd
Hume Avenue, Park West, Dublin 12
with associated companies throughout the world
www.gillmacmillan.ie

© Katie Hannon 2004
0 7171 3694 9

Index compiled by Helen Litton
Print origination by Carole Lynch
Printed and bound by ScanBook AB, Sweden

This book is typeset in Berkeley Book 11 on 13pt.

*The paper used in this book comes from the wood pulp of
managed forests. For every tree felled, at least one tree is planted,
thereby renewing natural resources.*

A CIP catalogue record for this book is available
from the British Library.

3 5 4 2

For DJ and Winnie Hannon

Contents

Acknowledgments

Politicians are understandably nervous of journalists brandishing tape recorders. To all of those politicians who let their guard down and shared honest insights into their often extraordinary lives, I am very grateful. Most of their names appear on these pages. Some do not. This book could not have been written without their cooperation.

Former politicians, their partners, and political and media handlers were also more forthcoming than I had dared hope. Thank you one and all.

While most of this book is based on interviews conducted with the author, some material was drawn from other sources. These include interviews conducted by Alison O'Connor of the *Irish Independent* and Stephen O'Brien of the *Sunday Times,* and the team of *Farmers Journal* reporters whose meticulous work in establishing the scale of councillors' expenses is reproduced in these pages.

I am also indebted to political authors Peter Murtagh, Joe Joyce, Stephen O'Byrnes, Michael O'Sullivan and Bruce Arnold.

Very special thanks to Jackie Gallagher and Jack Murray, who read earlier drafts of this book and offered invaluable advice, and to the wise and witty Liam Mackey, who did the same and a lot more.

Others who offered practical assistance or simply prodded me into completing this project when I threatened to run away include Siobhan Creaton, Alison O'Connor, Mary Murphy, Sam Smyth, Mark Brennock, Lorraine Curran, Marie O'Halloran, Maria Murphy, Martin Wall and the staff of the Oireachtas Library.

To IT genius Stuart Sheridan, who staved off my nervous breakdown when my laptop crashed, and his colleague Stephen Riggs, who also rowed in with a technical favour, thanks.

Thanks to all at Gill & Macmillan, especially Fergal Tobin, Deirdre Rennison Kunz, Aoileann O'Donnell, Nicki Howard, Cliona Lewis and Regina Barrett.

I am grateful to my former bosses in *Ireland on Sunday,* Martin Clarke and Paul Drury, for allowing me the time to do this.

And I am, as always, thankful to my family, for their unfailing support and encouragement.

Katie Hannon
March 2004

CHAPTER 1

Natural Born Politicians

'Oh, what pitiful people' – Dr Noel Browne

On a sunny Saturday afternoon in March 2003 the lobby of the Heritage Hotel in Portlaoise was littered with teenagers and twenty-somethings nursing hard-won hangovers. Most were college students just weeks away from their exams but academic advancement was, temporarily at least, the last thing on their minds. It was the Ógra Fianna Fáil Conference – the annual gathering of cadets of destiny who come to worship at the feet of the leader of the day and harvest tips from the grown-up politicos who move among them like demi-gods.

Some are in it because they got drunk during Freshers' Week and signed up for the Donogh O'Malley Cumann for a dare. A few admitted sheepishly that their commitment to the cause was fuelled by the hopes of the sexual opportunities that bonding sessions such as these might afford. There were, however, a disturbing number of fledgling fanatics: true believers who would gladly swap a night of passion with the squeeze of their dreams for the chance of an afternoon of policy wonking with Brian Cowen.

The elections for positions on the party's National Youth Committee and Ard Comhairle were fiercely fought. Rumours of candidates spending thousands of euro on their campaigns abounded. Posters for one blonde UCD student suggested that delegates should 'Put Your Tic In My Box'. She didn't get elected.

In the crowded lobby that day Minister of State, Brian Lenihan came upon a party colleague counselling two young women who were in a state of considerable distress. There were tears. They had failed to get elected to the National Youth Committee and were worried that this would damage their chances in the local elections. In his efforts to convince them to run, their mentor was assuring them that it wouldn't.

The Minister of State couldn't help intervening. 'You're like a drug peddler,' he admonished his colleague, 'these people should be doing their exams. You shouldn't be encouraging them into politics.' Lenihan was joking, of course. But when he recalled the moment weeks later he admitted he had voiced an instinctive reaction. 'That man was feeding them more of the toxicity of ambition!' He was laughing as he said it, but it betrayed an ambivalence about political life that is common even – or perhaps particularly – among those destined to ride the wave all the way to the Cabinet table.

Politicians frequently refer to politics as a drug and to themselves and their colleagues as hopeless junkies. It's easier to admit to having succumbed to a force greater then themselves than to attempt to rationalise their career choice as one entered into knowingly and freely.

Since the election of the twenty-fourth Dáil in November 1982, a total of 2,428 candidates contested six general elections. A few, like the legalise cannabis campaigner Ming the Merciless, put their names on the ballot paper to garner publicity for a cause and enjoy their requisite fifteen minutes of fame. But that still leaves about 2,400 candidates blessed with the heart-stopping humility to ask thousands of strangers for their number one preference and armed with the breathtaking arrogance to believe that they deserve it. Over the last twenty years, 951 discovered that their unswerving self-belief was not widely shared. In fact, so few people agreed with their estimation of themselves that they got less than twenty-five per cent of the quota and lost their deposits.

Some, like Sean O'Fearghail, stubbornly refuse to accept the expressed opinion of their fellow citizens. Having become a member of Kildare County Council in 1985 he went on to contest the general election in 1987. He was trounced but he was young and energetic and eager to try again in 1989. And again the enthusiastic Fianna Fáil hopeful was left for dust. Three years later he gathered up all his courage to face the challenge once more. And once more he was rejected by the voters. He had almost five years to prepare for the 1997 general election, and he might have made it too but for the late decision to add local radio presenter Christy Walsh to the Fianna Fáil ticket. Walsh polled just 662 first preferences and became the only Fianna Fáil candidate to lose his deposit in that election. But his intervention meant that O'Fearghail had to content himself with the consolation prize of being the best-placed loser.

One can only imagine the steely determination it must have taken to wearily dust down the posters and gather the troops to start knocking on doors for Election 2002. He made it. But, having finally realised his long-nurtured ambition on the fifth attempt, Sean O'Fearghail has made scant impact on the national political scene. Most journalists covering parliamentary business would have difficulty picking him out of a line-up. Yet Sean O'Fearghail is a natural born politician, a classic example of the species. Because it is not something that you do. It can't be measured in electoral successes or by notches on the jamb of the Cabinet room door. It is something that you are. Some of the most senior and respected women and men who have been elected to Dáil Éireann are actually not natural born politicians at all. These impostors do a passable impression of being true politicians. At least one was so convincing that he rose to the office of Taoiseach.

Politicians tend to bridle if confronted with Enoch Powell's oft-repeated assertion that all political careers end in failure. Some cite Garret FitzGerald as an example of a politician whose dignity, reputation and principles survived political life. But the truth of the matter is that Garret was never the real thing. Relaxing in his Ranelagh red-brick sixteen years after he resigned from politics, he recalls his twenty-seven years in the Dáil in terms that would baffle most of its inmates and enrage more than a few. Politics, he says cheerfully, was 'just a phase'. And the fourteen years he spent in office as minister and Taoiseach? 'Only a temporary interruption'.

His political reputation survived because he knew when to cut and run. And when the time came he did just that without so much as a backward glance. A true politician would sooner saw off a limb with a blunt penknife. Despite a family background steeped in politics and despite his obvious talent and skills in the field, Garret always regarded politics merely as something that he did. It never defined him.

His attitude to political life is unusual but not unique. Some do manage to dabble with the drug without becoming hooked. Shrewd observers of the political scene reckon that about two-thirds of those who play the political game are not so lucky. They are lifers. Utterly at the mercy of the beast. They forgot how to tell the dancer from the dance a long time ago. Some submit willingly, embrace their addiction, and enjoy the trip. They love the proximity to power, the celebrity, the thrilling intrigue, the nail-biting number crunching.

Dr Noel Browne believed that some politicians immersed themselves in politics in an effort to fill an emotional void. The psychiatrist turned politician told *Hot Press* magazine in 1986: 'You have the politician who is obsessed with the business of getting to the top and staying there and the politician who is interested in changing society. To me they are two different things.'

'There are politicians who need politics emotionally. I could think of some who lost their parents when they were young or something. Like, indeed, de Valera – his two parents disappeared one way or the other. I think that conditions their life afterwards – this need for recognition, this need for adulation and spotlights and so on, determines their attitude to the struggle in politics.'

A study of the twenty-four men who became British Prime Minister between 1809 and 1937 revealed a startling pattern. No fewer than fifteen of them had lost one or more parents by the age of fifteen.

The number of senior serving Irish politicians who were bereaved relatively early, in traumatic circumstances, is also striking. Jim McDaid says his earliest memory is of seeing his father's coffin being carried out the front door of his house when he was five years old. Charlie McCreevy was just five when his father suffered a fatal heart attack. Gay and Jim Mitchell were raised by their widowed mother. Ivan Yates' father died of lung cancer when he was eighteen. As the eldest son in a family of six, Jackie Healy-Rae was forced to take on adult responsibilities when his father was bedridden with a back injury when he was eleven. Brian Cowen, Enda Kenny, Mary Coughlan, Denis Naughten and Mildred Fox were all elected to the Dáil in their early twenties following the sudden death of their fathers.

Tras Honan, the first woman Cathaoirleach of the Seanad, isolated the day in Carlow in 1937 when her mother Carrie died aged thirty-three. Tras was just nine years old. Had she lived, the senator told a journalist almost fifty years later, she would have had memories of a happier, warmer childhood. Her mother would have loved her, pushed her, steered her to university and a happier life. But a happier childhood might have dented the edge, she surmised, that pushed her, at the age of forty-seven, to run for a Seanad seat, to become the first woman Cathaoirleach of the Seanad and, at the age of fifty-seven, to throw her hat into the ring for the Presidency.

Browne differentiated between those who are driven by emotional need from those who, like himself, are driven by ideological commitment. 'They're going different ways, really, because one is faced with compromise if he wants to survive, and the other knows that if he compromises he can't achieve his objective. And my experience of Irish politics is predominantly of the former. After a short time in the Cabinet observing these people and the way they would capitulate to every whim of the hierarchy, I began to feel "oh, what pitiful people."'

Largely cosseted from such personal and political tug-o-wars, the most content politicians are often to be found in the Seanad. Some are on the last lap, revelling in their new-found freedom after a long career in the trenches of front line politics. Others are on the way up, scrambling for a foothold on the well-greased pole. The senators with no ambitions beyond retaining their cushy number in the upper house are the happiest of all.

Irish Congress of Trade Unions President, Joe O'Toole has had plenty of time to observe the species over his fifteen years serving as an Independent senator. He knows that politicians are, by definition, egomaniacs. 'Once you put your name on a ballot paper that's a real statement of your self-worth. I just do not accept any shite over in Leinster House who says he or she is humble. We might all have much to be humble about but we've never found it. The fact is once you put your name on a ballot paper that's an egotistical action. You're saying to people "vote for me". And that's egoism writ large.'

When O'Toole was elected to the Seanad in 1987 he decided to leave his job as a school principal and become a full-time politician. He didn't tell his wife that his bold decision would hit the family budget to the tune of €5,000 per annum. He said nothing and borrowed to cover the loss. 'We had five kids heading for college. It was not a rational decision', he admits. And now he's one of the helpless addicts. 'There's no question but that you could be doing a lot more profitable things in different walks of life. But there is something absolutely addictive about politics. And it's different to an addiction to power. You can be addicted to politics without having any fucking power at all.' His eyes flash and his colour rises as he considers his profession. 'It's the moving and shaking and engaging and intrigue and conspiracies and plotting and one-upmanship and strokes which are an absolute dynamite cocktail. It's gamesmanship with real people. It's an extraordinary mix of sexy things – things that get the nerves going, that give you a bit of excitement.'

And, of course, for some there are few things sexier than a spot of masochism. 'You're always a lemming heading towards a cliff. There is always an election coming up which might shove you right over the cliff.' The Senator pauses to consider this bonus before deciding: 'And that gets you going as well...'

Others resent the endless hours, the outrageous intrusion, the thankless hordes, the crippling uncertainty, the constant, casual ridicule. Yet they are absolutely incapable of shouting stop.

If there was a twelve-step recovery programme, Ned O'Sullivan would gratefully sign up. Articulate and affable, Sullivan runs a successful menswear business in the north Kerry market town of Listowel, just a few doors down the street from the famed John B Keane's pub. Everyone from local professionals to fashion conscious farmers head to O'Sullivan's to get kitted out and chew over the affairs of the nation. The county councillor has been a familiar name on Seanad and general election ballot papers since 1989. He has no illusions about his peculiar predicament. 'I'm a failed politician. I tried again and again to get elected and I failed. But it's like being a gambler. You always want to stay in the pot. To have one last go. Once you're in it you're hooked. There's just no getting out of it. It's like the mafia.'

Ned was just twelve years old when a local Fianna Fáil activist called to his house to invite him to a cumann meeting. Years later, the popular draper was flattered into standing for election to Listowel Urban District Council. He won easily.

Looking back now he believes he was encouraged to run in the 1989 general election by party rivals who feared that he might become a threat and wanted him to spend his load early. He wonders if his subsequent failure to secure a nomination to run for the Seanad could have something to do with his impudence at performing better than he should have on that first outing. When he refused to accept a party nomination to run in the 1992 election on the grounds that he was being used and taken for granted, pleas from Fianna Fáil headquarters quickly turned to threats. He recalled the then general secretary, Pat Farrell telling him coldly: 'if you don't run you will be a long time waiting for another Fianna Fáil nomination.'

He went public about his decision not to stand but was talked into changing his mind. The Taoiseach, Albert Reynolds came down to the square in Listowel to personally launch his campaign. He just about held his own in the election that followed ten days later.

He was sidelined in the 1997 election and by 1999, bruised and disillusioned by an eight-year bitter war of attrition with his constituency party colleague Dan Kiely, he came to the conclusion that he'd never see the inside of the Dáil or Seanad chambers. He issued a statement through a local journalist announcing that he was leaving politics altogether.

Three years on, sitting in his comfortable living room on the outskirts of Listowel, he recalls a warning from a Fianna Fáil colleague that he should have paid more heed to. 'John O'Donoghue told me a long time ago that I wouldn't succeed in politics because I wasn't ruthless enough. "You have to be ruthless," he said.

'When you're in politics, everything else in life becomes secondary... it takes away from the good things in life. It coarsens you. It toughens you. I'm not the Mr Nice Guy that got elected in 1985. The enmity of the day can be very intense. It draws out the bitterness in you. If you go in with a gentle, cultured trait you'll lose it – or you'll lose out... I socialise with people with no interest in politics. I envy them their naivety.'

It was a considered diatribe against the essence of political life delivered from the heart. Having been bullied, threatened, sidelined, overlooked and out-manoeuvred by his own, he could now see clearly that he had spent the best part of forty years at a mug's game.

You would think he would be glad to have finally found his way out of the maze, that he would be on his knees every night giving thanks for his great, if belated, escape.

You would be wrong. Because Ned O'Sullivan did not, could not, walk away. He has already decided that he will be a candidate in the next local elections. Before I leave his company he tells me cheerfully: 'I am facing into them more enthusiastic than ever.'

Over the course of researching this book I spoke to many more politicians off the record who bemoaned the day that they had been trapped. Even the politicians who protested their contentment with their lot would refer to politics variously as an obsession, a man-trap, a religion, a disease. Some spoke of how they tried to shield their children from it, as a coal miner might hope for something better for his offspring. One talked of how he was careful not to dis-cuss politics in front of his teenage kids. He had stumbled blindly into it as a teenager himself and the next time he checked he had mortgaged a once promising life and would never stop making the repayments. He knew he was lost to it but he was going to do everything in his power to protect his children from it.

Maurice Manning was shocked by his initiation into party politics when he ran for Fine Gael in the 1981 European elections. The politics lecturer had been involved with Fine Gael as a student, working on the 1965 general election campaign as a volunteer in the information office. He drifted away until 1981, when he offered his services to his friend, the dynamic new party leader Garret FitzGerald. He was asked to run in the Dublin constituency and he enthusiastically stepped up to the plate.

'I hadn't been on the council and I didn't realise the extent to which politics at every level has a whole range of warring factions in each constituency who spend more time fighting each other and seeing conspiracies everywhere and eating up huge energy on internecine battles. That came as a total surprise to me. I thought we were all in this together.'

When it became clear that Manning was going to be a permanent fixture on the scene, the daggers were quickly drawn. He was nominated to run in the Dublin North-East constituency, where some supporters of the incumbent Fine Gael TD, Mickey Joe Cosgrave, took grave umbrage. 'The word parachute wasn't used then. When they wanted to do me down they couldn't call me the imposed candidate because I had come through convention. So they called me "the headquarters candidate" which was just as bad. That tag would stick with you. What I wasn't prepared for at all was the sheer nastiness at meetings. There were some people who were almost psychotic in their malevolence. Who would start rows at every single meeting. They would insult people and query the motives of everyone who opposed them.

'The other thing was the way your own side would do you down. It took a while for me to adjust to being a TD. I actually did get a whole series of clinics going and I'd spend my Saturdays sitting in one smoke-filled pub after another. Not many people came along.

But I was doing my work, even if I wasn't very good at it. But right from the very beginning, sane people from the other side of my own party (Mickey Joe Cosgrave's camp) got out the word that "this guy has no interest in the people, he's a hopeless intellectual. So he doesn't hold clinics." I can laugh at it now but it hurt at the time. The person who gets a name for getting up early can stay in bed all day. This was the same. I got that name very early. It wasn't true but it suited everybody – both my opponents and my own party. And it wasn't just in the constituency battlefields that blood was regularly spilled. 'I was utterly shocked when I got into the parliamentary party where I thought we'd be all one happy band of brothers. The reality was a sort of concerted move by a certain number of people to oppose everything Garret did. There were people who simply resented the fact that he had made Fine Gael a professional party and he had walked on a lot of corns in the process. And he was never one of the lads so there was a lot of resentment.

'The moral issues came up then. Some felt quite genuinely about them. Others simply used them as a stick to beat Garret. What surprised me was the extent in which people would take pleasure in tripping up the party leadership and making life difficult for them. That was absolutely perplexing. That so much time was wasted on this warfare at local and national level.

'There are people who are by nature part of the awkward squad and will take pleasure in making life difficult for the leader of the day. In the latter years Austin Deasy didn't give a damn about anybody. He had a safe seat and an almost Paisleyite capacity to be destructive without ever being constructive.'

Austin Deasy, the former Fine Gael Agriculture Minister, admits that he was bored senseless during the last fifteen years he spent in politics before retiring in 2002.

'Bloody-mindedness was the only thing that kept me in there. I know there were a lot of them who wanted to see the back of me. And I wasn't going to give them the satisfaction!'

His theory is that politics is 'seventy-five per cent balls and twenty-five per cent ability' and, from where he was standing, those vital appendages have been in short supply in his party for the best part of twenty years.

'We got this influx of people who jumped on the bandwagon in the Garret days. They had no allegiance to people or politics. They were only in it for what they could get out of it for themselves.

Some of them might have had a lot of intellectual ability. But they had no backbone. They were marshmallow politicians. Soft-centred with no substance. Some of them meant well, but a lot of them were only there for the ride. From about '87 onwards, I couldn't pick out anybody I could look up to. They all took the soup in the end.

'I found the last twelve to fifteen years in the Dáil very boring. I got fed up repeating the same old tunes. I wasn't getting anywhere. The calibre of the people in there was so bloody awful. All you had was a crowd of sleveens who were licking-up to the leader. In the old days the people who were in the Dáil may have been less educated and less articulate but they had sounder motives for being involved in politics.'

Alan Shatter is of the view that politics is 'a very unnatural existence for anybody.' And yet he chose it. As one of the most sought-after family law lawyers in the country, Shatter had all the wealth and prestige he could care for. And yet he spent twenty-one years beetling from his legal practice on Ely Place to the back-benches in Leinster House.

Just over a year after the electorate finally called time on his dual life for him, he is scathing about the system and the people who participate in it. He desperately wanted to be a minister, and considered himself to be more than qualified for the job. But he was not a man who made friends easily. His razor-sharp intellect was respected, but his searing sarcasm and apparent arrogance meant he was both feared and loathed by many of his colleagues. They might have warmed to him more if they knew he had designed women's wet-look PVC clothing and sold them in the Dandelion Market to keep the wolf from the door when he was a Trinity undergraduate. But then, as he mused himself in retrospect, most of the relationships he forged over two decades in politics were superficial.

'I think particularly in a multi-seat constituency you have to be a mé féiner. You have to run your own show while remaining within the party system. The real rivals are within your own party.

'It's very strange because most of your relationships in politics are superficial. Especially in the context of dealing with people in leadership positions. Relationships can be real for a period of time and it can be difficult to distinguish what's real from when you're simply being manipulated and used by people in leadership positions. So there is a lot of falsehood in personal interaction in politics.

'There are various aspects to politics that I personally never took to. That I never will take to. The superficiality of relationships within politics. The reality that even people you may perceive as friends may equally perceive you simply as a rival. A lot of the communication that goes on between people in politics isn't genuine. You can live in a very unreal world.'

While Phil Hogan insists that most politicians are there to do the State some service, he admits that the profession does attract more than a few naked narcissists.

'There are a number of people in the Dáil that get up in the morning and look in the mirror and say "I am a TD and isn't it great! And I have so many people prepared to vote for me. And I am the subject of intense scrutiny by my electorate but also of intense appreciation."

'There is a naive, sick group of people who think that way. Those people are on a treadmill, from 8am to 12 midnight, with no life. They are a breed that doesn't contribute anything to the welfare of the nation.'

They are a breed apart.

CHAPTER 2

Handlers

'What the fuck am I doing here?' – Fergus Finlay

Whether in government or opposition, politicians like to surround themselves with men and women (but mostly men) whose job it is to keep them out of trouble. Their relationship with their elected masters tends to be complex. Employed for their intellectual prowess and political nous, they advise and counsel on matters of policy and politics. But mostly their value is as expensive security blankets, giving their bosses the comfort of knowing that they do not walk alone. They have never been sprinkled with the magic dust of an electoral mandate (and some politicians make sure that they don't forget that), but they have a level of access and influence that the biggest first preference tally in the country can't buy.

It comes at a price. For Labour advisor Fergus Finlay, the most surprising thing was the crucifying pressure.

'I've never experienced anything like it. I started on Budget Day in 1983. There had been a huge row about how big the deficit would be. There was a huge public row between (Alan) Dukes and (Dick) Spring. Within a month of my starting we had to stay up all night one night writing a right of reply to a piece that was going to appear in the *Kerryman* about Dick Spring being an abortionist.'

For Finlay, the all-consuming feeling was of being out of one's depth. At just thirty-two, Dick Spring was the country's youngest ever Tánaiste and a relative newcomer to national politics. 'Dick Spring was in complete awe a lot of the time of Alan Dukes and Garret FitzGerald. These were trained economists, masters of the state craft et cetera. Dick was a barrister. I can remember one long discussion one night about public service pay issues when it suddenly dawned on me that Dick Spring didn't know what an increment was. He didn't know that every public service salary was on an incremental scale. And really there was no reason why he should have known.

'He had very little choice a lot of the time except to fall back on truculence. It was the only way of dealing with an argument: "okay, I see the logic of the argument, now fuck off." That made for very intense pressure.'

The Labour Party was unhappy in government. It was a time of cutbacks, which meant a constant battle with its socialist soul and the backbenchers who considered themselves its custodians.

'There was constant unremitting pressure. Late nights. Endless hours of work. To the point where Willie Scally, John Rogers, Joe Reddington, Sally Clarke, Dick and myself were frequent habitués of Jury's Coffee Dock at three or four in the morning – either on the way in or on the way home. It was almost a twenty-four hour job.

'I remember thinking at least once a week – "what the fuck am I doing here?" I'd say he did too. I'd say it was exactly the same. You were pulled in every direction all the time.

'Barry Desmond was born to be Minister for Health. He just adored the job. Whereas all the rest of us hated the job and craved for a couple of minutes where people weren't going at you all the time.

'In retrospect I'm surprised that Dick Spring didn't break. Or that other people didn't break in that three-or-four-year period. There were endless splits in the administrative council of the party. The rows with the militants. Being hammered all the time by the Left. The constant demands for more cuts from the Department of Finance. Northern Ireland was bubbling over at that time too.

'That four-year period was surreal. People can't do that kind of thing for their lives without becoming completely bonkers. Garret ran ten-hour Cabinet meetings. People would totter out pale with exhaustion at the end of these meetings, completely unable to remember what they said in the first six hours of the meeting. That's a recipe for complete personal breakdown. I think some of them did have elements of breakdowns.'

Finlay recalls one member of that Cabinet who 'would go straight from the Cabinet to the bar and get absolutely blotto and insult all around him.'

'It was madness. But it was a pressure valve. It was them against the world.'

Yet they seemed to forge a tremendous solidarity. There is a photograph of the four Labour ministers taken on the day they resigned. Barry Desmond and Liam Kavanagh have tears in their eyes.

'They were very, very close to each other. The had an incredible feeling of solidarity and pride in having done their best.'

Didn't the national debt double during that period in office? 'It was an amazingly difficult four-year period where they had worked their asses off. And there is satisfaction in that. You didn't let the country down. You didn't feather your nest. But there is no joy of achievement.

'In the aftermath of that election there was a tremendous slough of despondence. They just all went down and buried themselves. For six to nine months I don't think Dick lifted a finger. He was just worn out and exhausted, emotionally and physically. As a party we had the bailiffs at the door. And he couldn't do a thing about it.'

That was when militant Labour made their move. 'Emmet Stagg was elected against the tide and he came in bouncing full of energy and everyone was saying yeah, whatever. It was a glorious opportunity and of course he seized it. I'd say that if somebody had given Dick a better offer at that stage he'd probably have walked away. But then the Kerry thing took over. The Kerry thing of "I won't be beaten."

'I think the reason it's so hard to understand politicians is because of that stubborn thing. They don't want to be beaten. They don't give in. If they're going to give in, they won't stay long in politics. If you want to run a political system you do need people around who have that stubborn "I won't let this beat me" thing.

'Where a lot of the rest of us would say "what's the point? I'd rather have a family life, I'd rather play a perfect round of golf, I'd rather write a book," they have this thing about not being beaten, particularly by people whose motives they distrust. My political enemy is the guy who's after my job and that is almost never the leader of the opposition. That's going to be one of my own. And I don't trust his motives. Plotting. It's the nature of the beast.

'Generally speaking, when you get to the top in politics you stop plotting and the minute you stop plotting you start going down. Getting there and staying there are two very different sets of skills. The hunger is a difficult thing to understand.

'The difficult thing to understand with Dick was that it wasn't a pleasure. I don't ever remember a time when he sat back in his chair and said "Jeez, I love this job" the way Jed Bartlett (in *The West Wing*) might.'

Viewers of the popular political drama set in the White House might imagine that this is how Government Buildings works. That people tear around trading witty and erudite banter, pausing only to consider serious policy issues and wonder aloud if they dare risk doing the right thing.

Finlay says that they'd be sorely disappointed. 'People don't think about politics here like they do in the States. You get politics as process here. Here winning and losing is an awful lot about what politics is about. What you do with it doesn't matter as much. That's wrong and disastrous and it should be the other way up.

'I can't remember who it was that said in Ireland politics is about possession of the ball. It is the weak thing about Irish politics. There are times when the purpose of politics becomes very clear to you. I think getting rid of Charlie (Haughey) was a clear purpose. As was the Downing Street Declaration and the Framework Document. But too much of politics is about the process of winning and losing.

'Politics is really like a rugby match. Rugby, classically, is a game that is about possession of the ball. You can do nothing unless you are in possession of the ball. It's very often like one of those very sterile rugby matches where you trundle the ball up and down the field but nobody ever gets to cross the try line. Because you're really only interested in not losing the ball.'

Or being ejected from the club. This very exclusive club which guards its status jealously. Finlay recalls that 'on several occasions during my time in politics, it's been said to me "come back to me when you've 7,500 votes and give me that bit of advice."

'For many people membership of the club becomes extremely important. It is a club that when you join it gives you the privilege of being apart, and being different. It has changed over the years. There was a time when membership of this club entitled you to wear a long black coat and a hat and to be respected and treated with deference. Now membership of this club entitles you to be ridiculed as often as not. And to have derision heaped on your head. But still people want to belong.

'The thing they all have in common with each other is that it was very hard for any of them in the end to say "Liam Lawlor, you're a disgrace, get out." Because in the end of the day he was a member of the club too. It's almost like being caught cheating in the golf club. Somebody has to tell him but it shouldn't be me. He's a lovely fellow really. We're inclined to forgive our own. I've never understood that. Maybe if I was elected I would feel that way immediately.'

Finlay admits that at one stage he harboured hopes and dreams of joining that club.

'But when you're there and you're working on other people's elections, the idea of going off to get elected yourself would be seen as treachery. As a betrayal.

'If a by-election had come along and someone had said to me "Fergus, will you stand?" I'd have run like a shot. But of course when by-elections come along fellas are knifing each other to get into the queue. That was never going to happen.

'In some ways it's easier if you're an adviser. If you're good at what you do, you learn how to make the civil servants respect what you do when you're in government. You act as a fulcrum between them and the minister. You interact more with the civil servant than the minister does, you learn more than a minister, you have more leisure than a minister has to be able to do it.

'I can remember sitting in on meetings in the Department of Foreign Affairs that went on for a couple of hours, with people that you would sit in awe of, and thinking "wouldn't it be great if other people could sit in here and watch this process?"

'But at the end of the day you don't get to make decisions. You get to influence decisions to a greater or a lesser extent. But you don't get to make them. I've never been in the Cabinet room. I've never argued my corner in front of fifteen Cabinet colleagues. I've never had to defend myself against the Minister for Finance.'

Finlay accepts that they did have a fair idea before each Cabinet meeting of what would happen behind those closed doors. 'But then things happen inside and you never figure out what went wrong. Like the infamous tax amnesty. There was going to be no tax amnesty. And then there was a Cabinet meeting and there was a tax amnesty and we never knew why. I don't think even people in the Cabinet room quite knew what happened.'

Of course the adviser's experience – and thus their view – of the political world can be dramatically coloured by the political fortunes of the party that hired them. Internal party strife is a given. Party unity is a fiction. Or, at best, the briefest of temporary arrangements. There are cycles. Every so often the ubiquitous backbiting and fantasy positioning climaxes into something more serious. A heave is plotted.

Survivors of the anti-Haughey heaves of the Eighties in Fianna Fáil are now almost misty-eyed with nostalgia for the bad ol' days. For Fine Gaelers, the heaves against John Bruton and the legacy of Michael Noonan's brief tenure at the helm have yet to be sanitised by the passing of time. Indeed, several of those interviewed for this book expressed the view that Fine Gaelers simply don't have it in them to heave with ease.

Those Eighties battles blooded the Fianna Fáilers who went in with bare knuckles flailing. The battles that would tear Fine Gael asunder appear to have utterly devastated their participants. One handler who witnessed this at close quarters went so far as to admit that he feels psychologically damaged by the experience. He describes the deep sense of vengeance in the party as a hidden lava flow. 'It was always going to burst up eventually. Politics dehumanises people. It can be a very callous, devious, nasty business. When you see it close up it is very brutal and hurtful.

'I suspect that there are professionals all over the country dealing with people who lost their husbands to politics. Relationships that have cracked under the strain. How could a relationship possibly survive somebody spending six out of seven days in the week totally ignoring their partner except when they need them as an appendage for some political function?'

After years watching politicians at close quarters, he believes a great many of them are 'actually certifiable'.

'You have to be driven. You have to be burning up with a desire to change the world. What's interesting is when all that changes. When all that gets corrupted by the process. At what stage does it knock all of that out of them so that they become cynical, bitter, twisted megalomaniacs?

'It's not just the TDs that are mad. There's a lot of madness at other levels too. One of the reasons young people are turned off is when they get to the back of the hall and they see the horror unfolding before them on the top table. They don't see an intellectual occasion.

They see all kinds of bickering and backbiting. They see all sorts of machinations within the local branch.

'You have to have a little bit of insanity to be in politics. It's a very unnatural state of being. Very few people stay entirely sane or are well-rounded and balanced human beings at the end of the process.'

He named a number of sitting politicians. People he worked with closely whom he variously described as 'bonkers', 'incoherent', people who would 'change sides without blinking in any shift of power'. In more than one case he reckoned that politics was no more than 'occupational therapy' for the individuals involved.

'I saw at very close quarters where people were politics junkies. Not just in terms of the national scene. (It was about) power within the party. Power generally. People do become addicted to it. The adrenalin rush. The sound of one's own voice. Getting the press release picked up. Getting the front page. Being involved in a bit of a controversy.'

There are some people in politics who, while appearing to be taking a hammering from the media, are actually secretly enjoying it. Press officers know that type only too well. 'There's an element of sadomasochism to politics,' says one. 'It's because they can't resist being the centre of attention. They may be a pariah nationally but they're a celebrity back in the local pub. Celebrity is a very powerful drug that some people find very hard to resist.'

This former political handler thinks politicians are almost uniquely self-destructive: 'If you were to do a mental health audit of people in politics you'd have to start by asking why people would put themselves through this gruelling, time-demanding profession at its most basic level. Take being a TD: when we know how destructive it is of family life; when we know how destructive it is of personal relationships; of people's health. Why aren't these people certified? Or why aren't they so aware of themselves as a group that they haven't tried to come together to repair that and make it better so that they have reasonably decent lives?'

He thinks he has the answer. 'It's because politicians don't value time. Fundamentally, the system is corrupted by a lack of value of time. They don't value their own time, so they don't value their staff's time. So everybody works all the time, in constant campaign mode. Where do you get the time to think? So many of them are borderline catatonic.

'Fine Gael was dripping with bitterness. Dukes is the coldest, most closed human being I've ever met. He has managed his bitterness better than most of them have. There's a lot of very damaged, bitter human beings trying to come together to produce a series of political messages and they are psychologically incapable of doing it. Post the Bruton and Noonan era – I've never seen anything like it. I feel psychologically damaged after living through all of that. God knows what they feel like.'

Another political advisor believes that politicians are just different from regular folk.

'I think it takes a particular sort of personality to put up with the total invasion. Whether they're involved at local or national level, they always have to be available to all the wankers in the world. You can't tell them to feck off. You can't just say I'm on me holidays, I'm at home, I'm with my family, I'm at Mass, I'm at a football match. If you're not that sort of personality I don't think you could do that for very long.'

He, too, believes that there is a touch of insanity about the political drive.

'Most ordinary, sane, rational people would say: I'm getting out of this, I need to separate myself from what I do, I don't want to be a piece of public property. Add to that the fact that every now and then people decide to dump you without there necessarily being any relationship between the dumping and your performance. You have to have a particular resilience of personality to decide to go back for more.'

Which the true politician almost invariably has. 'They simply sit and wait for the next chance to subject themselves to the same thing. Whereas you or I would say "I'm off, that's given me a message, I've had enough".

'I think what buoys them up and keeps them going is a bit like some people's fascination of the red light of media – there is a charge they get out of the whole political process. They get a charge out of the limelight, out of being in there, being near to power, giving power, dispensing things. That's the drug. For most people politics is a drug that they absorb early on. And those who don't tend to come to it, dip in and get out.'

Rehab chief Frank Flannery, who has worked with Fine Gael on a voluntary capacity for over twenty years, says he has 'quite a good opinion of politicians as individuals.'

'I have asked myself how many would I employ as key executives in an organisation. They are not by and large that kind of people. They are not structured, organised people. And they're not necessarily leaders. They are not executive types.

'The best executive types hardly ever go into politics. Politicians wouldn't make good executives. Politicians are more lone rangers. They have their mobile phones and some have their laptops. And they have an arcane methodology of dealing with their queries in their clinics, but essentially they are loners. Every politician sees their future as primarily dependent on her or himself. That is their essence. It is a quintessentially insecure place to be.'

A one-time president of the Union of Students in Ireland, Flannery says he found the constant campaigning and lobbying to be rather arid compared to the buzz of doing something real and making things happen.

'Politicians are not frustrated. They are kind of free people. They are very much a master of their own destiny. They don't really have a boss other than themselves. There is the election but that can be years away and that's a testing time, but other than that they are kind of masters of what they survey. By and large, they have reasonable control over their constituency organisation. I think they like it. It's a free ranging life.

'I think that by and large there is a strong correlation between progression and talent. And those who claim there isn't tend to lack the talent. You can have the likes of Alan Shatter and Jim Higgins being left on the backbenches. But that was because they supported coups against their leader. In business terms that would probably get you fired. In politics, it interrupts your career progression.

'Politics is more about power than anything else. In former arenas people got themselves killed for making the wrong political decisions. It's about exercising the levers of power. That more than anything else is what drives politicians. They have this yen for public service – they all think they can do something to change society for the better and they want to exercise power to do that – but they also love the trappings of politics.

'They love being TDs. They love being somebody, being recognised and singled out. Then they get a big buzz out of being ministers, every one of them, their staff buzzing around them, the car at the door with a driver at the wheel and somebody carrying their bag. That wouldn't attract me at all, but for the political person it's just the ultimate buzz.'

He believes the Fine Gael organisation went into serious decline from 1990 onwards, when it lost faith in the voluntary side of the party.

They used to be known as the Scruffy Murphy set, a group of key Fine Gael strategists that included the lawyer Enda Marren, public relations gurus Pat Heneghan and Bill O'Herlihy as well as Flannery himself. They would meet over a pint in Scruffy's, a pub located in Dublin's south city business district, and plot strategy for the party. They enjoyed open access to the party leader of the day, but were resented by many of those lower down the party's food chain.

As Flannery recalls it: 'They stopped trusting that whole apparatus of voluntary advisers. They felt they had too much influence. The net effect of it was that they got rid of them at a time when both Fianna Fáil and Labour began to develop that side. So that huge coterie of young, dynamic professionals that were around Fine Gael were disbanded and not replaced.

'They thought they could do it with a very thin head office in Mount Street. So it became a very thin gruel. Which has led to the progressive failing of the personality of the party from being very vibrant, policy-driven, modern and liberal to something very milk and watery. That's what happens when you neglect the basics.

'It also became fixated by its own problems. So they just became worse and worse. It became like the last days of the Roman Empire with various warlords fighting over the vestiges of what was in many cases imaginary territory. Territory they once had that they thought they still had.

'When you take the pursuit of power away from attachments to ideology, it becomes quite a volatile and uncontrollable thing. And I think that happened in Fine Gael to a large extent.'

CHAPTER 3

The Start

'Oh my God, what have I done?' – Dr James McDaid

I t's almost midnight. A handsome young doctor is standing on the pier at the tip of Fanad Head. He is wearing a sharply-tailored suit. There's nothing he can do about the inappropriate attire. He'd been enjoying a dinner in Portsalon when the emergency call came. The trouble is that this was nothing like the kind of emergency that he is used to dealing with from his years as a busy GP and skilled surgeon.

He'd been tipped off that there was some commotion down at Fanad Head. A patrol boat had arrested a boat on suspicion that it was fishing with illegal nets. He was dispatched to the pier to stand around looking authoritative when the skipper came ashore, to assure this total stranger that he was on the case.

Jim McDaid still has a vivid recollection of the night he lost his virginity as an elected TD. His first act of political patronage, performed just a week into his first Dáil term in June 1989, was tinged with embarrassment and confusion.

'I felt like a fool. I stood there thinking: "what am I supposed to do here?"'

But he'd been warned. Back at Portsalon they were adamant: 'Oh jaysus, you'd better go down. If they heard that you were here at a dinner and you didn't go down...'

The doctor-turned-TD took a deep breath and went to talk to his skipper constituent. Unsure of what he should say, he listened. He doubts if he ever got a vote for his troubles. 'It was strong (Niall) Blaney territory,' apparently.

McDaid had never attended a Fianna Fáil cumann meeting before he agreed to run on the party ticket in Donegal North-East. The first party meeting he was ever at was the convention that nominated him. The day after his victory dance at the Mount Errigal Hotel 'the fear and apprehension crept in'.

'What did I know about this? I mean, particularly me, because I didn't know anything about it. I remember the day after that victory dance sitting down and thinking about the night before, about the crowds that had turned up, the feeling of being put up on shoulders, the back slapping and everything. And I thought "oh my God, what have I done?"'

What he had done was swap a solid medical career for a life less ordinary. And the road less travelled turned out to be pock-marked with potholes and liberally studded with landmines.

Within two years a chance photo would see him branded a Provo fellow traveller in the Dáil, a political brickbat that put his life in danger and forced him to resign from a Cabinet that had yet to meet. He would get the call to serve at Cabinet again – only to be unceremoniously dropped after one term. He would see the most intimate episodes of his personal life splashed across the tabloid press in excruciating detail. His profile would win his estranged wife a book deal and a platform to wash the lurid linen of their failed marriage on the *Late Late Show*.

Back in Letterkenny, the medical practice he helped build is thriving. His former partners earn three times his current salary. They only have to work every eighth or ninth weekend.

Jim McDaid could be forgiven for being disillusioned. Bitter even. But he's not.

'By 1989, I had no more mountains to climb in medicine. I was thirty-nine and politics was a new challenge.'

He tilts back in his chair in his sparse office in Government Buildings as he considers what might have happened if he had passed on that one. 'I have no regrets,' he says. He says it with such firmness that you sort of believe him.

The first woman to be elected to the lofty position of party leader in Ireland never set out to be a politician. When the Tánaiste and Progressive Democrat leader Mary Harney was growing up in the 1970s, politics was only considered an option for women if they happened to be the daughters or widows of former public representatives.

'It wasn't something that in my wildest dreams I imagined I'd be,' Mary Harney says now.

Her promise was apparent from a young age. She shone at public speaking in secondary school. Her father was very active with Fianna Fáil locally, and the young Harneys would hand out leaflets during elections. Politics was an interest but not a passion.

When she surveyed the plethora of clubs and societies that thrived in Trinity College in the Seventies, she plumped for the St Vincent de Paul Society and devoted her free time to working with Traveller children.

She was over a year in Trinity before she attended her first Fianna Fáil cumann meeting. It was a modest affair. There had been mass resignations from the cumann in protest at Des O'Malley's Offences Against the State Act. So when she joined, Harney was one of just four members. Which is why she was elected treasurer at her first meeting.

She became very active in the party's newly established youth wing, Ógra Fianna Fáil. The bright young thing quickly made a name for herself. Invitations to speak at national conferences and to be the voice of young Fianna Fáil on radio and television piled up. Her role as auditor of the History Society meant that she was meeting and greeting all the senior politicians who were invited to address it.

In early 1977, the inevitable happened. She was asked to run for the party in her home constituency of Dublin West. Brian Lenihan assured Jack Lynch that he'd get her through the convention, but in the event she was beaten to the nomination by Liam Lawlor.

When the then General Secretary of Fianna Fáil rang to tell her that she was being added to the ticket in Dublin South-East, the eager young candidate was non-plussed. 'I said "where on earth is that?"'

Nevertheless, she threw herself into this first electoral battle with gusto. She had a £40 donation from her parents, a bicycle and a hazy notion of the constituency boundaries. Years later, Michael McDowell confessed that at the height of the campaign he had seen her canvassing on the side of a street that was actually in the neighbouring constituency. Being director of elections for the Fine Gael candidate Garret FitzGerald at the time, McDowell didn't feel the need to put his future party leader straight.

This was also the campaign in which Mary Harney got her first proposal of marriage. As a career move.

Another young gun on the campaign trail, Peter Leo Gibson, was casting about for an idea to gain some much-needed media profile. He came up with a cunning plan and put it to his running mate. They would get engaged. The publicity would be mighty. She recalls that he was a nice guy, if a little flamboyant. She turned him down. Years later she heard that Peter Leo Gibson had joined the PDs. Was she sure the indecent proposal was motivated purely by politics? 'It definitely was for the publicity... the things a woman refuses!'

Despite the massive swing towards Fianna Fáil in that election, the young Trinity student parachuted into unfamiliar territory garnered just 1,599 votes.

And that might have been it. She graduated from Trinity and began working in the United Dominions Trust as a researcher, assessing clients for loans. She planned to do accountancy. Then one Monday in August she answered her phone and was told to hold for a call from the Taoiseach. Jack Lynch came on the line and asked her if she would accept a nomination for the Senate. As soon as she put the phone down she was convinced it had been a hoax. She'd been drinking with friends over the weekend and immediately suspected that one of them — most likely George Birmingham — was behind it. She rang him up and declared 'I know it was you.' George, who would go on to become a Fine Gael TD himself, was completely at a loss.

It wasn't until Martin O'Donoghue rang her up later that day and asked if the Taoiseach had been in touch that she really let herself believe it was for real. Her life changed dramatically from the moment she accepted the nomination. The normal twenty-something social life disappeared, to be replaced by residents' and cumann meetings and clinics.

Asked if she enjoyed the change, she responds pragmatically: 'Well, I was very focused on wanting to get there.

'With a lot of people who pursue careers that are unusual you find that it's in their twenties that they make the biggest sacrifices. That's the decade that can determine when you get married, who you meet. They're the choices people make.'

If she hadn't been elected in 1981 she would not have run again. By then she was thinking of a career in the Law Library. 'I might have done the Bar. I've often regretted not doing that.'

But she did get elected. And coming from her background, Leinster House was a particularly intimidating place. When TDs came calling to the Harney household her mother would send down to the shop for the lettuce, ham and tomatoes, and a bottle of whiskey would be produced. It was always a big occasion. And yet, while her father was excited and proud of their politician daughter, her mother was ambivalent.

'My mother would have preferred if I became a teacher and went home in the evening and looked after my children and had the meals ready for my husband when he came home from work. She always said that. "Be a teacher. A secure pensionable job."'

Over twenty years after she first entered the Dáil she heard a recording of an interview she gave on the day. And gasped. 'God, that wasn't me surely. The innocence of it all! I was going to change the world.'

Some truly believe their political path was predestined. Dublin North-Central TD Ivor Callely can find no other reason for his in-explicable avid interest in current affairs television programming while aged no more than three-and-a-half. Then there was the incident with a soothsayer, which his proud mother only revealed to him after he was first elected as a public representative.

It happened before he started school, when Ivor was little more than a toddler accompanying his mother on the bus into the city centre. Just before they reached their stop a woman approached them and told them she was a fortune teller. She pointed at Ivor and declared with certainty 'that man there is going to be the President!'

Ivor tells this story with wide-eyed wonderment. 'There was always a fire in my belly about politics. I don't know where it came from,' he says. Despite there being no real family interest in politics, he got active in Fianna Fáil in the early 1980s, at first joining Ógra Fianna Fáil and then holding every possible officer position before going on to stand and win a local authority seat against the odds in 1985. He succeeded in taking a Dáil seat on his second attempt in 1989.

'I had friends within the Haughey machine who were attracted to me for one reason or another and offered some assistance and guidance to me. I was seen as someone of the organisation and of Dublin North-Central, so I was very much of the people. I could relate to the people. I am very much a home-produced TD. People like to produce their own.

'In Dublin North-Central I am seen as someone who came through the ranks. I was a member of Ógra Fianna Fáil and I probably held every position at every level in the organisation, from ordinary member to social secretary to secretary to treasurer or chairman.'

He was clever enough to find ways to rise above the herd. In politics, delivering bags of money to the party coffers will usually work. Under Ivor's direction his cumann generated the biggest intake in the country in the Fianna Fáil national draw for two years running.

He was a man on a mission. 'What I saw here was something we could peak at. I joined, I became active on the ground, active in the promotion of the party, active in organising social activities, bringing in a wider group to the cumann.'

With one goal in mind? 'I certainly joined Fianna Fáil with the intention that I wanted, and I felt I had the courage, to try and make some changes. I saw that there were gaps and vacuums in the system with people saying "that's the way it is, that can't be done". I believe that you can do things. I have this "I can achieve" attitude.'

Some political careers really do appear predestined. Garret FitzGerald was brought into the Dáil by his father when he was just eight years old. He recalls being in awe of the place. When he was fifteen the priest who ran the debating society in school, Fr Burke Savage, told his young charge that he should get involved in politics and aim to be Taoiseach. Most teenage boys would probably have thought this an overly extravagant ambition. Garret FitzGerald took it in his stride. He remembers thinking that 'it seemed rather a worthwhile thing to have a go at.'

The world was at war when he volunteered for his first political job. He worked at Fine Gael headquarters addressing envelopes for the 1943 general election campaign. By then he was seventeen and preparing to start college. His father was about to bow out of political life after a career which had included terms as Foreign Affairs Minister and Minister for Defence. For his older brothers politics wasn't really an issue. The founding fathers were still in place. But Garret was young enough to think of the politics of the future.

An early humiliation – realising that he was the only one in a class of girls who didn't know about the assassination of King Alexander – made him resolve to read the newspapers every day from that moment on. He became deeply engaged in the Spanish

Civil War and the politics of World War Two. He still has notes he copied out to use in the schoolyard to argue the case against the Germans in 1939. He was thirteen. There was, he recalls, a 'particular ambience' around his home, where the leading lights of the national movement would gather for gossip and politics. The Mac an tSaois, the McGilligans and the Blythes were all regulars.

In 1948 he canvassed Waterloo Road for Fine Gael, the Commonwealth Party.

'And then of course it became a republic, which I found rather trying so I gave up on Fine Gael for seventeen years after that,' he says breezily.

He was working in Aer Lingus by then and felt he shouldn't be involved in politics while with a State company.

His father never wanted his children to go into politics. 'He was disillusioned. They had been out of office for fifteen years by the time he died. He was very depressed about it all.'

He was also aware that his father disapproved of seats being passed from father to son. 'I remember mostly in my late teens that was in the period after Liam Cosgrave came in. It was clear to me that he believed that in politics you made your own name. You didn't do it on the strength of your father's name.'

Ruairi Quinn was also an early starter. He reckons that he was already highly politicised by the time he was reached fifth year in the fee-paying Blackrock College. He hung around with Stevie Coughlan, whose father was the Labour TD for Limerick. Coughlan had read an article about the Oxford Union or the Cambridge Union converting itself into a mini United Nations. They decided the school debating society could do with a shake-up.

Ruairi put together a dossier from *Time* magazine and the embassies of twenty countries and arranged the society members into teams representing the various member states. Stevie Coughlan was the Secretary General while Ruairi took on the representation of Portugal because it gave him an opening to discuss colonialism. Another student who is now an eminent solicitor represented Cuba, resplendent in an Afghan coat.

'Some people grew up in houses where music was very prominent, others where sport was very prominent. In our case politics was a very regular subject for discussion.

'The Ireland that I saw – the oppressive Catholicism, the oppressive insulation, isolation, was unacceptable to me. So I said to myself either I stay here and try and change it or I go. And I didn't want to go. So that was basically it.'

He grew up in a house where education was all. Although he lived close enough to cycle to school, he became a boarder in sixth year so that he could more fully immerse himself in the rarified regime at Blackrock. He recalls that the six Quinn children could get away with almost anything in their house, as long as they got their exams.

Canvassing in the general election in 1965 affected him profoundly. The poverty of the inner city slums appalled him.

'It was like walking on to an O'Casey set in the Abbey, except with the smell added. I remember the smell of urine all up and down the whole of Gardiner Street.'

He was narrowly defeated the first time he stood for election in 1973. He got elected to Dublin Corporation in 1974, and in 1977, against the power of the Fianna Fáil landslide, he made it to the Dáil against the tide.

'A lot of young people get interested in politics and participate in election campaigns. I was just more tenacious – and also lucky.

'An awful lot of everyone's opportunities in life are about being in the right place at the right time and seizing those opportunities. Okay, there's an element that you make your own luck but if you're not out running around the pitch you're not going to catch the ball. Of course the ball doesn't necessarily come to you and if it does you sometimes drop it.

'Getting elected. Being recognised. Becoming a public representative. Being chosen. Emerging from a tight contest. It's a very public exercise. You fail very publicly or you succeed very publicly.

'The buzz of having the title, having the power. Yes deputy, no Minister and the recognition of that, that people will talk to you because you're a councillor. That they'll reply to your letters.

'I had been writing in to the National Gallery looking for support for the campaign to open up Merrion Square and the letters were never answered. But when I wrote in as Councillor Ruairi Quinn I got a reply. The title is an empowerment to get access, to become an advocate, to get responses. Plus the applause. There is a certain similarity between actors and sports people and politicians. You know, show me a crowd and I'll make a speech. There is definitely something in that.'

For others, a political life is thrust upon them. In 1982 Jimmy Deenihan was captain of the legendary Kerry team that was then gearing up to win a record five-in-a-row national championships. Although his father had been politically active, the young P.E. teacher harboured no political ambitions. He planned to do an MA in physical education in Berkeley College in California once his football career had ended.

Local Fine Gael activists sounded him out about running for the party in the February general election. He said he was too committed to the football. Then fate stepped in. He broke his leg that summer and when he went back teaching in September he even had doubts about being able to continue teaching P.E. after his injury.

The government fell on a Thursday in November. Frank Quilter, a Fine Gael activist, called to his school to ask him if he would run this time. He asked the career guidance teacher in the school for advice.

On his way home he called into John B Keane's pub. The late writer was a staunch Fine Gael supporter and a good friend. He warned him that he should be aware that it was a very rough game before he committed himself. But he also said that he should run and promised to propose him at the convention if he decided to give it a go. And so it was that the writer proposed the sports hero at the selection convention two nights later. He was duly selected.

'I was surprised. When I put my name forward I hadn't really thought that I would end up on a trailer outside a church gate the following morning introducing myself to the electorate.'

Why did he do it? 'As I taught history along with P.E., I understood politics. I had a lot of admiration for Garret FitzGerald. He was an inspirational figure. I felt that if I gave the same commitment to politics as I gave to sport and teaching I could do okay. I liked the challenge. If you want a challenge, no other vocation in the world gives you the kind of challenge that politics does.'

CHAPTER 4

The Bottom Rung

'If you take away local democracy, you might as well have a dictatorship' – Councillor Tom Quinn

A year after the devastation of the 2002 general election, a Fine Gael handler confided that he had a cunning plan for the 2004 local elections. He would impose an extra candidate on every ticket in the country in a bid to maximise the Fine Gael vote. Vote management would not be an issue.

This was obviously a high risk strategy. It might help to increase the Fine Gael percentage of the vote on paper, but it could split the vote so much as to cut the number of Fine Gael councillors actually elected. No matter, he said. The idea was to get people back into the lost habit of voting Fine Gael. 'The 280 councillors we have at the moment have done us feck all good anyway,' he remarked.

Ireland has a system of local government strikingly different from that of other modern European democracies. Still governed by the principles of the 1898 Act, so little power is invested in the elected members that local democracy is in reality neither democratic nor particularly local.

The European model is based on the French system of departments which oversee a vast number of communes and municipalities, each with considerable administrative powers which are jealously guarded.

Our local authorities and urban district councils are in reality little more than talking shops where most of the power rests in the hands of unelected county and city managers.

While central government has relinquished the power to decide when elections to local authorities should be held or postponed – they must now happen every five years – the Minister for the Environment can still move to suspend a local authority and replace it with appointed commissioners if councillors fail to strike a rate. The single most important task entrusted to local authority members is the drawing up of a five-year development plan which the manager and his officials are obliged to implement.

Ironically, the other power they most controversially evoke is the corruption of these plans, putting pressure on planning officials and voting through Section Fours to make exceptions for their constituents.

Councillors love being councillors and many hang on to their seats for decades in the less volatile electoral environment of local government. They do so by acquiring an encyclopaedic knowledge of their bailiwick, a good working relationship with council officials and a reputation for getting things done. Their smaller electoral bases are easier to manage and massage. Which is just as well. Because for a local councillor, there is nowhere to hide.

As one senator who has sat in the kitchens of hundreds of councillors begging for their votes in several senate election campaigns noted: 'The thing that impressed me most about councillors is their level of knowledge of what's going on on the ground. If there's a problem in any family in the area – any problem – they know about it. They keep their antennae up for anything coming down the tracks.

'Councillors are hugely representative of their areas. They are elected in the main by people who know them personally. People who slag off councillors and call them gombeen men should think about what they are saying. What they're really having a go at is the people they represent.'

He describes a typical afternoon in his local county council office. 'There might be half a dozen or more councillors waiting for a chat with the planning officials and a few more going into the housing section.

'It's nearly like a trading floor at times. Not the buzz and excitement but lads wandering between offices, trying to get a file re-opened here, a word in an ear there.'

When they're not servicing their constituents, councillors are attending meetings. Councillors are martyrs for meetings. An enthusiastic councillor with a bit of time on his hands can eke out quite a handsome living from this business of attending meetings. There's the monthly council meetings, of course. But then there's also the plethora of committees and boards that are established to enquire into or oversee all manner of projects, developments and enterprises.

In South Tipperary, the first meeting of the newly-elected council in 1999 appointed councillors to a total of thirty-five committees and boards. These included six separate water supply committees and five drainage committees.

Every local authority has a raft of Strategic Policy Committees which frequently spin off into sub-committees and sub-committees of sub-committees and working groups.

An ambitious councillor might be elected to a Regional Authority from which they could go on to be elected to either the Border, Midland and Regional Assembly or the South and East Regional Assembly.

Local authorities also send representatives to local Port Authorities, Vocational Educational Committees and, until they are abolished, regional Health Boards. It doesn't end there. There's the tyranny of having to travel somewhere hot and foreign for conferences on how foreigners do things in hot places. And when summer swings around and the council chambers fall silent for a few months, our tireless councillors do not rest, attending all manner of summer schools and seminars the length and breadth of the country until their conference expenses budget is completely exhausted.

In 2002, councillors lost their amateur status and went professional. For openers, the Minister for the Environment decided that they should be paid an annual salary of €12,500. They also get at least €4,500 as a yearly allowance. A chairmanship of a Special Policy Committee is worth another €5,000 a year while the chairmanship of a local authority itself comes with an annual allowance of €28,000 in a full year. That ambitious councillor who got himself elected to the regional authority could pick up another €8,000 in allowances and expenses. A director of the Cork Port Company collects an annual stipend of €10,000 while membership of a Health Board could yield more than €20,000. After that every councillor has a conference budget which can be worth up to €5,000 in the course of a well-travelled year.

It all adds up, as a comprehensive study of rural councillors' allowances and expenses undertaken by the *Farmers Journal* in

2003 starkly illustrated. The trawl of councillors' expenses payments using the Freedom of Information Act revealed that the Irish taxpayer spent over €25 million financing rural councillors in 2002. It unearthed fifty-four councillors who had collected more than €50,000 for their part-time positions, and another 229 who collected more than €40,000. The figures are inflated with a once-off back payment of up to €15,420 paid to councillors in 2002. But they do not include the hefty expenses collected for membership of Health Boards and Vocational Education Committees.

The top earner, Cllr Jimmy Maloney of Foxford, collected a stunning €75,058.40 in allowances and expenses when he was chairman of Mayo County Council in 2002. He stoutly defended his impressive take. 'A study trip abroad is educational and necessary to make an informed decision, whether it be about planning issues or land-fill issues,' he said. 'If Mayo wasn't represented in the St Patrick's Day Parade in New York there would be uproar.'

Cllr Paula Desmond of Cork County Council, the second highest earner at €74,618, at first dismissed the survey as 'silly season journalism' before going on to complain that she had to give up her practice as a solicitor to devote herself full-time to her duties as chairperson of the Council and was subsequently looking for a job.

Cllr Tom Quinn of Mayo County Council received €62,910.85 in allowances and expenses in 2002. Cllr Quinn pointed out that he was the furthest away from the council chamber and travelled the 100-mile round trip at least once a week. He was also chairman for half the period in question when he said he attended over 100 meetings in the county at his own expense.

'If you take away local democracy, you might as well have a dictatorship,' he insisted.

Ask any current or former council chairperson how it is or was for them, and expect a lengthy diatribe on the stresses and strains of a job that gobbles up all personal and family time. But whether it is the high public profile, the packed social diary, or the chance to lord it over their councillor colleagues, the truth is that most councillors would kill for the chance to get their hands on that chain of office.

One councillor swears that the chairmanship of a local authority was bought for cash in his presence in the late-1990s. The author has no reason to disbelieve this story. The councillor in question asked only that the details of the time and place be omitted lest his identity become known.

He says he took no part in the haggling. But he was witness to the event nonetheless. The transaction made him feel so dirty that he felt he needed to have a shower as he left the council chambers that day.

The would-be chairman had been looking forward to donning the chain of office for a long time. There was a loose arrangement in place on the local authority and he understood that he was next in line. He had political ambitions beyond the council chamber and the chairmanship would be a vital stepping stone towards their realisation.

'He wanted the chairmanship so bad, he was like a child,' is how our narrator recalled it.

Just one vote stood in his way. One councillor was threatening to renege on a deal that had been done the previous year. 'He was a man who wouldn't stay bought,' apparently. So the market was opened up again. Four councillors gathered in an office beside the council chamber to broker a deal. Those present included the man who needed the vote, the man with a vote to sell, and two council colleagues. The would-be chairman's opening bid was a promise to appoint the councillor to a couple of the more lucrative committees. But this time the councillor wasn't biting. He wasn't saying it out straight but it became clear that he wanted cash up front. Eventually the would-be chairman cut to the chase. 'Let's make it simple,' he said, 'How much is it worth to you?' The councillor named his price. 'He went down to the bank at lunchtime and withdrew the money. It was £2,500 in cash,' according to our source.

'I wanted to have a shower after that. I wasn't thankful to the man who brought me in to witness it.'

Planning officials are under constant pressures from councillors who are under constant pressure from constituents to have exceptions made to the county development plan for once-off houses. The best councillors are constantly tic-tacking with the planners; suggesting ways in which plans could be tweaked to fit in with development rules, making cases for constituents who desperately need a roof over their heads. They will often reach honourable compromises.

But sometimes the planners insist on holding the line. Which means that councillors may be forced to reach for their most deadly weapon – the Section Four. At times like these a conscience can be a major liability. Or as one councillor put it: 'If you have a principle you're at a disadvantage. If you're cynical about it it's much simpler. I have to examine my conscience on Section Fours. I wouldn't be too thrilled about some of the Section Fours that have come up. But I voted for them because I knew I'd need a majority down the line when I'd have a Section Four.'

For all the talk of low standards in high places, the years of investigations carried out by the Planning and Payments Tribunal have raised more questions about politicians at local authority level than they have about those among the political elite.

Councillors agree that they are vulnerable. 'There's room for more corruption at local level,' one noted. 'These guys are in your face every day.'

'There was a situation up to the mid-1990s when each councillor had control of about £20,000 worth of grants. A pattern emerged. Some councillors were spending their grants outside their electoral areas. A suggestion was made that councillors were getting a few bob out of it themselves. The system was quietly changed.'

Fianna Fáil Cllr Tom Nolan reckons he holds the record for having the shortest ever tenure on a local authority. Nolan, a used car salesman with his own business in County Offaly, is named after his late father, who was appointed Minister of State by Charles Haughey in 1979. His brother Enda sits on Carlow County Council, while the other brother, M J Nolan, is a Dáil deputy.

Tom Nolan was co-opted on to Offaly County Council in early 1991 having won a convention vote by a convincing forty-six votes to five. However, just three months later, at a convention to select candidates for the local elections that summer, Nolan came up against a new candidate with strong GAA connections. He was rejected by the same delegates who had embraced him just three months earlier by a resounding forty-five votes to six.

'A personal thing happened and I lost four precious weeks and other people got their feet under the table. The convention is lethal. If you're going to fight people or they're going to take on certain tactics, you want to be willing to do that. I mean, everything goes out the window.'

After the convention Nolan was told that party headquarters would be adding his name to the list. He says he declined for personal reasons and because he predicted that a long-sitting councillor was likely to be squeezed out and he didn't want to be blamed. 'I knew if I had been added in '91 I would have been an outcast in the party. I would never have got any further. I would have been finished.'

Instead he worked through the organisation. He rose to secretary of his cumann and then to cumann chairman. Later he was elected secretary of the Comhairle Ceanntair and was then selected as a delegate to the Comhairle Dáil. By the time the selection convention swung around in 1999, he had his homework done. 'I turned the tables around.' Having spent the previous eight years trying to represent his area without a mandate, he was duly elected to the county council.

'My only platform had been that it was known that I was a councillor for a short time. And some of the public forgot that I wasn't elected. When I was out and about people would come up to me. They would hear I'd done a turn for someone. That helped me get back.'

His efforts to act as advocate for his neighbours were not always appreciated by the council officials. He particularly recalls being pulled aside by one official during one of his frequent visits into the council offices and told that they could only do work for elected members.

'When I was elected, one of the first people I sought out was that official. I took great pleasure in walking up to him and saying "now I'm f-ing elected, can you do that and that and that and that and that."'

Nolan agreed to forego his place on council committees last year for the chance to be chairman, which, he says, 'was a great honour for a blow-in.'

As chairman he featured prominently in the *Farmers Journal* list of top earners for the year. He defends his earnings robustly, arguing that they don't come close to compensating for the crucifying workload a council chairman must carry.

'As I told the local reporter who phoned me about it, I should have got twice as much. This is the first year that the allowance has been taxed. On top of that I'll give you copies of my mobile phone and land-line bills. I have nothing to hide. I was out seven nights a week. Genuinely, I should have got double what I earned and it still wouldn't be enough.

'I have three step-children who nearly don't know me at this stage, and it's got that bad that I went in the other night and the dog bit me because he thought I was a stranger.'

Nolan insists that most councillors work very hard and put in long and often thankless hours in the service of their constituents. However, he is prepared to admit that there are too many committees under current local government rules and says the issue needs to be addressed. The number of committees on Offaly County Council range from the special policy committees and County Development Board to the Barrow Drainage Board and Portarlington Burial Board.

When a local authority holds its first meeting after an election, the first item on the agenda is the election of a chairman. Then they get down to dividing the spoils of victory. If one party has a clear majority, they will ensure that they have a majority on every committee of importance. If the biggest party needed help in electing the chairman, those supportive members will have to be looked after. By the time all the places in all the committees are filled, each councillor could well find himself on as many as seven or eight. While some committees are more trouble than they are worth, others, such as the Midland Health Board, and the Vocational Education Committee, are much-prized. As Nolan explains: 'These are the ones that the public are coming to you with the most problems.'

The Regional Authority, which brings together councillors from all the local authorities in the region, can provide valuable networking opportunities for councillors with political ambitions beyond local government. Tom Nolan was co-opted on to the Regional Authority and Midlands and East Tourism, which incorporates seven counties.

While councillors have an unenviable reputation for lavish junketeering, Tom Nolan claims that much of the excesses of old are now stamped out. Offaly County Council does not encourage foreign travel. Each member gets an annual budget of €4,000 to cover expenses for attending conferences. Whether and how they use it is up to them.

'There is junketeering but it depends on the county,' Nolan explains, 'A culture builds up. It got ingrained years ago and it's still happening in some places. But the trend is very much going away from that.'

He is surprised to hear the tale of the chairmanship that was bought for €2,500.

'If I needed the vote of, say, an Independent member to be

elected to the chair, I might talk to him. But it's like the fella in the dentist's chair who puts his knee between the dentist's legs and says: "we're not going to hurt one another now are we?" If you're in that type of a situation I'd walk away from it.

'If I wanted a vote to be chair in a situation then, yes, if there was something I could give that particular member that they wouldn't get otherwise, certainly, I'll talk to them. But not to the point of buying a vote.

'It would fall back on you. If you're going to do business with people like that, you're gone. The day that you think that's over and done with, that's the day it's only starting to rot.'

CHAPTER 5

Pounding the Pavement

'I love tramping the streets' – Bertie Ahern

It can now be revealed that it was none other than Charlie Haughey who christened them. Chris Wall recalls bumping into the then Fianna Fáil leader at a function almost twenty years ago. Haughey smiled when he saw one of Bertie Ahern's closest political allies ambling towards him. 'Ah, I see the Drumcondra Mafia has arrived,' he murmured.

The name stuck. The story of the band of fiercely loyal men that gravitated towards Bertie Ahern over two decades ago and pledged themselves to the task of ensuring that he would consistently return one of the highest first preference votes in the country is now the stuff of Fianna Fáil legend.

The Drumcondra Mafia calls Bertie 'the bossman'. They revere the self-effacing Dub as something akin to their messiah. No matter how pressing the affairs of the nation, no matter how unreliable the Government jet, Bertie will always try to fix his schedule so that he is back in Dublin every Sunday night to meet the lads for a pint in one of his few favoured locals in Drumcondra.

It's not just for the sake of keeping in touch with his roots. Or to be sociable. Or even to get a break from the political maelstrom. Especially not to get a break from the political maelstrom. It is over a modest number of pints in Drumcondra that Bertie takes the pulse of his constituency. And, by extension, of the country. It is here that constituency generals deliver the latest reports from the field, where his army of canvassers are engaged in a relentless intelligence gathering operation.

The Dublin Central Fianna Fáil machine is the most ruthlessly professional and efficient constituency operation in the country. It demands unquestioning commitment from its volunteers, who devote huge swathes of their time to being Bertie Ahern's representatives on earth. When I phoned Chris Wall as part of the research for this book, he mentioned that we were neighbours. Despite the fact that we had neither met nor spoken previously, he could name the street that I live on. I joked that if he knew my house number I'd get really scared. He admitted that he couldn't tell me the number off the top of his head, but he was certain he could pick it out if he was standing on the street. He wasn't even impressed with his party trick. He knew me because he knows Dublin Central intimately. I was on his register.

As a young amateur athlete, Chris Wall ran against Bertie's older brother, Maurice. When he moved to Drumcondra his wife decided to canvass for Bertie. When he dropped her at the constituency headquarters, then run from the Ahern family home on Church Avenue, he realised the family connection. On the fourth night he said he would tag along with his wife for a walk. Twenty years later, being there for Bertie has become his raison d'être.

Back in the early 1980s, the Fianna Fáil operation in Dublin Central was run by Tom Houlihan. A miller by trade, the über-organiser had been one of the stalwarts of Charlie Haughey's operation in Dublin North. Following the chopping and changing of constituency boundaries, he came in to help the ambitious young sports enthusiast in Drumcondra.

Wall recalls the first time he walked into Bertie's mother's home in Church Avenue: 'In the sitting room every wall was covered with lists of every street in what was then Dublin Central. They were marked "canvassed, dropped" or whatever was done. That was all listed. Handwritten out.'

The system was simple, if time-consuming. When canvassers finished their rounds at 9pm, the cumann responsible for each ward would fill in a form indicating which houses had been covered. Someone else had the job of collating this information. The charts on the walls would be colour-coded. If streets had been canvassed once, they were coloured blue; twice-canvassed streets were coloured red; and three-time canvassed streets were coloured green. Any queries raised on the doorsteps were then numbered and acknowledged so that future canvassers could back-reference them.

'It's run like a business. As far as I'm concerned we are constantly carrying out market research. Market research is knocking at your door and distilling all the stuff we pick up and deciding "this is an issue".

'The current issue happens to be law and order. That's fed into the system. So the bossman knows this from these constant door-knocking exercises carried out by all the cumann people.'

While the entire operation is now computerised, the methodology remains the same. Canvassers have to try and guesstimate how well – or poorly – their candidate will do from gauging the reactions they get on the doorsteps. All of them carry electoral registers, which are marked after each encounter.

'You have to pick up that sort of stuff, and be able to the best of your ability to form an opinion on whether these people will vote for you. You mark a register. Its accuracy depends on who's marking a register. From knocking on doors it's not easy but it is possible to establish the likelihood of support.

'You have to try to track what the local issues are. The truth of the matter is that when it comes to people's votes – with the exception of those who are totally committed to a party – it's all to do with local issues.'

Wall insists that rather than engaging in a cynical exercise to take the temperature of the constituency and win votes, the canvassers are offering a real service.

'I accept that we support a particular individual. But that individual is elected to provide a service to his constituents. Now his workload may take him away more than he wants to be away, so he has to have his back-up. That's the way it's done.' Not every politician does it this way. 'No. The operation in Dublin Central is superb. The reason it is so good is that originally it would have been in a constituency that had Charlie Haughey and George Colley, both of whom had superb operations.'

Indeed Haughey's intelligence network was so comprehensive that it is said he had a named person on every single street whose job it was to keep his office acquainted with all relevant local gossip. It makes Bertie's adoption of the 'boss ward' system look almost shoddily lax by comparison.

There are about forty cumann with an average of forty members in each in Dublin Central. Not all of them would be in a position to engage in the odyssey of door knocking that the constituency demands. Those that do are divided into 'various different goal seekers,' according to Wall.

'In some instances you'd probably have the young buck who wants to be a TD and he has a few friends with him knocking on doors. Then you have the party members who are just party supporters. They don't care who's on the ticket. They're the essence and the continuity of the whole structure.'

This breed is particularly important in city constituencies where fluctuations in population levels see frequent boundary alterations. Dublin Central has had different boundaries for the last consecutive five elections. In the last election the goal was to get local doctor Dermot Fitzpatrick in on Bertie's coat tails. The fly in the ointment was Nicky Kehoe, the Sinn Féin councillor whose constituency work-rate made him a serious threat.

Bertie loaned his running mate one of his oldest and closest aides, Paul Kiely, to direct the operation and police the vote management arrangements.

When constituency boundaries change some loyal cumainn find themselves cut off from their candidate and forced to contemplate supporting the chosen candidate in their new ward. This is a tricky time. In some cases, people have canvassed for the same candidate for years. Their loyalty to them can be personal rather than political or based on party affiliations. The party bosses must move in swiftly to prevent vital cogs in the constituency machine from rusting away.

A new plan of campaign for the newcomers to the constituency will be drawn up. Efforts are made to ensure that the cumainn all represent roughly the same number of votes. In more sparsely populated pockets in the constituency, some cumainn will not be able to make up the numbers to justify their existence. If any of these find themselves in Dublin Central after a boundary change, they will be forced to amalgamate with a nearby cumann. Which, of course, can cause ructions in the internal politics of a cumann. Where once there were two officer boards, there is now one. Where once they could send three delegates apiece to conventions and other party gatherings, now they can send just three delegates between them. The modest nature of the political prizes at stake is no guard against the bruised egos and epic power struggles these developments can trigger.

When the plan is in place, a meeting of the Comhairle Dáil is convened. The Comhairle Dáil is the highest tier in the constituency organisation and all cumainn will be represented when it meets. They are basically told how the wards will be divided, who their individual bosses are, and how Dublin Central operates. They have little choice but to take it on the chin.

Making the right impression on the doorsteps is an art in itself. Pleasing all of the people all of the time is a delicate business. Chris Wall described how he tries to work out the priorities of a voter from their age, address and accent.

The changing face of inner city communities where what we used to call yuppies have bought up huge swathes of the red-brick terraces which were once the preserve of the working classes and the elderly can be a challenge. Oxmantown Road, which runs between the Phoenix Park and Stoneybatter, poses a particular problem for even the canny canvasser.

'When I'm knocking on doors on Oxmantown Road and a young person answers the door, the chances are that they're some-body who's moved in. If it's an older person, chances are they are long-time residents. But if I'm not careful and I say something to you that's not kosher from an Oxmantown Road point of view and you turn out to be the daughter or grand-daughter of a long-time resident, I'm finished. I may as soon pack up my case and go away. You've got to make absolutely sure that you don't cause anybody any upset.'

With the local elections just a year away, Chris was canvassing between two and five times a week. A group of about sixteen can-vassers would cover about 500 houses in about three-and-a-half hours. But experienced canvassers prefer to work in smaller groups that are more easily organised. Sixteen-strong groups can prove too unwieldy depending on the urban terrain being canvassed. The ideal is considered to be three to four groups of not more than six persons. The bulk of people are expected to hit the streets between two and five times a week. At the height of Bertie's campaign for re-election in May 2002, there were 200 canvassers swarming through Dublin Central every evening.

During the feverish pre-election period, most campaign workers would canvass every night without a break. Some would canvass twice on Saturdays. In non-campaign mode it's a slightly different operation. They are not so much begging for votes as researching the market. But the pace is still sweltering. On a typical Saturday a full year before the local elections, there would be six different groups of canvassers out in the constituency with, on average, seven people in each group. This kicks off once Patrick's Day passes and the weather picks up. The comfortable shoes are not put away until September.

During the winter months canvassing is more strategic. If a particular issue crops up that is upsetting residents in one area, the word filters back to St Luke's and Bertie will be advised to drop around on a Saturday to register a presence and lend an ear. In tightly-run constituencies the cumann secretaries are expected to convene nine to ten meetings a year. The Comhairle Dáil meets the first Monday of every month, eleven months a year. But your commitment to the party doesn't end there. Cumann members are also expected to be active members of other clubs in their parishes in order to keep a finger firmly on the pulse of their local communities.

'As far as we're concerned, the volunteer effort is paramount to the betterment of this society. So we would ask our people what club they are in locally. Some of these enthusiasts with ambition would want to be in nearly every club in the parish.'

It's not all sweetness and light out on the canvassing trail. Competitive canvassing is the order of the day. If one candidate's team hears that another candidate is heavily canvassing one area or attempting to take ownership of some local hot issue, a flying squad of canvassers can be assembled within the hour to head them off at the pass. The vote is managed meticulously. If canvassers get negative feedback on the doorsteps in any particular area, the previous election result will be consulted. Where once they relied on the tallymen to give an accurate picture of voting patterns in each ballot box, now a detailed list of who voted and where is available to everyone. Experienced canvassers can make a good stab at guessing who voted for whom. If the vote seems to be slipping between elections, strategies to bring it back up are employed on a street-by-street basis.

When the constituency organisation was in its infancy, Tom Houlihan had it all in his head. Wall wrote it all down, producing a thick volume, setting out how to micro-manage the constituency in excruciating detail. He believes that Bertie has it in St Luke's to this day.

In November 2003 *Irish Times* columnist Róisín Ingle wrote hilariously of her shock at discovering the Taoiseach on her doorstep when she answered her doorbell one Saturday morning. We must surely live in one of the only modern democracies where the Prime Minister makes unsolicited house calls at the weekend.

He does it, he says, because he is that peculiar breed of politician that thrives on meeting the people.

'There are three types of politicians,' he explains. 'There are those who hate constituency work and hate being out with the people. They are elected by them but they don't feel comfortable with them.

'There's those in the middle who do it on and off. They feel enthusiastic about it sometimes and they hate it other times.

'And then there's people who like being out there. Of all the things of politics that I like, I love being out there. It's my favourite bit of the job. I love tramping the streets. I love dealing with the ol' issues and stuff. I get a great sense of satisfaction out of that.'

It's the immediacy and the feedback that's the drug. 'You can actually do things quicker and meet people. You enjoy it and you feel appreciation and you feel some bloody use. And it doesn't go on endlessly trying to achieve something.

'You can actually do something, you can get stuck into it. Whether it's changing the traffic flow, building the scouts' den, getting a place for a park, or getting a site cleared for something or other. You can actually do it.

'I shouldn't be the one to say it, but in Dublin Central there are hundreds of things that I am directly responsible for doing on my own. That's the reality and I get a lot of satisfaction from doing that. Whether anyone else believes I did that or not, I know I did.

'And because you do all of them, then you get a vote. That's why I have a big vote. Because there are people and groups around all of those issues. Even though I can't be out as much as I used to be now. The last few years have been hard. But I still try to get out a few hours a week. That's all I'd manage now.'

It bothers him that he had to spread himself so thinly over the course of the last election. But what is truly revealing is his aware-ness of the precise amount of time, down to the number of minutes, he spent in his constituency during that election campaign.

'Other politicians can go out and do eighty or ninety hours (in their constituencies) during the elections. I can't. I was out around the country. In the four weeks of the campaign, we worked about 360 hours. We averaged ninety hours a week. And I spent seven hours and ten minutes in Dublin Central.'

CHAPTER 6

Dirty Tricks

'It's not like any other thing, this thing we do. It's like the
Sopranos' – Fianna Fáil Dáil candidate

L einster House is an intimate community where most of the
permanent inmates are at least on nodding terms with each
other. At times of crisis the numbers swell as battalions of
barristers and public relations gurus sweep in to shore up the usual
straggle of political groupies and hangers-on whose persistence has
earned them access-all-areas passes to the corridors of power. Many
of them get gigs as researchers in their party's press offices or as
advisors to ambitious opposition deputies, only to find themselves
on the Government payroll when the election goes their way.

There is one such person who is a familiar face around Leinster
House. He eats in the self-service restaurant most days and can
often be seen enjoying a sociable drink with his colleagues in the
Visitors' Bar. And yet most people are vague about what it is he
actually does. In fact he works in the Taoiseach's Department in
Government Buildings where his post is officially described as that
of 'researcher'. But that doesn't come close to describing the highly
unusual role this young man plays in the Fianna Fáil political
machine. His job involves keeping files on political rivals and media
figures, for use when in election mode or in times of crisis. He
reports directly to one of the Taoiseach's aides.

Much of his work involves clipping out press statements,
speeches or, best of all, off-the-cuff remarks reported in the local

and national press. Anything that might prove embarrassing or compromising down the line. Special attention is given to the pronouncements of party leaders. There is, I'm told, a thick file on the activities of Pat Rabbitte's old party, Democratic Left.

Anonymous letters and phone tip-offs alleging wrong-doing and chicanery by rival parties and politicians are all investigated and the results kept on file for possible future use. Intelligence from party hacks or councillors on the ground is similarly noted and stored.

Sometimes the results are spectacular. The Fianna Fáil dirty tricks unit had a hand in the wide dissemination of the tape of former Fine Gael leader John Bruton declaring that he was 'sick of answering questions about the fucking peace process' in 1995. Fianna Fáil researchers also dug up information about the Youth Defence leader Justin Barrett's trips to neo-Nazi events in Germany – when his opposition to the Nice Treaty was putting the entire EU project in jeopardy.

My source revealed that there are even files kept on journalists and 'opinion-formers' whose analysis and comment could be the making or breaking of a campaign. Their reports and details of their background are kept on file with a view to outing inconsistencies or highlighting potential conflicts of interest.

Dirty tricks go hand in hand with the political game, where the stakes are high and the players will do just about anything to win. Most politicians deny ever having played one. But then almost all have a story to tell of the time they fell victim to them.

Tony Gregory has always suspected that some members of Bertie Ahern's campaign team were behind a sophisticated dirty trick played on him during the 1981 general election. Bertie Ahern was a sitting TD going into that election, having been elected in the Dublin-Finglas constituency in 1977. However, it was the first time he was running in Dublin Central where he was sent in to undermine George Colley. It was a ruthless affair. Gregory recalls constituents telling him that Bertie's canvassers had asked them to vote number one and two for Fianna Fáil, but to vote Tony Gregory number three ahead of George Colley.

It was Gregory's first stab at a Dáil seat. 'I was the threat that had to be dealt with,' he believes.

While not directly involved in the campaign in support of the H-Block hunger strikers, he was sympathetic to their cause and had put down a motion in Dublin Corporation in support of the hunger strikers' five demands. The motion was defeated and Gregory walked out of the council chamber in disgust, an event that attracted some publicity.

The election followed just a few months later. On the morning of polling day he rose at 5am and set off to ensure that his posters had prominent positions outside every one of the thirty-two polling stations in the constituency. But somebody had been up and out before him. A flurry of new posters were littering the constituency. These posters bore the legend: 'Support the Five Demands. Vote Tony Gregory. Support the H-Block Hunger Strikers.'

The posters had mysteriously materialised overnight in all the areas in the constituency where such sentiments would go down like a lead balloon. What's more, they were pasted on shop windows and postboxes – again guaranteed to cause offence and lose votes. In some of the leafier middle class districts they were even pushed through residents' letterboxes.

Tony Gregory was forced to abandon his original mission and race around the constituency tearing down these liabilities. But the damage was done. Voters had seen the posters on their way to work. He lost that election by 150 votes to Alice Glenn.

'I've a terrible temper. I went up to the HQ of the H-Block committee like a lunatic. They thought I'd gone bananas. They said they hadn't put up any such posters.'

Then he heard that one of his campaign vans had been driving up Church Avenue – just up from the Ahern campaign base – that morning and had come upon a gang of people pasting up posters. They ran when they saw the van and dropped a sheaf of posters. These were the posters in question.

After the election he said within earshot of Bertie Ahern that he thought he would have won it if it hadn't been for Ahern's smear tactics.

'Bertie just said: "Now, Tony, you don't think I'd do anything like that". I just said that anybody putting up any shite about me in future will get a hatchet in the back of the head. I said I'll be driving around the area all night. I'll have a hatchet in the car with me. Spread the word.'

Over twenty years later, Gregory is clearly still furious over the incident and has never fully accepted Ahern's assurances. He took particular pleasure in the fact that it was Bertie Ahern who had to drive Charlie Haughey to his office in Summerhill the following year when he cut the famed 'Gregory deal'.

'He had to wait in the car for three-and-a-half hours while I did the deal. What a suck-in!'

Candidates are at their most vulnerable on the night before polling day. The media blackout on the eve of polling day is partly to guard against eleventh-hour smear tactics. But it also means that last-ditch dirty tricks are impossible to counter. Many TDs have discovered this the hard way. In 1992, when Labour was riding high on the Spring tide, it was Labour candidate Joe Costello who posed a major threat in Dublin Central.

Polls showed that, like most Labour candidates in that election, Costello was doing particularly well in the middle class parts of the constituency which were sure to register a high turn-out.

The night before polling day a leaflet was pushed through letter boxes in these areas declaring that Costello, a well-known advocate of prisoners' rights, 'works with murderers and rapists.'

In the event, the crude attempt to scupper his campaign backfired. He got over twenty per cent of the valid poll in that election and sailed into the Dáil.

The lengths to which some politicians will go to nobble a rival are breath-taking. It happens in all parties. Rumours are the easiest. Marital infidelity is the classic. Of course it helps if your rival really is having an affair. But that is not strictly necessary.

In the 1980s, when the Pro-Life movement was at its most frenzied, one Fine Gael candidate was widely rumoured to have travelled to England for an abortion. At the time, the Pro-Life movement was at its height and lapels were strewn with the tiny gold feet that were the movement's emotive symbol. If people had believed the unfounded rumour, the candidate's political career could have been destroyed.

One Fianna Fáil politician told of how his running mate, who was a senator at the time, launched a whispering campaign about his decision to give up teaching.

'He said I was a paedophile. He was telling people that I was forced to leave the school because I was interfering with the children. It was a survival thing. He saw me as the coming man.'

When he got cast iron proof of the source of the rumours, he dispatched a solicitor's letter warning his party colleague that he would see him in court. Because of the nature of the rumours, and the danger of the no-smoke-without-fire principle kicking in, he did not wish to go on the record and he didn't take the matter further. In any case, he's sure he's not unique.

'There are a lot of fellas like that in this game. Fellas who are living on their wits. They'd sell their mothers for a quota... There is every kind of a chancer in Fianna Fáil. It's not like any other thing, this thing we do. It's like the *Sopranos*.'

Bertie Ahern's right-hand man, Chris Wall is matter-of-fact when asked about the special tool invented for the sole purpose of tearing down a rival candidate's posters. 'Yeah, there's a hook that you can get to pull down posters. It's just like a meat hook that you put on the end of a brush handle.'

However, he is coy about the genius brain who invented it, or where one might go to acquire one. 'That's probably there since the days God was around. I honestly was never involved in that side of life.'

Developments in postering technology have made this age-old dirty trick less manageable. Now that the election posters are made of coriboard and fixed to lamp posts with plastic clips, tearing them down is a more complex affair. It would involve getting a ladder to snip the clip – and that's difficult to do covertly. Of course, the person most likely to tear down your posters is not your rival from another party, but your running mate. As Chris Wall puts it 'if there are three candidates going for two seats, there will be savagery.'

Nora Owen believes that 'by and large our elections in Dublin North were clean. There were never any nasty leaflets put out. Although at times there were rumours put out.

'At one election they put out a rumour that I was divorced. It was convenient that my sister Mary was separated. Some of our canvassers got it at the doors. People said they weren't sure about voting for a divorced woman. It came back to me on the query sheet: "Is Nora divorced?"'

On another occasion the TD heard that a friend had been asked if it was true that she was an alcoholic. It was, of course, the kind of snide aside that would be much more damaging to a woman politician than to her male colleagues.

'I was very, very particular about not going into a pub on my own. That's another difficulty for a woman politician. Enda (Kenny) would tell me that he'd be driving down to Mayo and he could do six pubs on the way. I don't think in my whole political career I went into a pub on my own. Never, ever, ever.'

Owen heard many other rumours about other candidates over the years and chose to ignore them. 'It's the price you pay when you put your name up there.'

Alan Shatter doesn't think he was ever the victim of a dirty trick. 'If I was, I was totally oblivious to it.'

There was, however, the minor controversy involving Shatter's balls. With three candidates chasing three seats in his constituency in 1981, they decided they needed something to get their newest recruit noticed. That was when they came up with the idea of Shatter's balls. 'I am the only person ever elected to Dáil Éireann on the strength of distributing his balls around Dublin South,' Shatter boasts to this day.

The 3,000 balls in question were, coincidentally, the exact colour of the PVC coats he used to sell in the Dandelion Market as a law student. He recalls getting an instruction from Fine Gael HQ to bounce his balls around his constituency colleague Tom Hand's bailiwick on the day before the election.

'The day before polling day we invaded two of these estates with about twenty people. Afterwards I called into Fine Gael's Dundrum HQ to collect polling cards. As I walked in, the Fine Gael director of elections was leaning against a fireplace and I could hear Tom Hand's voice saying: "Shatter's fucking balls are all over my estate! What are you going to do about it?"

'I took the coward's approach and retreated back out the door and left it for some other branch member to collect the polling cards.

'I had understood he was going to get some notice of this by HQ. I hadn't given him notice. It didn't affect his first preference vote. But the tactic worked because I got forty per cent of Tom's second preferences, and there was no reason why they should have known who I was. It does say something about the relevance of policy to politics.'

Tom Parlon was stunned by the intensity of the campaign the Fianna Fáil machine fought when they feared they might lose a seat in Laois-Offaly in 2002.

'Fianna Fáil had their machine. The intensity of the campaign towards the end was unbelievable. Every minute of every hour and every day there was someone ringing saying "so and so has been here, the pressure is on". Every pro-active move we made, there was someone undermining it out there. Every statement you made, there was someone pulling the rug from under you.

'It was fairly personalised stuff as well. Politics is a fairly ugly business when someone thinks his seat is going to go. Every bit of dirt that could be said about anyone would be said. I couldn't repeat what was said now. It was very personal stuff. There were all sorts of rumours and innuendo. You'd hear the most dreadful stories about yourself around the place.

'I would have heard them previously about other people and just taken them with a grain of salt. But when it's about yourself and your family, it's another story. That is one of the least attractive things about politics. People are so committed that as long as their guy and their party is winning, they don't care what they have to do.'

CHAPTER 7

The Parish Pump

'It's a beautiful feeling to get somebody something' – Ivor Callely

---

Frank Cluskey didn't like holding clinics. Doing his constituency duty in the pool rooms and lounge bars of Dublin South-Central was a pointless chore for the no-nonsense Labour legend. His friends and advisors would argue forcefully that holding clinics was a necessary evil if he wanted to continue to enjoy the amenities of Dáil Éireann. But Cluskey dug in.

He had a devastating theory about the business that eats up endless hours of (almost) every deputy's working week:

'A third of the people who turn up at clinics want you to do something that's fuckin' impossible,' he would insist in his trademark Dublinese. 'Another third want you to do something that's fuckin' illegal. And the rest of them are only fuckin' lonely!'

There are no statistics available for the number of sad souls who head to their local TD's clinic of a Saturday morning for a bit of company. But there is plenty of anecdotal evidence that Cluskey hit the nail on the head with the other two categories.

The few studies that have been done on the electoral benefits of filling potholes and putting flickering street lights to right indicate that it's a thankless business. Michael D Higgins accepts limited studies that show that about thirty per cent of people who attend clinics are not even on the electoral register. A further thirty per cent of clients do not bother to vote. When the numbers of clients who take their troubles to all the candidates in a constituency are taken into account, it is estimated that constituency clinics generate about one vote in every nine cases taken up. That is the maximum. But that doesn't stop them from trying. Every TD, senator and upwardly mobile councillor knows only too well of their constituents' enduring belief that a public representative can pull off all manner of miracles for them. That, in many people's minds, is what they are paid for.

The range of requests runs the whole gamut from the sublime to the ridiculous to the downright dangerous.

Noel Davern's all-time favourite pleading letter dates back to the 1980s. A constituent wrote to the South Tipperary TD outlining his precarious financial situation. He'd had a bad run of brucelosis. All his cattle were taken away. He could get out of this hole if he could raise the cash to buy more calves this year. And he had a cunning plan. If Mr Davern could see his way to having a quiet chat with Major Vivion de Valera, the proprietor of the *Sunday Press*, and extracting from him the exact location of the missing football in a forthcoming 'Spot-the-Ball' competition in his fine publication, the cash prize would cover him. And no-one need ever know.

Noel Davern is still tickled by the memory of it. 'I mean the innocence of writing that letter to you,' he marvels now.

But surely that letter was merely indicative of a time when people thought their TD could do just about anything? Davern gets a wistful look in his eye as he remarks: 'TDs could do a lot of things then. You're limited now by everything.'

So what did TDs do then?

'There were cases squared for drunken driving. There were speeding cases squared. They were always done on sympathetic grounds. On grounds that a man would lose his job over it and on the basis that he wouldn't step out of line again. The guards did it in the interests of the social circumstances. But you wouldn't even think of doing that now.'

Davern describes a more recent incident that reveals just how much the political climate has changed. About ten years ago a constituent came to him in some distress. He had been breathalysed and taken to the garda station the previous night. He pleaded with him to sort it out. Davern explained that there was nothing he could do, but his constituent was insistent, pleading with him to 'ring him at least'.

'I said I'll ring him just to ask him how bad you were. Is that clear to you now?'

It turned out that there had been a mix-up with the samples taken at the garda station on the night and no-one who had been arrested would be charged.

'I turned to him and I said "you're lucky" and explained what had happened. But he said "ah, you're only saying that. You did it." I was at pains to explain to him that I didn't do anything. Because if he was going around the place saying that about you now you'd be a social outcast!'

Davern is one of the longest serving TDs in the Dáil, having been first elected in 1969. He misses the old days, when his constituents had to push button A to get through to him from the only coinbox in the village. It seems to him that the job then was more about doing what he calls 'personal favours'.

'If somebody wanted to contact Social Welfare they couldn't do it themselves. You'd phone. You'd sort it out for them. All of that sort of thing is going now. Every child in the country has a telephone now. Everyone is capable of doing things now that they weren't capable of doing then.

'A fella might come into your clinic. He'd be humming and hawing about something. You knew very well if they'd nothing to talk to you about, they'd be wanting to touch you for a couple of quid. You'd always say to them "look, don't give me the bullshit, here's the money, I don't have time to listen to it." Or a fella would ask you for an entrance fee for a pub. In other words, if he could buy the first drink himself he'd gauge in the pub where he'd get another drink. He came to you for the independence to buy the first drink.'

Another big part of his constituency workload in his early years as a TD was requests to get constituents a bed in a hospital.

'You could get people beds in the old days. The most sought after places were the county homes. You would often be asked to get someone in there for a long term stay. Or knights of the road would come to you and ask to get in there for a couple of nights. You'd ring the matron and say "he's here in town, could he get in for a few nights." She'd say "get him to get a ticket from the guards and I'll take him in".

'Planning never was a problem, up to the late 1990s. You went in. You compromised on it. There was no question of a family not getting a planning permission for a farm. If a farmer needed money

– if they had a child going to university or something – you'd tell the planning officer that he was in financial trouble and he badly needed the permission. And they'd give it to him. A farmer wouldn't have cash any time of the year. T'was important that he sold that site.'

And did he get medical cards for constituents?

'You could do it back then. There were no set guidelines. Well, they weren't that clearly defined.'

As clearly defined as the guidelines now are, some politicians have still managed to carve out reputations for their ability to swing medical cards for their constituents. Politicians who have served on the Health Boards have an obvious edge. And few politicians have dedicated themselves to Health Board service with as much commitment as Fianna Fáil's Ivor Callely.

The Dublin North-Central TD served as chairman of the Eastern Health Board, the Northern Area Health Authority and the Eastern Regional Health Authority.

'If I wasn't chairman I was vice-chairman. If I wasn't vice-chairman I was chairman of the protocol committee. I always held a very high position.'

He knows everything there is to know about getting medical cards. 'There are guidelines there for the chief executive officers around the country on the issue of medical cards. But there is discretion. Medical cards can be issued on a medical need basis. A lot of people who make an application don't understand the system. When you start talking to people you understand that there's a need for them to have a medical card, but you just can't get the equation right. It's only when you start really talking to people that you start to work out the equation that will result in them getting a medical card.'

He admits modestly that he is seen as a TD who is very good at getting the equation right.

His approach to constituency work sounds vaguely theological. 'I'm a believer that you can do it. You need the courage to do it and the sincerity to understand that there are things that you can change, and there are things that you can't change, and you need to recognise the difference.'

Callely was the first TD in Dublin North-Central to open a full time constituency office, beating the then Taoiseach, Charlie Haughey, and long-serving minister, Michael Woods to the trick. He also designed his own 'mobile information unit' which he tows behind his car every Saturday morning to selected outposts in his constituency.

There is a funny (and most likely apocryphal) story told about a TD who liked to conduct his constituency business from the comfort of a mobile home, which had the added benefit of allowing him to bring politics to the people. He parked one afternoon on the edge of a new housing estate only to discover that the advance publicity had not generated much excitement. He took to knocking on doors to drum up a bit of business. The TD quickly discovered that there was a hot issue disturbing the residents of the estate. Several had noticed the mobile home that had recently arrived in the neighbourhood. He could not have come at a better time. Word raced through the estate that Travellers were about to set up a temporary halting site on their green belt. 'Could you get them moved on?' they wanted to know. According to Leinster House lore, never was a constituency concern so quickly addressed.

Ivor Callely's mobile information unit is no mere mobile home. It's a custom-made prefabricated office on wheels. The waiting room is equipped with a small radio to drown out the sounds of the confessions being heard in the consulting room through the partition. Constituents go in one door and emerge from another, unburdened and invigorated with a new hope. He designed it himself and spent about £5,000 having it constructed about ten years ago. The idea has since been copied by a number of other ambitious TDs. But none have managed quite so elaborate an operation as Callely's.

Representing a constituency of 100,000 people 'brings its complications,' Ivor admits.

'I have to meet their demands and their needs and what's in the wider public interest. Measuring it all up I would deal with thousands of my constituents' queries on an annual basis. You wouldn't be talking anything less than 5,000 a year.'

He is careful about giving away the tricks of his trade. 'There are sensitivities as to what I do work wise that I wouldn't want some of my colleagues to know. So I'm not going to spell it out. But somebody who is with me or somebody I meet will get a response from me extraordinarily quickly.

'My busiest clinic is on a Friday. I've had people with me on a Friday morning who said they got a letter from me before they got home. That's how quickly I work. When I was elected to the Dáil in 1989 I inherited a girl from the Fianna Fáil pool who is with me since. When I was elected to the Council in 1985 I was involved in the local tennis club. One of the members of the executive tennis club did some part-time typing. Those two girls are my mainstay. They know the way I think, what I'd do, they know when something comes in where I would go and how I'd do it. The three of us work as a great team.'

His office is open on Mondays, Wednesdays and Fridays. He has a clinic in the heart of his constituency on a Friday morning and an official clinic in his mobile information unit on Saturday morning. He also has a clinic on the northern side of the constituency once a month. He says he spends 'a fair amount of my week' on matters relating to the constituency.

'I love my work. I eat, drink and sleep it. I don't know how my wife and kids put up with me. But I get a particular pleasure when somebody comes to me who has been denied something. It galls me when I know that there's a need for that. I'll move mountains if I have to get that sorted.

'Whether it be a medical card or a hospital appointment, an enrolment in a school, whatever it may be. It's a beautiful feeling to get somebody something. When you can see their body language and their anxiety change.

'I think the stroke politics is dead and gone. I'm not interested in stroke politics. I'm not that vintage and that's not my modus operandi.'

So how does he explain all the pointless paper trails he generates in the full knowledge that his constituent can't be helped?

'In certain instances a person... you have to call it yourself... if I was talking to someone of your calibre who would understand the situation if I explained it to you, it would be okay. But if I was speaking to someone else, maybe what they want is for me to listen to what they have to say, and for me to be seen to make an attempt to assist them. And if that meant that I was getting a letter from a minister then they'd be happy. At least I'm seen to have gone through the process.'

And none of this has anything to do with shoring up your vote? He is unapologetic: 'Of course I do things to improve my vote.'

He also goes to almost as many funerals as a rural TD. 'People that I would know, people that have been in contact with me, if I see their death in the paper I would go to the funeral, or if I know some member of the family I would try to make an attempt to go.

'I don't think there's votes in going to funerals. But I do think that there are votes in getting a DART station or a leisure facility. The people who use the Clontarf DART station today, do they say Callely got it here? I don't know. The people who use the Westwood Leisure Centre, do they say I did that? I don't know. But what is clearly recognised is that I am a hard grafter. I'm up every morning at six and I don't go to bed most evenings until sometime around midnight. So I drive myself very hard. I drive myself seven days a week and I'm seen to be doing all the things in the constituency. That I'm not just focused on doing something when there are votes in it.'

Some of his political rivals would, naturally, disagree. They point to an incident some years ago in the constituency where they say Callely was caught red-handed trying to hunt with the hounds and run with the hare, attempting to garner votes from both sides of a development divide.

His apparent duplicity only came to light when a group of residents who were objecting to the development of the Shelbourne Football Club put in a freedom of information request for all the representations made to Dublin Corporation on the issue. They discovered that Callely, who had assured them that he was passing on their concerns to the planning officials, had, in fact, been at the forefront of pushing for the development in the first place.

The junior minister doesn't bat an eyelid when confronted by this. 'A football club approached me. I was happy to hear their represen-tation. I wrote in to the Corporation and said that I am led by the club to believe that this development is necessary to accommodate their plans. That went in. Their submission merited consideration of the planning authority so therefore you forward it in.

'When it became public knowledge, a group of residents on the other side of the Tolka wanted to object. They wrote me a letter indicating their concerns. I'm not going to cherrypick. They had some valid points. So what I did was send their communication to the planning authority, which I thought was the fairest thing to do. Knowing that the person that would be adjudicating would have both of my letters.

'What one person did was make political play of it. Here's Callely riding both horses. I favoured the club development. And I'm delighted to say that the planning managers on the technical planning merit of the application granted the permission. I met with the club. I never met with the residents. I wrote a letter back to the residents saying that I would bring their concerns to the attention of the planning officers. And that's what I did.

'Over the years I've gotten the most bizarre requests. And requests that you know are offside. Having said that, I believe that it's important to listen to people. There is usually an issue behind it.'

Kerry Independent TD Jackie Healy-Rae lights up at the mention of his constituency workload. 'Any day that I can sort out a fella's headage payment, if I can get a (hospital) bed for someone, if I can get a medical card, or put it right if it's gone wrong, or if I can get a road done that there's no hope of getting done, I'll definitely get more of a kickback out of it than the fella I'll do it for.

'Tis a sort of the sense of achievement, and of being able to get the thing done. That's what I think it's about. Because if you weren't interested in the result you couldn't be interested in fighting to get it sorted.'

Most politicians vigorously protest that they enjoy their constituency work. That it keeps them in touch with the issues on the ground and the problems faced by the ordinary citizenry. They are loathe to acknowledge (presumably in case a constituent should overhear) that they find the bulk of the work hugely tedious. For ambitious politicians it is regarded as a dubious means to a largely unconnected end.

It falls to retired politicians to come clean. The former Fine Gael minister Ivan Yates also says that he got 'a great kick' out of his constituency work. 'There is great job satisfaction in getting things done. It actually made it all worthwhile to see the smile on some-one's face.'

But what wearied him was the level of repeat business. 'It was the same people coming back with more and more problems.'

Yates freely admits that he milked the constituency clinic system for every last vote he could squeeze out of it.

'Safe seats don't come for free. You've got to work at them. I knew the rules. The whole clientelist system didn't bother me. That was the game. I played the game. I was quite happy to maximise the number of people at my clinics, to maximise my constituency correspondence.'

Yates set about building up his power base in a business-like manner. 'I had a target of meeting between fifty and seventy new people a week in the beginning. Austin Deasy told me that's how he got started against Eddie Collins in Waterford. He actually had to set a target, go into a pub, try and meet and personally get to know fifty to seventy new people a week.

'I was always on the edge of that number. It was an endless charm offensive. I was at that for twenty years. As you get better known you can always work on the basis that they know you. One of the difficulties I had was that I had a difficulty remembering names. It required quite a bit of skill to be personable and on top of your game as regards names. Someone might twig it. Or you'd call him boss, or whatever.'

Twenty years of glad-handing takes its toll. By the late 1990s Yates found that he no longer had the stomach for it.

'I found as time went by that it got to the level of prostitution. This business of knocking on doors throughout a summer when there was no election, canvassing for problems. I just felt that was a step too far. The rules of the game were changing. There was a new ratcheting up of competitiveness and I accepted that for what it was. But I felt that this was a prostitution of the politicians. I felt it was degraded.

'If there was a referendum campaign on I would hand out cards with my clinic times along with the leaflets. But at least there was some pretext for doing it. But what I call the "cold calling" I found distasteful. I felt uncomfortable doing it.

'Once the rigour and drive of holding your seat and the drive of knocking out a wage and a career is gone, what is the function of a TD? I found myself spending seventy per cent of my time being a community worker and a social worker. I had to be honest with myself, as I came to forty, and ask if this was what I wanted to do for the rest of my life. And the answer was "no way!"'

His Fine Gael colleague Alan Shatter has a reputation of being one of the few TDs in Leinster House who did not have to concern himself with the minor details of his constituents' lives. Other TDs envied him his affluent constituency of Dublin South, one of the few where they reckoned a high profile family law lawyer with a formidable reputation as a legislator could get elected without doing the donkey work. Nuala Fennell, Shatter's constituency and party colleague in Dublin South, admits that the constituency work was a doddle.

'The kind of constituency I was in was the kind of place where you'd get a phone call to say "would you ever get on to the French

embassy and stop that pâté de foie gras because it's very cruel."
That's not an exaggeration.'

There were pockets of poverty in the constituency and Fennell
used to do a clinic once every two months in a disadvantaged
estate. 'The party faithful used to tell me to stop wasting my time
because FG never got a vote there.' Indeed the one chance she had
of getting a vote was scuppered by a clever Sinn Féin manoeuvre.

'Those women had no phones and at that time they were way up
on the side of the mountain and it was pretty remote. I got a few
phones put into the estate and the very next day Sinn Féin had a
circular out claiming responsibility for them!

'I went to things in the constituency and I worked for people in
the constituency because I reckoned that you're elected for that. It's
part of the job description and it wasn't very arduous.'

Alan Shatter, who lost his seat in the Fine Gael wipe-out in
2002, protests that he actually did 'quite a lot' of constituency
work. 'I just didn't go around beating my drum about it,' he says.

He admits that he closed down his constituency clinic in 1989
after ten years of listening to his constituents' tales of woe. 'Around
the time of the mid-1980s you'd get the odd person who'd come
with a real problem. But because of the type of constituency it is,
most people with real problems would phone you or write to you.
They didn't need to meet you. And where they did, they didn't want
to come down to a constituency clinic and hang around. They'd
make an appointment.

'It reached the stage by 1986 or 1987 when it was quite apparent
that there was a group of people who didn't really have political
problems. They really needed a psychotherapist.

'They'd visit me every two or three weeks with all sorts of issues.
I even had one guy who felt it was his obligation to wander around
the streets of Rathfarnham to identify light bulbs that were broken
or weren't working so that he could bring me a list of them. It
became quite insane.

'So I stopped opening a clinic and distributed literature around
the constituency saying the clinic was closed but they could come
to me. And when it came to elderly people I would just call to their
homes on the drive into Leinster House or on the drive home in the
evening. There were quite a few elderly people over the years who
had their wills done free gratis.'

Some years ago Ruairi Quinn drove down to Cork on a Friday

evening for a political function. He had a policy of fitting in party work on occasions such as these.

He recalls: 'As we were leaving Connolly Hall, Finbar Cregan, who kind of ran Connolly Hall, and therefore ran the union and therefore ran the world, came over. "There's an old boy inside now and he wants five minutes of your time and Jaysus if you don't give it to him he will bad mouth Toddy all over the parish and we'll all be destroyed."'

In the interest of sparing the local deputy Toddy O'Sullivan from this ignomy, Quinn went to meet the supplicant. The weary Quinn was subjected to a meandering story involving a dead brother, a nephew who had married badly in his view and had also died, culminating in an allegation that city hall and a local firm of funeral undertakers were engaged in a sinister conspiracy to over-populate a burial plot. He had brought along a heap of paperwork to support his claims.

In the interests of getting home before dawn, Quinn eventually interrupted him with the précis: 'As I understand it there is a grave and in that grave amongst all the other people there is your grandfather, your brother and now his son – your late, recently-deceased nephew.'

He said 'that's right boy, you got it.'

The puzzled politician wondered what it was he wanted him to do. On this point his tormentor was perfectly clear: 'I want him out, he's in there without my permission!'

Taken aback by this turn of events, Quinn wondered if the elderly petitioner was perhaps worried that there would be no space for him should he shuffle off this mortal coil. He found himself enquiring politely: 'Is it a very small grave?' 'Oh no,' came the reply, 'tis a grand big grave. I just want that fucker out. He shouldn't be in there.'

Quinn went through the papers to double-check that no Labour Party colleague had committed to doing anything in the macabre case before embarking on a new strategy. He asked the irate Corkman if he was aware of the current cost of burials in the city. He was assured that he did, and that it was indeed a desperate price.

Quinn recalls: 'I said I can tell you now with authority that to exhume somebody costs you exactly 14.4 times as much.'

'He looked at me and said "I'll pay."'

At that Quinn gave up and did the unthinkable. He told Toddy's constituent that he was asking the impossible and that he couldn't help him. He appeared unphased. He said 'I thought as much. But seeing as you're here, I've another problem... .'

Much of the burden of the constituency workload is shouldered by politicians' long-suffering secretaries. They are as familiar with the intricacies of the social welfare code and the exact length and breadth of the housing lists as their bosses. But, occasionally, they too are flabbergasted by the demands that come their way.

One secretary to a high-profile politician recalls taking a call at 5pm one evening just a week before Christmas from a woman who was in some distress. The caller explained that she was ringing from the hard shoulder of the Naas dual-carriageway. Her car had broken down and she wasn't an AA member. She was in a pickle. So she rang Leinster House, asked for the office of a TD she thought looked kind on the TV, and explained her predicament. His secretary was non-plussed. What did the caller think the TD could do for her? The caller said she thought he would help her because she liked the cut of his jib on the news. She appeared to want the TD to drive out to the Naas dual-carriageway to tow her home. The secretary remembers: 'She was gobsmacked when I said no.'

More recently, the same secretary was contacted by a constituent in search of elephant manure. She had a problem with wild cats and was told that spreading elephant turds on the lawn would keep them at bay. On this occasion, the TD was able to help. Negotiations were opened with Dublin Zoo and the deal was done. The lady got her dung. We will never know for sure if the TD got her vote.

Tom Parlon, the PD Junior Minister elected to the Dáil for the first time in 2002, is still getting used to the constant demands that are made on his time. And space.

'If you only go to have a pee in the jacks there's a fellow come in beside you. That happens all the time. It's a great opportunity. They have your attention for two or three minutes. What can you do? You can't walk away. You're committed!

'I was dreading the prospect of doing these clinics. But I find people show up. They don't waste your time. The biggest problem is that you end up with a big book full of problems. You get a great feel for what the issues are out there. You know what the county council is doing. You know what the shortcomings in agriculture and education are. It is just a pure education and I think it's essential. The politician that doesn't do his clinics doesn't know what's going on.

'The downside is you spend so much time worrying about someone else's problem and the fact that you didn't do something for someone. And that someone is going to ring you back tomorrow. All that stuff is going though your head and bothering you. I might go down to Doheny's and have a few pints and meet a few people and forget all about it. But on the way home you're saying "fuck it, I'm after spending two hours there and I have forty phone calls to make."'

He opens his book and reads the results of a typical clinic.

'A lady in about planning permission for a site. Her husband has a small business doing guttering. They're building a house and they want to put the workshop beside the house.

'Another lady on about planning permission. A farmer who is an organic farmer looking for a grant with the local meat processing firm to process organic beef. He's already supplying a bakery with his organic milk.

'I had a guy who rang to say he's going to give me four complimentary tickets to my golf classic. He can't come and play his team.

'A delegation from a local school where a school leaves the baby and high infants off at two o'clock. School transport only brings them home at three o'clock, but the teachers say they are not babysitters. It's almost gone into civil war and I'm invited to go in and seek a solution.

'Four landowners and businessmen affected by the next phase of the motorway from Portlaoise down south. They were wondering about the rollover relief. Is it likely to happen in the next four years? Should they invest further in the farm?

'Two pharmacists in from Birr concerned about the deregulation. The new report is out. What's going to happen?

'A lady on about her son whose just gotten out of milk and he wants to get an extra suckler quota. What will happen with the CAP? A guy on about the local Teagasc office that is about to close as part of Teagasc policy and would I make representations to keep it open?'

How does he go about sorting out such a myriad of problems?

'I've had to build relationships with ministers. There is a degree of competition when you're a small junior party. What I find is that if you scratch my back I'll scratch yours.

'Any minister that gets on to me asking would I ever do such a thing, I make a big effort to see that it's done. And then when I need to go back and say what about this other thing I get my calls returned. There's an element of building up a bit of trust.

'We have a new county manager in Laois. The first opportunity I had I made an appointment to see him. I've made representations on his behalf to the Department of the Environment for his new sewage treatment scheme. And so on. And now when I want something I can call him.

'Likewise, I was at a function for a retired county engineer in Tullamore on Thursday night. I was the last to leave. I was chatting and having a few drinks with the engineers. You just have to build up the relationships. It takes an awful lot of time, but unless you do it, it won't happen for you.'

CHAPTER 8

Conventional Wisdom

'Fuck off back to Dublin!' – delegates at a Galway East
selection convention

There are thousands of party activists throughout the country. They are men and women who live and breathe politics, whose dedication to the cause knows few bounds.

Some see it as a route to a seat on the Council or, joy of joys, a shot at the Dáil. But most are content with the kudos their association with the local TD brings and are content to stay beavering away in the background.

They join the local cumann or branch of their party of choice, take the minutes at meetings and handle correspondence. They put up posters and knock on doors and spend polling day ferrying elderly widows to the polling station.

I recall a beautifully-groomed middle-aged widow at a PD dinner who told me she canvassed for Michael McDowell. She had been a member of the Dublin South-East branch of the party for many years. 'It's a marvellous hobby,' she explained.

Others see it as a duty. They are committed party people who fervently believe that the well-being of their constituency – of the country – is utterly dependent on their getting their candidate into the Dáil.

For their troubles they get a few privileges. A day out in the Dáil Visitors' Bar once a year. An invite into the presence of their party leader at annual dinner and dances. At election campaign time they get a few drinks and a plate of curly sandwiches at the end of a hard canvass. They get grief and bunions, and the thrill of being part of a winning team or the character-building experience of sharing a humiliating defeat. Some of the rewards are more tangible. If they back the right horse, they can get a nice little earner out of it. A seat on a State board that carries considerable status and a modest stipend. Or perhaps a place on the visiting committee of a prison located at the absolute other end of the country in order to maximise the generous mileage expenses.

Fine Gael TD Jim O'Keeffe undertook an investigation of the composition and role of Prison Visiting Committees in 2003. Requests for information under the Freedom of Information yielded a massive volume of petitions to the Minister for Justice to have party hacks appointed to these visiting committees. It is clear from these letters that the only qualification required for these posts is dedication to the party or devotion to a deputy. The sheer level of political industry devoted to getting loyal hacks on to one of these committees was staggering. I put the box containing four years' worth of this craven correspondence on my bathroom scales. It weighed in at just over a stone.

Party activists are intensely political people, but their access to the levers of power is limited. They are largely forced to sit in the stands while the power games are played out on the field of dreams by the few brave and bold enough to put their names on the ballot sheet. The only time they get to step into the limelight is at selection conventions. They may not be the players, but they can be the team selectors. It's a role that is jealously guarded. The frequent attempts by party headquarters to dilute it are fiercely resisted.

Back at headquarters, party organisers regard the constituency organisations with a mixture of fear, exasperation and despair. Some constituencies are run by organisation overlords, Svengali figures whose power extends into every branch or cumann. In some cases, old enmities can kill off promising careers at birth.

In Waterford, one young political hopeful found his attempts to launch a political career blocked at every turn. Martin Cullen's grandfather, a former director of elections for the local Fianna Fáil strongman, fell out with the party in a bitter row over his candidate's successor. Cullen's father subsequently won a seat as an Independent on Waterford City Council. Cullen longed to return to the fold, and put out feelers that he wanted to join Fianna Fáil in the early 1980s.

'You have to be accepted into a cumann and I couldn't find a cumann that would accept me. There was no welcome on the mat. I suppose some of them thought I might be a threat to a few local councillors. I wasn't even thinking in terms of national politics at that stage.

'The indications were that it would not be something that would be easily achieved. In the end I decided I didn't want to go some place where a whole group of people didn't want me.'

In many constituencies, it is the long-serving TD who pulls all the strings. This is the most dangerous scenario for party headquarters. The inherent paranoia of the political game means that even the most secure TDs get jittery at the prospect of inviting an ambitious colleague to join them on the party ticket. The core party vote is a finite commodity. A talented, hard-working party colleague would put him in clear and present danger. Better to find a mediocre also-ran, who might manage to mop up the core vote in the other end of the constituency and be eliminated early enough to bequeath his second preferences en bloc on the day of the count.

In recent years the culture has been challenged. The party bosses are exerting even more pressure.

Jim McDaid almost did himself an injury in his efforts to help Cecilia Keaveney win a by-election in his constituency in 1996. In 2002, long-standing Fianna Fáil TD GV Wright was forced to be so generous to his running mate Jim Glennon that the newcomer actually out-polled him in Dublin North. The main motivation in running such extraordinary risks with their power bases is the carrot of ministerial preferment. Or at the very least, the chance to become the chair of a Dáil committee. The flip side of that coin is that the failure to pull in a running mate can cost a TD dearly.

A TD who is perceived to have been less than supportive of the party strategy in their constituency will be left to rot on the backbenches while colleagues they regard as less talented are presented with their ministerial stripes.

Fianna Fáil garnered their best election result in the country in the Carlow-Kilkenny constituency in the 2002 general election, winning three out of the four available seats with fifty per cent of the first preferences cast.

Liam Aylward had toed the party line to get MJ Nolan returned to the Dáil after a gap of five years. John McGuinness, who narrowly beat Nolan to the fourth seat in 1997, was not as enthusiastic. Party headquarters took a particularly dim view of his attempts to campaign for votes in the Carlow side of the constituency, Nolan's allotted bailiwick. When the dust settled, Aylward was duly appointed Minister of State at the Department of Agriculture and Food. The former laboratory technician took responsibility for the animal health, welfare and customer service briefs. John McGuinness, a company director in the real world, was left to stew in his own juices on the government backbenches. Like a severed head stuck on a railing in the town square, his plight serves as a powerful reminder to all who pass that there is a terrible price to be paid for insubordination.

While this carrot and stick approach can be a powerful motivator in encouraging sitting TDs to back strong running mates and divvy out a chunk of their vote, sometimes the stomach-churning insecurity is so great that a TD will risk political purdah rather than open the door to a potential challenger. Five years in the wilderness of the backbenches on €80,000 per annum plus expenses may well be better than five years teaching geography to insolent teenagers on half the salary and none of the perks.

In recent years party bosses have moved to neuter the power of Dáil deputies in selecting their running mates. The traditional Fianna Fáil convention format where the sitting TD was automatically re-selected is a thing of the past. Now TDs have to contest the convention themselves. As one party mandarin explained: 'That gives them less time to make mischief. Not all TDs are like that but some are absolute blackguards for it.'

In the last election some Fianna Fáil chiefs believe rightly or wrongly that Brian Lenihan pulled a fast one on them by holding his constituency convention earlier than anywhere else. Deirdre Doherty Ryan was selected to be his running mate. She had been elected to Fingal County Council in 1997. The redrawing of the constituency boundaries lost her a lot of ground and she polled just 2,300 first preferences.

'Brian Lenihan got away with a lot,' is how one Fianna Fáil insider read it. 'Deirdre Doherty Ryan is a nice lady but she didn't have a hope. We were sold a pup. At the time he had his convention we didn't rate Dublin West as a constituency that we were in play in. As the months went by we realised we were in play in every constituency. And by then it was too late.'

In Dublin South-West, Brian's brother Conor was dealing with what he regarded as unfair competition from his running mate, long-standing councillor Charlie O'Connor.

Fianna Fáil headquarters were determined to get O'Connor elected. As one campaign worker recalled: 'The very heavy intervention from Mount Street (HQ) drove Conor Lenihan insane.' On the eve of polling day leaflets imploring the electorate to give their number one preference to Charlie O'Connor, signed by the Taoiseach, were dropped into strategic locations in the constituency.

For Lenihan, this was the last straw. He felt he had played his part in the two-candidate strategy and was now being taken for a chump. He was so incensed when he learned of this development that he angrily sought out an associate of O'Connor's director of elections. A frank exchange of views followed. In the heat of the campaign, no offence was taken. In the event, both Lenihan and O'Connor got elected, registering the highest vote swing to the party in the country in that election.

The Dublin West slip-up was a rarity in Election 2002, which Fianna Fáil chiefs regard proudly as 'the most professional and interventionist general election campaign ever mounted.' In the main, constituency conventions were carefully managed. The party strategy was ruthlessly imposed. Every constituency was vigorously polled so that by the time it came to call a selection convention, headquarters knew exactly which candidates had a chance of getting elected and what mix of candidates would maximise the party vote. Unfortunately, their moles in the constituency organisations were indicating that the convention delegates would have other ideas. As these are the foot soldiers who would be expected to wear out shoe leather on the campaign trial, their views could not just be summarily dismissed. But neither could they be allowed run roughshod over years of meticulous polling and planning. If cajoling has failed, the only hope of thwarting the delegates' intentions is to cap the convention. While three candidates will eventually run, the delegates are told that they may only select two.

In some places that didn't work very well. In Tipperary North the Defence Minister Michael Smith went along with the strategy, only to endure the humiliation of deselecting himself. Maire Hoctor and Tom Harrington were selected to fly the Fianna Fáil flag. The polls showed that Hoctor and Smith had the best chance of taking two Fianna Fáil seats. One Fianna Fáil handler later revealed: 'I couldn't tell you the grief we had to get Harrington off the ticket.'

The party's national executive is the governing body. Under the party rules, it has the power to deselect any candidate that is selected at a convention – or add any candidate to the ticket if they failed to get the support of enough of the delegates on the night. The danger is that a candidate who is deselected may decide to run as an Independent candidate – and take the rump of support that got him through the convention with him.

So, a lot of time is devoted to persuading candidates to step down voluntarily. 'You meet him. And you talk to his wife. And you listen to loads of shit. And sometimes people are reasonable. But not always.'

Harrington would not budge and was deselected. Headquarters held their breath but he didn't run as an Independent.

The Galway East constituency was a particularly hairy affair. The constituency boasts a very independent-minded old-school Fianna Fáil organisation. For party headquarters it was very frustrating. The Fianna Fáil core vote was massive yet the results on the ground did not reflect it.

The convention was to be chaired by Michael Smith. Fianna Fáil General Secretary Martin Mackin and the party's political organiser John Mullen accompanied the veteran minister into battle.

This is one account of what transpired: 'It was held in the Temperance Hall in Loughrea and never was a place more in-appropriately named. It was the most intemperate place on earth. They were used to selecting four candidates themselves. Michael Smith was saying things like "I'm just the messenger now from the national executive". All you could hear was this rumble, rumble, rumble from the crowd. They were all spoiling for a fight. You could cut the atmosphere with a knife.

'Then he said it: "I'm here to select... two candidates". The place went wild. 500 people roaring. Shouts of "fuck off back to Dublin". The local journalists were all sitting at a little bench like a school bench. They were all laughing their heads off.

'We thought we were literally going to have to go out the back door with the hillbilly music playing in the background. "Fuck off back to Dublin!" In the end we told them we had to have a special consultation. And then we told them they could select three. That led to more roaring. A lot of it was stoked up by Paddy McHugh and his people.'

'We agreed to select three. There was absolute war. Mayhem. But we calmed it down. There was a whole load of people on the ticket. It went right down to the absolute wire and Paddy McHugh was pipped by about two votes. He lost fair and square.'

Of course, all the candidates had earlier signed the party pledge declaring that they wouldn't run on an Independent ticket. Why do they bother? 'It's meant to exert some moral pressure. And it also allows party HQ to say "what kind of a person is this? A person who signs a solemn pledge in front of the organisation and then breaks it with impunity.'"

Paddy McHugh ran as an Independent and was elected to the Dáil with 7,786 first preferences, beating Fianna Fáil's Michael Kitt to the fourth seat.

CHAPTER 9

The Day of Reckoning

'Just for a second I thought "there's going to be a mill here!"' –
Tom Parlon

T his author understood the rewards of having connections with the Fianna Fáil organisation from a very young age. In an audacious combination of cronyism and nepotism, the future chairman of the Fianna Fáil Listowel comhairle ceanntair offered me the position of personation agent for the party at the polling station in Knockalougha National School. At thirteen, a tenner and the thrill of a close encounter of the third kind with the electoral process seemed like an exceptionally good deal. Thanks Dad.

Knockalougha National School had officially closed its doors to schoolchildren about ten years previously. For polling day it was heated, as it had been during decades of school days, with a big open turf fire.

I remember looking up personation in my dictionary. According to my Collins Concise English Dictionary, personation is the assumption of another person's identity with intent to deceive. I was solemnly told that as a personation agent my job was to ensure that no Fine Gael or Labour supporter attempted to vote illegally using someone else's name. It was not entirely clear what I should do if a Fianna Fáil supporter were to request a half-dozen ballot papers.

In order to ensure that everything was above board, everyone who voted was to be marked off my register. Of course my real raison d'être was to supply the local constituency organisation with a list of those who voted so that the tallymen could identify the party loyalists from the turncoats when that box was opened at the count centre the next day. It was only upon reading *The Boss* by Peter Murtagh and Joe Joyce years later that I realised that my spell as personation agent in Knockalougha coincided with the most infamous allegations of double voting in Irish electoral history.

Pat O'Connor, a solicitor and election agent for Charlie Haughey, was accused of attempting to vote in two different polling stations in the same constituency. So were a number of members of his family. Some of them were even formally challenged by personation agents. No-one had told me that I apparently had it within my power to demand that a prospective voter take an oath on a bible along the lines of: 'I swear by Almighty God that I am the same person as the person whose name appears as X on the register of electors now in force for the constituency of Kerry North and that I have not already voted at this election and that I had attained the age of eighteen years on the date of coming into force of this register.'

Efforts to keep the allegation out of the news until the polls were closed involved Fianna Fáil activists attempting to buy up all available copies of the *Evening Herald* on sale in the constituency. It has also been suggested that a bicycle thrown into a generator caused a power cut just as the six o'clock news was about to be broadcast.

The case against the O'Connors eventually collapsed when the prosecution failed to prove that they had actually voted twice (although it was clear that they had actually requested ballot papers twice). The main player in the drama was, however, known as Pat O'Connor Pat O'Connor for the rest of his days.

As it turned out, I was woefully poorly qualified for my position, so there was no danger of such a high drama stand-off in Knockalougha. I knew most of the electorate to see, but could put a name on very few of them. Thankfully, the presiding officer seemed to know everyone and I simply marked off my electoral register after the presiding officer had done his. There were fewer than 100 people on the electoral register for Knockalougha. It was a slow day.

Another former personation agent described how he operated a method of establishing who voted for whom during his day at a quiet polling station. He put a fresh sheet of paper on the shelf in the polling booth after each voter had voted. Voters invariably put their ballot papers on top of this white sheet. The indentations left behind meant that there was no such thing as a secret ballot in that polling station. It's not clear whether this was done out of boredom or was encouraged by the grown-ups as a way of getting the earliest possible tally.

Ironically, my abiding memory of that day was the extraordinary ceremony that surrounded the opening of the package with the ballot papers in the morning, and the sealing of the ballot box with string and wax and the official seal once the polls closed.

Of course, the reality is that in a country polling station the politics of the vast majority of those who roll in to mark their ballot papers is an open secret. The local party workers ensure that the electoral register is kept bang up to date. As the hardened party faithful would vote for their party's donkey before they'd give the nod to the other party's Jack Kennedy, it is often second or third preferences that are up for grabs. Special favours that should have steered a stray preference their way are noted. Efforts are made to ensure that the offspring of families with strong political allegiances are eligible to vote the second they turn eighteen.

The blow-ins and the few local political floozies are well known. Once the box is opened at the count centre and the tallymen do their thing, the sincerity or otherwise of doorstep assurances are instantly unmasked.

The extent to which identities are purloined for voting purposes is one of the great unspoken features of the Irish political system. It is ludicrously easy to do, particularly in city constituencies. There are few safeguards in place to prevent it and little appetite among the main political parties to tighten up the rules. With our low voter turnouts, by polling day the country is awash with polling cards that are not destined to be used. Given that it can take prolonged letter-writing campaigns and endless phone calls to eke one single vote out of a constituency clinic, the notion that thousands of votes are never cast is infuriating to your average candidate.

Sometimes it is over-enthusiastic supporters who take it upon themselves to go the extra mile – and vote an extra time – for their candidates. In other instances, there are organised campaigns to subvert the electoral process.

A friend, let's call him Harry, described one such campaign back in the 1970s. A student at University College Galway, Harry was a 'Stickie', an active member of Official Sinn Féin. He recalls the thrill of multiple voting in two elections during that period. Galway, as a student city, was ideal territory for rampant personation. Canvassers knocking on doors in the city's flatland were instructed to scan the hall tables in the communal areas for abandoned polling cards. By the eve of polling day, organisers had quite a stash. Because most members of the student body were known to the activists, it was easy to figure out which polling cards could be used undetected.

The borderline cases were put into a separate pile – to be used within an hour of the polls opening and before any self-respecting student was out of the scratcher.

Harry recalls a gang of about ten volunteers meeting up in a flat on the night before polling day in 1977. The polling cards were divvied out and instructions issued as to what time the cards should be used.

'Somebody was to drive us around the polling stations and tell us where we were and who we were supposed to be,' Harry recalls. Their greatest fear was that they would be spotted making a number of entrances to a given polling station by the party hacks stationed outside the doors.

'Although, to a certain extent, we had a good cover. The kind of people Fianna Fáil and Fine Gael had manning the polling stations at that time thought all students looked alike. As far as they were concerned, we were all long-haired layabouts and they paid us little or no heed.'

Just in case they might be spotted, they would try and vote a number of times in the same station – what Harry called 'single-entry multiple-voting' – during the tea-time rush. 'I remember managing to vote three times in the same polling station without ever leaving it. We felt it was safer than trying to run the gauntlet of the lads outside three separate times.'

As the day wore on it became clear that they were not the only party at it. 'I particularly remember running into a fella I knew was a Fine Gael supporter at more than one polling station.'

By the time he used his own vote – you always kept your own polling card till last in case you lost your nerve – Harry reckons he had cast a ballot paper at least twelve times.

He remains unrepentant. 'We had no qualms about it. Part of it was the buzz of getting away with something illegal. It was great craic.'

One young man was apprehended attempting to vote using a name that was not on his birth certificate that day. Word of the arrest swept through the personating classes and everyone raced to the pub that night wondering who had been caught. Everyone assumed it would be a 'Stickie'. It transpired that it was a Fine Gael supporter. He left the country for the summer and the summons was never served. He is now a very respectable lawyer.

One Dublin TD describes how a constituency rival's election agent organised people to canvass working class areas. If they were told the residents weren't going to vote, they asked for their polling cards. They targeted busy polling stations where the officials were simply too busy to notice if faces seemed strangely familiar.

'During the most busy time fellas would go in, vote, come out and change their jackets, and go in and vote again,' according to this TD.

After the lull of election day, the candidate and their supporters must brace themselves for the emotional rollercoaster ride that is the count.

The Government's plans to introduce electronic voting was met with howls of protest from the very people with the least to gain from the single transferable vote's agonisingly slow progress through an army of counters' fingers under the old system. While candidates complain bitterly about the trauma of the long wait, the truth is that the day of the traditional count is the jamboree of the Irish political system. Exhausted from the weeks, and sometimes months, of pounding the pavements, emotionally drained from the highs and lows of the campaign trial, and burdened with a whole new set of promises to keep, candidates have taken to inventing diversions to keep themselves occupied and away from the count centre until the tallymen can put them straight about their likely fate.

For many, the loss of a seat, or the failure to gain one, is as deeply shocking as a death in the family. If they must grieve in public, they prefer to cry alone. But there is no shortage of takers for the advance party. Because, as every political animal knows, nothing can match the frisson of pent-up excitement that runs through a hall when the wax seal on the first tin box is cracked open and all those little creased ballot papers come tumbling forth.

As more and more boxes are opened, and the neat bundles of fifty votes start to stack up, the powerful cocktail of agony and ecstasy that swirls around a count centre in a volatile constituency can be intoxicating.

Tom Parlon rates the day of the count after the 2002 general election as one of the best of his life – even if it did almost erupt into violence. He can still hear the ear-splitting cheer that rose from Brian Cowen's entourage when the returning officer announced that he had topped the poll.

'When I came in second, my crowd just went berserk. Then they announced that Cowen had been elected and his crowd gave another almighty roar. There was real passion in it.

'My crowd were looking at them and just for a second I thought "there's going to be a mill here!" Genuinely. There was that sort of rawness about it.' Parlon instinctively moved to defuse the situation. 'I started to clap. Two more joined in. And then others joined in. But just for a second it was that intense. You wouldn't know if all hell was going to break loose.'

While the first-past-the-post system in Britain sees MPs elected with massive margins, the single transferable vote system can see seats won and lost on the basis of a handful of votes. Such scenarios inevitably end in recounts. And that's when the real fun begins. Political veteran Micheál Martin reckons he learnt more about the single transferable vote system during three long, tense days of counting and recounting the votes in his Cork South-Central constituency in May 2002 as he battled to save the seat of his colleague John Dennehy.

'It was an awful, awful three days. I learned more about Proportional Representation than I'll ever learn again. It was devastating for John to lose by two votes. We gathered the troops and decided to be in there at ten the following morning.

'The human resources that have to go into a recount are incredible. The key thing is that you need at least twenty experienced people who can spot a problem in a ballot paper. Kathy Sinnott's people weren't as experienced on the first recount but by the time the whole thing ended they were, if anything, more robust than us.

'When Kathy saw me inside in the square pen looking at the perforations, she said this is a terrible thing he is doing. She took it personally. But I was thinking of having to go back to the boss and explain this mess.'

Every ballot paper must be stamped by an election official before it is handed to a voter to be cast. If for some reason the stamp didn't register the vote is declared invalid.

By all accounts the rows that raged over the depth and width of indentations in Cork South-Central left the tales of the hanging chads of Florida in the shade. A magnifying glass was produced for the second recount. Pristine ballot papers were held up to the light as the candidates and their agents desperately chased the shadow of an indentation of a stamp.

The other common error is that the bundles of fifty turn out to be one short or have one too many. Martin was warned about this by a contact who had run counts in the past. 'He said watch out for the fifty-ones and the forty-nines.'

The turning point came when they discovered that a bundle of fifty votes for John Dennehy actually contained fifty-four votes. He duly became the last member of the twenty-ninth Dáil to be declared elected. By just six votes.

While just four mislaid votes proved to be crucial to Dennehy, there was one other occasion when counters managed to mislay an entire ballot box full of votes.

Tom Nolan, a former chairman of Offaly County Council, is an exiled member of the Nolan political dynasty of Carlow. He will never forget the count in the Carlow-Kilkenny constituency in 1981, when his father, a staunch Haughey-ite, was beating his Fianna Fáil colleague Jim Gibbons by 180 votes on the final count. It was almost an exact reversal of the final count twenty years previously, when Gibbons beat Tom Nolan by a similar margin. At the time, Nolan walked away. It was a Fianna Fáil seat. But two decades later, Gibbons was not going to let go so gently.

The way Tom Nolan Jnr remembers it, 'Jim Gibbons walked in at three in the morning and demanded a recount.'

Tom had a row with his father. Their tallymen suspected that something was up. Tom agreed and tried to convince his reluctant father that they needed to alert the party leader. He eventually persuaded his father to part with Charlie Haughey's home number. He rang Haughey and the man in Kinsealy sent in the troops. 'At eight o'clock on Monday morning there were senior counsels and junior counsels and there was every feckin' counsel you could think of down in Kilkenny.'

When the returning officer stepped up to the podium, Haughey's solicitor, none other than the man who would come to be known as Pat O'Connor Pat O'Connor, introduced himself as Minister Nolan's representative and demanded a full recount. The recount got underway. 'All the boxes were stacked up into a corner. When they were all taken down, the last box, which would have been the first box stacked, was the Rathanna box – and the seal was still intact.' Rathanna, as Tom Nolan explained, was a village 'at the bottom of Mount Leinster in Carlow, where Daddy and Mammy were born.'

His eyes still dance at the memory of the moment. 'The returning officer called us in and said "we're after finding an unopened box". I looked at the box and saw Rathanna on it and I let a yahoo out of me.

'We were told that all the boxes were opened. If we had demanded an inquiry into this there would have been very serious implications. There was virtual civil war between the camps at that stage. There was an added element because of the Haughey-Gibbons split. I told them I was going out to announce it then and there. I said there are 240 votes in that box and there are 230 of them for Tom Nolan.'

And so it was. 'Daddy is dead and Jim Gibbons is dead. It's all history now. But I can still see it. The box right in the angle.'

CHAPTER 10

By-election Bonanzas

'You just wouldn't believe what goes on' – *a Fianna Fáil insider*

In the pantheon of election stunts, one desperate last-ditch stroke has gained a special place in the cynical hearts of the Irish electorate. On the eve of the Dublin West by-election in May 1982, the Fianna Fáil Minister for the Environment, one Ray Burke, arranged to have some trees planted in a new housing estate in Clonsilla after canvassers reported residents' complaints about their lack of foliage. Two days later, when the returning officer confirmed that the Fianna Fáil candidate Eileen Lemass had suffered a shock defeat at the hands of a Fine Gael newcomer, the trees were uprooted and carted away.

(It's worth noting in passing here that the by-election itself was the result of another Fianna Fáil stroke. It was called to fill the seat vacated when Charlie Haughey, desperate to shore up his minority government in the Dáil, dispatched a Fine Gael TD, Dick Burke, to Brussels as EEC Commissioner.)

The minister's brief foray into the landscaping business is now little more than a footnote in a rap sheet that runs to several pages. In 2003, Ray Burke accepted the dubious honour of being the first ever Irish politician to be denounced as corrupt by the Planning and Payments Tribunal .

While the sheer breathtaking brazenness of the tree stunt marks it out, it was really no more than another example of the chicanery that comes of the crazed scramble for votes that by-elections inevitably unleash.

By-elections draw out all that is venal and unlovely in political life. The normal checks and balances that keep a constituency from boiling over into a seething mass of jealousy and rivalry are stripped away.

At national level, every by-election is seen as a crucial vote of confidence in the government or the party leader. If that party leader happens to be in government, no amount of taxpayers' money is too much to spend on securing their reputation.

In that 1983 by-election, along with the disappearing trees, the electorate of Dublin West were showered with largesse. On 22 April, despite the hair shirt times, the Minister for Finance announced a £45 million PRSI tax concession. The children's allowance increases which were due in July were brought forward and paid in May. Schools and sports centres were promised. A major US forklift plant was announced for Blanchardstown. There would be 2,000 more gardai, with an unspecified number of them to be sent to man the new garda stations promised for Dublin West. There was to be an action programme in crime prevention and a new legal aid clinic in Ballyfermot. On the final Sunday before polling day, mass-goers counted twenty-four members of the Oireachtas lined up outside Ballyfermot Church to plead for their votes.

Nevertheless, the government candidate failed to be returned to the Dáil.

Time and again, constituencies which have come in for the by-election treatment astound the politicians with their ingratitude. Since 1997, there have been a total of twelve by-elections. The government party has won just two of them.

One former Fianna Fáil advisor who worked on a number of by-election campaigns shudders at the memory. 'By-elections are the greatest waste of taxpayers' money in western society. You'd have a dictatorship if you had to run by-elections on a regular basis.'

The first hurdle that party bosses have to surmount when a by-election looms on the horizon is the stampede of ambitious local activists and councillors in pursuit of the nomination. The competition for a by-election nomination is exponentially more intense than the scramble for a nomination to run in a general election. They naturally see a by-election as a glorious opportunity, their one chance to make a stab at a Dáil seat with no sitting TD ahead of them to soak up the core vote.

'All of these people start positioning themselves before an election and you have to get them off the pitch. You just wouldn't believe what goes on,' our insider confides. 'The haggling is unbelievable. People want to get appointed to boards, they want school playgrounds tarred, or commitments on sewage schemes or whatever.

'Really you should take a steamroller to them, but you have to play along with them. Because of the way Fianna Fáil is organised, they control the cumainn. You couldn't go into the convention without knowing the outcome because you would get some hairy-assed man from the mountains who was put up just to upset the apple cart. So you have to guarantee the outcome before you start. By-elections are very tricky. Very expensive. They're just awful.'

Happily for the government party, the taxpayer picks up the vast bulk of the bill for these political jamborees.

'The first expense is buying off the ones who are on the pitch. They all believe that they can be Taoiseach. They all believe that if they get the mandate from the people they are as equally entitled to be Minister for Finance as Charlie McCreevy. They all believe that they are equal and that others are made more equal only by selection.

'I don't believe that they go into it just to mess things up. A lot of them go forward because they are talked into it by fellas who fire them up. Those people would be screwing up the system deliberately. But the candidates that emerge all believe they have the potential to be it.'

Which makes it all the more difficult to dissuade them. 'There is much soothing of brows and telling them that they're great fellas but that this isn't their turn. Then there are others who are quite resolute about what their price is to go. It's not unusual for their wives or brothers to be involved at this stage in this process.'

Once the candidate is chosen and the convention is strong-armed into doing the right thing, the organisers turn their attentions to the electorate.

Experienced organisers know that by-elections are less about making promises, and more about getting things to happen. As one Fianna Fáil insider with experience of a particularly frantic by-election in recent years wryly commented: 'Constituencies should kill off a TD in their own interests, because it is only in the run up to a by-election that things happen in extra-fast time, projects that are languishing get finished, projects get started that never would have started. If it's managed well by the constituency they can really reap the benefits.'

His job was to ensure that everything that could be done was done for the constituency in the four weeks in the run up to polling day.

'People identify to you what the issues are. You then go to the relevant Department and say "what's the story about such and such a project?" They might say that the money is there but the contracts haven't been signed or whatever. So you basically say "get your fuckin' finger out!"

'Nothing illegal happens. The Minister knows that this is a political priority. If it's do-able it should be done. Things are planned or promised and the only thing holding it up is people fluting around. When there's a by-election, those things get unlocked.'

Local TDs or ministers are most often given the job of Director of Elections. This can, of course, present even the most loyal party men and women with a serious conflict of interest. The better the candidate, the less enthusiasm the Directors of Elections is likely to drum up to secure their victory. They get the gig anyway to assuage local sensitivities. But in many cases the office is purely titular. Party HQ is careful to keep a beady eye on their directorship. A fleet of TDs and senators is drafted in from outside the constituency to police the canvassing arrangements. HQ is only too aware that in times of tensions in the party, canvassing teams can quietly go on strike. Or put in such a lacklustre performance on the doorsteps that they represent an electoral liability.

If a heave is underway against a party leader, a poor by-election result is almost certain to hasten his or her demise. When news of a double defeat in two Cork by-elections was relayed to Jack Lynch while on a visit to the United States, the wife of the Irish ambassador recalled his reaction. 'His face drained,' Elizabeth Shannon reported. 'He was pale and shaken. He told us that he could not believe his own beloved Cork could do this to him. It affected him deeply.'

Of course it was not his own beloved Cork, but his own beloved colleagues, that had let him down. As he took in the disastrous news, he intimated that he believed it was the end of his leadership of Fianna Fáil. He was right.

When the by-election in Tipperary South was set for June 2000, the knives were already out for the Fine Gael leader John Bruton. As one supporter of Bruton who was intimately involved in that campaign noted: 'Some people did nothing in that by-election in order to hasten the departure of John Bruton. But, unfortunately for them, Tom Hayes went within 500 votes of taking the seat.

'The vote was there to be won for the party if people had put in a bit of an effort. But the result in the ballot boxes in the areas that were assigned to some prominent members of the parliamentary party would indicate that they hadn't done much.'

As usual in by-election campaigns, high profile party figures were drafted into the constituency to jazz up the candidate's campaign. They were each 'given' a tranche of about 1,500 voters and warned to canvass them a couple of times. They were also to organise a leaflet drop through their letterboxes, make sure that the posters in their area were prominently displayed, and get their support out on the day of the election.

The party hadn't expected to do well in Clonmel, where the ultimately successful Independent candidate Seamus Healy was strong. However, when it emerged that the second-biggest party in the country had received exactly one vote in a particular ballot box in the town, tempers flared. The electoral area had been assigned to a veteran politico. Afterwards, Phil Hogan, the Fine Gael Director of Organisation, approached him and asked him if he had bought a drink for anyone in Clonmel during the campaign. He didn't respond.

John Bruton reshuffled his front bench the following month. While he didn't exact all-out vengeance for the attempt to oust him by stealth, he ensured that those who showed their loyalty were rewarded.

Niall Blaney is the father of Fianna Fáil by-electioneering. His political and organisational skills were legendary. Jackie Healy-Rae still has an old photograph of his hero and 'colossal friend' on the wall in his Leinster House office.

'He was one of the best organisers and the best motivator at times of elections that I thought I'd ever meet. We'd a crack team in charge of by-elections. So much so that I fearlessly say to you that in the parties I know now, including Fianna Fáil, none of them have a clue about running a by-election.

'We had a system going of canvassing everything in the wide earthly world. We put certain people in charge of strategic key spots where we didn't win the vote the last time out. To the areas where we wouldn't have a big vote we'd always pay particular attention.'

The idea was to fight tooth and nail for every last vote. Jackie recalls canvassing in a by-election in Galway West for Máire Geoghegan-Quinn. He had targeted one lady who insisted she wasn't going to vote for anybody. On polling day he decided to have one last go and went out to her little white-washed farmhouse. She didn't commit to voting for the Fianna Fáil candidate but was willing to accept a lift to the polling station.

'She was very slow getting into the car. After a good struggle to get her in, didn't a hen start craking after laying an egg inside up on a high fence. The poor lady started shouting "cairce, cairce, cairce!" She wasn't going to go to vote until the egg would be taken out of the nest.

'I had to go out and go up the ditch and get the egg. She had to get out of the car, open the door, and put the egg into a basin of eggs up on the dresser. When we got out of the car at the polling booth, she said, "seeing that you did for me with the egg, I'm going to vote openly for Máire Geoghegan-Quinn". I'm perfectly convinced that that's the way I got that vote. You go every inch of the way.'

Blaney was a hard task-master and no messing was allowed on his beat. Healy-Rae recalls another day on that by-election campaign when Blaney asked Bobby Molloy for the register he had checked on the canvass that day. Molloy demurred and said he had given it to someone else on the canvass.

'He queried him very tightly. Blaney said "Bobby what you'll do now is pack your bags, get out of the campaign and go back to where you were yesterday."'

'Now I didn't know where he was yesterday. But Jesus, weren't there races in Galway. And didn't Molloy escape for the day and Blaney found out. He sent him home and wouldn't let him back. He sent a new team the following day. That's the way he did it. I saw him do several things like that.'

Jackie brought a touch of razzmatazz to the campaign trails, specialising in grand finales with torch-lit rallies and spectacular episodes of pyromania. He is misty-eyed about a particularly hard-fought campaign in Galway back in the 1980s: 'We used to have sods of turf and the pikes and all that stuff. But what we did in Galway was I went flying around the square with a can of petrol. One of the lads at the other end put a match to it and up went the whole square. We did it in Mallow as well. That was the final rally. When people would be stunned into silence.'

CHAPTER 11

Leinster House

'It's the most exclusive club in Ireland' – Joe O'Toole

The most taxing job of the gardai assigned to stand sentry at the Kildare Street gates of Leinster House is redirecting tourists to the National Library to their right. Or the National Museum to their left. If approaching from the Merrion Square side, a startling number of taxi drivers mistake the nearby Government Buildings for the Dáil.

The mix-up is understandable. The meeting place for the houses of parliament is modest by international standards. It doesn't help that the sweeping Leinster Lawn which until recently graced the Merrion Square façade has been tarmacadamed over for use as a car park.

Leinster House was built as a town house for James Fitzgerald, the twentieth Earl of Kildare, in 1745. It was sold to the Royal Dublin Society in 1815 and made over to the State in 1924.

The gates at both entrances are kept open while the Dáil is sitting, a symbolic gesture underpinned by the constitutional requirement that the houses of the Oireachtas (an old Irish word for general meeting which has been adapted to mean parliament) meet in public.

In practice, members of the public are only allowed to pass through them if they meet strictly-applied criteria. Only serving and former TDs and senators, their staff, civil servants attached to

Leinster House, cleaners, caterers, gardai and a small number of journalists with permanent resident visas can swan past the eagle-eyed
ushers who guard the gates. Others can only gain access if invited by
a member of the Oireachtas and supplied with a visitor's pass.

On sitting days the corridors of Leinster House are thronged
with gaggles of visitors. It's particularly popular with the very young
and the very old who avail of a free tour guided by a knowledgeable
usher. They are shown the original marble fireplaces, the Waterford
Glass chandeliers, the beautifully-restored old ballroom that now
houses the Seanad, and the modified lecture theatre that serves as
the Dáil chamber.

The walls are packed with portraits of all the national heroes
before and since Independence. Life-size portraits of former
taoisigh have pride of place, while pictures of the former cathaoirleach of the Seanad are hung along the corridor that links the two
chambers. Some years ago it was agreed that the former Leaders of
the Seanad would also have their photographs placed on the wall
for posterity. It was done, I'm reliably informed, at the insistence of
one Donie Cassidy, the then Leader of the Seanad.

The traditional final stop on the tour is the Visitors' Bar, where
they can expect a round of refreshments on the tab of their
constituency representative. The Visitors' Bar is situated around the
corner from the Dáil chamber. A nifty TD could make it from
her gin and tonic to her seat for a vote in about twenty seconds.
Not many do anymore. The Visitors' Bar has become a lonesome
hostelry. It is hopping at mid-morning when the Dáil staff break for
their elevenses and the Dáil reporters and political correspondents
straggle in for their requisite coffee and scones after the Order of
Business. Business might pick up again for a leaving do for a Dáil
secretary, and can get quite exhilaratingly packed on a Wednesday
night if some hint of political moving and shaking is on the cards.

Other than that it is frequented by the constituency delegations
– complete with crates of Coke and bundles of straws if it's a school
group, or rounds of brandy and ports if a TD is entertaining a gang
of senior citizens. The only feature that sets it apart from the
many other hotel bars in the vicinity are the extra strong mints and
packets of Anadin prominently displayed for sale by the till.

The Visitors' Bar backs onto the Members' Bar, which is reported
to be its architectural twin. We have to take their word for it
because there have been very few occasions when mere mortals got

in to that secret garden to have a peek. The bar staff, some of the most canny political observers in the country, are tragically discreet about the foibles of their clientele.

Even the usually expansive Senator Joe O'Toole almost has palpitations at a casual inquiry about the place.

'The Members' Bar? Nobody talks about what goes on in there. It's a rule!' I only wondered if it was a direct copy of the Visitors' Bar. 'I have no idea,' said a man who is no stranger to both establishments, 'It's a rule. You never speak about what goes on in there. How do you know I've ever been in the Members' Bar?!'

'It's a clubby comfort zone. It's the haven, it's the escape. It's like the hare running into the escape. That's the Members' Bar. It's the most exclusive club in Ireland.'

Dáil folklore has it that there were two great revolutions in the Members' Bar. The first cultural revolution – fiercely resisted – was the introduction of tea and coffee. People are fuzzy about the details but most agree that the great outrage occurred about twenty-five years ago. O'Toole wasn't around then but he's heard the stories. 'There was a huge opposition to it. The people who regularly frequented the Members' Bar said this was just an opportunity for gobshites to come in in the middle of the day to check on who was drinking. Then, of course, they ended up serving sandwiches. There were nearly calls for people's resignations!'

TDs and Senators who regularly frequent the Dáil bars have formed themselves into an unofficial grouping known as the 'bar lobby'. Although dominated by Fianna Fáil members, it's always prided itself on its ecumenicist principles. Inside those walls, party loyalty lines blur. What sets them apart from the rest of us is what bonds the brotherhood in the privacy of their clubhouse.

The sisterhood never really gained a firm foothold. Women would be welcomed into the company but have never been considered full members of this laddish lobby. Back in the 1970s and even the 1980s, the bar lobby had dozens in its ranks and no heave could hope to succeed without the backing of its influential members. But that's all changed utterly now. The core of the bar lobby numbers no more than a dozen hardy annuals. It still has a few influential members, not least the man tipped to be a future Taoiseach, Brian Cowen.

But one thing hasn't changed. The only people who are excluded in the Members' Bar are the deputies who are slow to buy their drink. As one veteran put it: 'It's like it says in the catechism. It's an indelible mark. You can never buy it back!'

One man who bore this indelible mark was the late former-Taoiseach Jack Lynch. Back around the time of the Arms Crisis in the early 1970s, he entered the bar just before the Christmas recess to find a half-dozen of his finest deputies lined up along the counter sipping what appeared to be coffees. He remarked that everyone was very well behaved for the festive season. One of them offered the party leader a drink and he graciously accepted a glass of whiskey. He then asked the barman to put up 'the same again'. His company interpreted this as an act of opportunism on the part of a cheapskate looking for a very cheap round. The look on his face when the barman came along and poured a measure of whiskey into each coffee confirmed their suspicions.

Gerry Crowley, a deputy representing the Cork East constituency, took it one step further.

'You can't beat a Mallow,' he said conversationally.

'A Mallow?' wondered Lynch.

'Fortified coffee,' Crowley replied with a straight face.

To this day, new deputies looking for a morning pick-me-up quickly learn to ask the Dáil bar staff for a bustling market town in east Cork.

Noel Davern, the doyen of the bar lobby, complains that the craic is gone out of the place now. 'It's politically incorrect now to be taking drink. Or to be seen to be taking drink. There are very few characters now. They see themselves as perfect. Or think that they need to be perfect. So they can't take a drink. I don't think the public are like that. I think the public would rather see a fella who knows what's happening on the ground enjoying himself and having a drink. But they don't do it anymore.'

Apart from Davern and Cowen, the other card-carrying members of the lobby include ministers John O'Donoghue and Michael Smith, northsiders GV Wright and Dermot Fitzpatrick, country deputies Liam Aylward and John Cregan and, representing the Senate, Eddie Bohan.

The night the Arms Crisis came to a head, Brian Lenihan Snr bumped into Noel Davern. The stifling stress in Leinster House was getting to him. 'Come on,' he said, 'we'll go for a drink and get out of here.'

At the time the politicians' home from home away from the Dáil was The Junction on Kevin Street, where you could always be guaranteed a few pints after a late sitting in Leinster House, and eat curry with spoons from the place next door on the way home. It was here that Davern heard the shocking news that ministers were about to be sacked.

Shortly after that night, the Sinn Féin party split and one half moved their office to Kevin Street, right beside the pub. The Garda Special Branch were staking out the new office so after-hours drinking became a more complicated affair and TDs drifted away from a once-favoured hostelry.

Another favourite watering hole for Fianna Fáil politicians was Bill Ahern's on Fleet Street, where the Tipperary proprietor would make his patrons generous country ham sandwiches to keep hunger at bay and thirst at a maximum.

Joe Groome, a member of the Fianna Fáil National Executive, had a residents-only dispense bar in his hotel on Parnell Street, but that too became a place where people gathered.

In more recent years, Fine Gaelers have been left bereft by the sale of Dessie Hynes's fine establishment on Baggot Street, the scene of much banter, plotting, and, if the stories are to be believed, illicit liaisons over the years.

It is indeed ironic that it is only now, in the wake of new laws that extended the opening hours of pubs, that our legislators appear to have given up their quest for the perfect late night lock-in.

CHAPTER 12

A Safe Port

'There's great freedom there' – Billy Kelleher

S eanad Éireann has a most diverse range of members, in emotional as well as political and social terms. Every newly-elected Seanad is a patchwork quilt of political personalities. There are the smug half-dozen senators who keep getting re-elected by the university graduates; the pointy heads with personality. There are the smug lifers who keep getting nominated by the same public bodies and re-elected by the same well-serviced councillors. There are the raging-but-relieved former TDs who lost their seats in the general election and scraped back in having endured the ignominy of a bruising Seanad campaign. There are the very relieved former TDs who lost their seats in the general election, failed to win a Seanad seat, but got named as one of the Taoiseach's eleven nominees. There are the bright young things bristling with enthusiasm for the career they have just launched. And there are the laid-back politicos, with long Dáil careers now behind them, for whom the Seanad acts as a sort of decompression chamber to stave off the dreaded return to the real world.

There are sixty members in every Seanad, of whom six are elected by the graduates of Trinity College and the National Universities of Ireland, and another eleven are nominated by the Taoiseach of the day. This ensures that the government parties always have a majority in the Upper House. That leaves forty-three to be elected from five panels of candidates representing Culture and Education, Agriculture, Labour, Industry and Commerce and Public Administration, by an electorate composed of the 900 or so city and county councillors.

In order to stand, a Seanad hopeful must get a nomination from either their party or from the myriad of public bodies with nominating powers – some of which only come to life at the necessary moment every few years in order to perform this worthy duty.

For candidates still reeling from a devastating defeat in the Dáil election, the prospect of taking their shattered confidence on a national tour for a Seanad election campaign can be overwhelming. The Seanad campaign is a gruelling endurance test in which candidates clock up thousands of miles in a race against time to meet as many councillors as is humanely possible inside a month.

Some old soldiers speak of crying tears of exhaustion as they got lost for the twentieth time down a boreen in west Donegal or south Kerry. Others describe shaving in the toilets of pubs and petrol stations, stocking up on fresh shirts, socks and underwear in Dunnes Stores, waking up shivering in their car on a country road to nowhere.

The councillors hold court in their kitchens, listening as the candidates assure them of their bona fides, amused or engaged by their attempts to dredge up some local connection, their efforts to flatter their wives, to praise their baking, to make their mark, to get a firm number one vote or a possible number eight.

Most councillors vote along party lines. After that, they vote for the candidate that can be trusted to remember the good turn and keep them in the loop down the line.

One senator tells a (most likely apocryphal) story to illustrate the lengths to which Seanad hopefuls will go to secure a number one vote from a councillor.

When talk would turn to the greyhound bitch in the yard and the fine litter of pups she would be likely to have, according to this source, 'any decent aspirant senator would have to step up to the plate at that point to make an offer for the pups'.

One senator with an impressive electoral record is said to pile on the pounds in the run up to every Seanad election. 'He would have a quota of about eighty votes and he would try to take a full quota of councillors and their families out to dinner,' according to Seanad lore.

Senator Francie O'Brien, a farmer from County Monaghan, has retained his seat on the agricultural panel since 1989. His reputation for acquiring GAA tickets for councillors is legendary. Indeed, one colleague swears he has spotted him outside Barry's Hotel on All-Ireland day, purchasing tickets to pass on to a councillor and his entourage. This same senator is alleged to have picked up a hitch-hiker at Newlands Cross when driving to Kilkenny only to discover that his father was a councillor in Clare. He insisted on driving the young man to his door.

With so narrow an electoral base, many Seanad seats are won and lost on tiny fractions of votes. Once a candidate gets a nomination and succeeds in getting elected, they make damn sure that any issue that is to do with the body is looked after all the time. And that all calls from councillors are instantly returned. Indeed news that a councillor has dropped into Leinster House can cause a mini-stampede in the narrow corridors as senators race to the Visitors' Bar to stand their round.

As one senator reveals: 'There are lads that come up here once a year to be treated like lords. One fella will take them down to the Members' Restaurant for a bit of grub, and after that he'll sit in the Visitors' Bar for four or five hours without ever having to put his hand in his pocket.'

Union chief Joe O'Toole has been a senator since 1987. He admits that 'the whole Seanad system is unrepresentative and undemocratic' but he likes the diversity. 'I do not support the view of many of my colleagues in the Seanad who demean people in the Seanad who want to be in the Dáil, or who demean people in the Seanad who weren't elected to the Dáil, or who have finished their career in the Dáil.

'The original idea was that it would have senior people. I think that it needs a good mix. I think it is important to have people who have aspirations to go into government and I think it's important to have people who were in government. And it's important to have people like myself who have no aspiration whatsoever to be in the Dáil.

'It works quite well. There's no doubt about it but that it is a very useful House. It approaches things in a different way. There isn't the same level of party political hounding that goes on in the Dáil. You're much more likely to get a rational debate. What it can't do is permanently reject the Lower House. I absolutely support that idea. I do not like the idea of the legislative gridlock that takes place in the US and elsewhere. I think it is a perversion of democracy to have two houses of equal status. There has to be one that is superior. The other's role should be to modify, to engage, to reform.

'There are people in the Seanad – and they're all in the Seanad – who think the Seanad should have more power. These people haven't read the rules. There's enough power for people to do what they want to do. If they want to be in government, the Seanad is not the place to be. But if you want to influence decisions, you're in the right place.'

As debatable as that may be, the Seanad is definitely the place to be if you want to speak your mind. With just one reporter covering proceedings in the Upper House, and little interest in the national press in his reports, Senators can get all manner of things off their chest, safe in the knowledge that nobody will ever know.

As former senator Billy Kelleher TD says: 'You can say a bit more in the Seanad. You can step outside the party line a bit. There's great freedom there. If you do that in the Dáil, your phone rings off the hook with journalists asking if you're going to vote against the Bill.'

With a built-in majority of eleven, it would take a particularly careless whip to allow the government to lose a vote. But it has happened.

Joe O'Toole remembers another story of a particularly close call which led to the only documented case of a senator announcing to his colleagues that he was going commando. A row erupted just as the Seanad was about to wind down for the night and Senator O'Toole took to filibustering at length on an issue relating to agriculture. As O'Toole extrapolated at length on a subject about which he knew little, the senators quietly slipped away one by one until, too late, the Fianna Fáil whip realised that they would lose the vote that was required to shut the proceedings down.

'Eventually, they decided that they had to get people back in. The nearest man was Donie Cassidy who was staying in his hotel in the city centre. The then Leader of the House, Mick Lanigan, rang him. Donie, getting this call at 2.30 in the morning, thinking the House had closed three hours earlier, told Lanigan to fuck off, accused him of being drunk, and hung up,' according to O'Toole.

Several further attempts were made to reach him until he eventually picked it up again and was left in no doubt but that Lanigan was serious.

'He was in such a panic he hopped straight out of bed and into his trousers. He came running into the House with seconds to go before the vote to a chorus of "what kept you?" "What kept me?" he is alleged to have responded, "I came straight over! I'm not even wearing my underpants!"'

CHAPTER 13

A Day in the Dáil

'Having considered the matter fully...' – Ceann Comhairle

Visitors to Dáil Éireann are given a handy wallet containing ten separate pamphlets setting out everything you need to know about the Houses of the Oireachtas.

The pamphlet on Teachta Dála is one of the more expansive ones. It states: 'A typical day's work for a deputy to Dáil Éireann includes researching and preparing speeches for debates on social, economic, financial and budgetary issues, drafting amendments to and examining proposals for new legislation, contributing to debates on Bills and other important matters, voting on issues in the House, attending Question Time, participating in the proceedings of Committees and making either oral or written representations on behalf of constituents to Ministers or Government Departments.'

Just reading that is exhausting. And a tad misleading. Because the truth of the matter is that Dáil life can be remarkably un-demanding for an under-ambitious backbencher. If one takes away the mountain of constituency work – much of which is self-generated – there can be few jobs with such generous pay and conditions where the workload is so light.

Jim McDaid recalls the incredible lightness of being he experi-enced when he was first elected to the Dáil. Having been plucked from his full-time medical practice in Letterkenny, it took some time for the tyranny of the constituency clinics to kick in.

'I had nothing to do. I didn't have any work. I had an office here with nothing on my desk. I used to spend hours in the chamber. I had a seat immediately opposite the Ceann Comhairle's – the last seat on the top row. I used to sit there listening to practically everybody that was speaking.

'I sat there for weeks and weeks and weeks, dreading my maiden speech. My Dáil colleagues used to ask me why I was spending all my time in there. But the fact of the matter was that I didn't have any clinics, I didn't have any work.'

The record shows that it took a full fourteen months for TDs to clock up a modest 100 sitting days following the 2002 general election.

By the time the Dáil broke for the 2003 summer recess, the Oireachtas had passed the grand total of thirty-three pieces of new legislation. Debate on twelve of those new laws was guillotined in order to get the Bills passed and dispatched to the President for her signature in the final few frenzied days before the Dáil recessed for its twelve-week summer break.

Once the Government has approved proposed new legislation, the Bill is introduced by the relevant minister to either the Seanad or the Dáil. It then begins its laborious passage through the four further stages of its consideration, getting passed between the Dáil and the Seanad and the relevant Oireachtas Committee, where TDs and senators scrutinise its strengths and weaknesses and propose amendments.

That's the theory. But the reality is that most backbenchers would rather leave legislation to the ministers and their opposite numbers on the opposition front benches. Studying and understanding Bills to the degree where one can propose amendments is a tedious and time-consuming business. They have their constituents to service – constituents who would not thank them for spending time amending section three sub-section twenty-one of some bill they have never heard of, when they could have been battling to secure traffic ramps on their cul-de-sac. The media take little interest in run-of-the-mill debates on legislation and as a consequence the standard of debate is often shockingly low.

One senator who lost his seat in the Dáil remarked to this author that he could not see how the Seanad had gained a reputation as a place of great and worthy rhetoric.

'I've heard some of the most ill-informed debate on legislation and matters of public interest since I went in there. It's actually quite shocking,' he said.

For some years now just one journalist has taken an on-going interest in the proceedings of the Upper House. If Jimmy Walsh isn't in the press gallery, the proceedings of the Seanad are like the proverbial tree falling in the forest.

The decision by the government to introduce the controversial Freedom of Information legislation in the Seanad in 2003 packed the press benches for the first time in recent memory. The Leader of the House, Mary O'Rourke couldn't resist enquiring acidly of a long-serving political correspondent: 'You found your way alright then?'

While ministers have a team of civil servants available to them to draft their Dáil speeches and suggest responses to tricky questions, the front bench spokespeople who must respond to them are afforded few research facilities beyond the poorly-stocked Dáil library and an over-worked press office. Most gallantly struggle to construct speeches that highlight the inadequacies or outrages hidden in the government legislation. But backbenchers pressed into service by the whip to fill up the time allotted for debate are generally less industrious. If it contains a provision they railed against at their parliamentary party meeting, a government backbencher will already have lost the argument by the time it makes it to the floor of the chamber. The best they can hope for at that stage is that they will be spared the ignominy of having to speak in favour of it in the debate. That job will be often entrusted to the safe hands of those colleagues who know little and care less about it.

Rather than going to the bother of researching the proposal upon which they must speak, a government backbencher can fall back on an old trick. He can go the Oireachtas internal computer system and pull down a copy of the speech delivered by the relevant minister when the bill was first introduced. All that is then required is to judiciously cut and paste whole chunks of it, top and tail it with a few standard platitudes, check the word count, and pass it off as his own work.

Many others don't even take that limited amount of trouble. They rely on the press office to do the job for them. Watching them stumble over long words and awkward constructions in the Dáil chamber, it is painfully obvious that we are witnessing the first time that the TD has laid eyes on his copy.

Opposition backbenchers must also do their duty. They can cut and paste from their party front-benchers' response when the bill was introduced. The cute ones spot an opportunity to make a tenuous connection between some personal hobby-horse and the proposed legislation, and use their Dáil time to get some matter of constituency business aired on the floor of the House. A transcript of the TD's intervention will then be sent to the local newspaper and radio station to assure their constituents that their representative is standing up to the big boys in Dublin. Unless it is of particular interest to their constituents, or is causing problems for the party nationally, most backbenchers remain blissfully ignorant of the provisions of the legislation upon which they vote.

When the Dáil is sitting, its working week begins at 2.30pm on a Tuesday, when the Ceann Comhairle dons his silk-trimmed black robe and rises to his feet to say the official prayer. The assembled deputies rise with him, bow their heads, clasp their hands together and intone solemnly: 'Direct we beseech thee O Lord, our actions by thy holy inspiration, carry them on by thy gracious assistance that every word and work of ours may always begin from thee and be happily ended through Christ our Lord. Amen.'

By the time they are saying the 'Amen' the stragglers are bounding down the steep steps of the chamber, clutching a bulky grey document in which the questions the Taoiseach and his ministers have been asked over the course of the previous week are listed.

The week's business kicks off with the Taoiseach's Question Time. The questions are frequently vague and general, the opposition's apparent obsession with the Taoiseach's diary being a regular opener for ten marks. Being specific can complicate matters when it comes to sliding some current Government embarrassment into the supplementary. Note that this part of the Dáil's business is called Question Time and not Answer Time. This is no coincidence.

The focus is very much on style over substance. It's a rare occasion in the modern Dáil when the primary purpose of these twice-weekly showdowns is to elicit information. That's what telephones and the Freedom of Information Act are for. Question Time is about asking loaded questions in such a probing and righteous manner that any reply from the Taoiseach sounds shifty. Opposition leaders fantasise about the day when their killer question is so devastating that the Taoiseach responds by breaking down, weeping uncontrollably, and declaring that his entire political career has been a sham. The Taoiseach is in the hot seat, but it's the opposition's time to shine.

John Bruton, who was responsible for having television cameras introduced to the Dáil chamber, now wonders if their presence hasn't contributed to the decline in the quality of debate. Recalling his tenure as leader of the opposition, he candidly admits: 'I wasn't interested in the substance of the question that was asked of Bertie Ahern as much as, you know, would I get it into a sound bite that RTÉ might use? I was worried about looking right, if I was facing the right way, that sort of thing.

'One was pressured in that direction when in fact one should have been concerned solely with giving the question and getting the answer.'

Once the Taoiseach has held the line for forty-five minutes, a minister will step into his place to field his priority questions. The questions are split between those nominated for written answers and those that must be answered orally. While each day's question paper contains hundreds of questions, just five questions are nominated for a priority answer.

Ministers appear for Question Time on a strict rotation. As it will have been at least five weeks since the minister was last subjected to this grilling, there is much to discuss. If the Ceann Comhairle is firm and the opposition deputies aren't too rowdy, a minister can get through up to twelve questions in the allotted hour. The answers to the hundreds of other questions over which scores of civil servants have toiled for three days will appear in the Dáil's internal computer system by 6pm. (They used to appear as soon as they were ready. But the story goes that a certain Dáil deputy was outraged to have his thunder stolen on local radio when a constituency rival got on the airwaves first with the response to a pertinent parliamentary question. As that deputy happened to have sway in the Ceann Comhairle's office at the time, the 6pm threshold was introduced to ensure that all self-publicists could be at the starting gates at the same time.)

After that little unpleasantness is dispensed with, the Taoiseach returns for Leaders' Questions on matters of national interest. This is where the opposition leaders can demand that the Taoiseach account for himself over some scandal that broke on *Morning Ireland* a few hours earlier, or feign outrage over the latest economic data. As it is the slice of Dáil time most likely to get aired on television, the chamber fills up to witness opposition leaders at their most bolshie and bombastic for these precious twenty minutes.

At 4.36pm, the Taoiseach is invited to rise to his feet again to outline the order of business for the rest of the day's proceedings. But not before a raft of opposition TDs get to their feet to demand that the Ceann Comhairle evokes Standing Order 31 and suspends the business of the Dáil in order to allow debate on a matter of vital national importance.

A Leinster House novice seated in the public gallery might get excited at this point. The general air of this bit of procedural nonsense is calamitous. The sky is falling and the Dáil must drop everything and deal with it. Be not afraid. It's most likely to be something they spotted on the front of the *Irish Times* on their way in on the DART.

The Ceann Comhairle patiently waits for the last TD to solemnly outline the reasons for his demand before stating, equally solemnly, that 'having considered the matter fully' he is denying the request.

He has, on a few mischievous occasions, acceded to the request, which is great fun. The opposition party that demanded the debate is left with a swathe of Dáil time to fill, and not a prepared note to cover their discomfort. But usually the Standing Order 31s are dismissed to make way for the Order of Business.

On obstreperous days there will be a great deal of argy-bargy over the time allotted for certain debates, or the failure of the government to allow time for what the opposition considers to be the burning issues of the week. When the Ceann Comhairle asks if they are agreed on the Order of Business they will shout in unison 'Votáil!', and spend fifteen minutes having a vote they cannot hope to win. They do this to Make a Point. On some especially bad-tempered days, giddy with dissent, they make this point over and over again, often until they have used up the equivalent of the time they were demanding.

Once they have settled down again the floor is thrown open to all-comers to try to catch out the Taoiseach with a question related to promised legislation. This is when the TDs can be at their most adolescent, dressing up smart-ass digs as questions, flinging abuse at their colleagues across the Dáil chamber, arguing with the Ceann Comhairle over points of order.

Every so often in the career of a backbencher it is necessary to get expelled from the House. It gets them a mention in the national media, makes them a hero in the constituency and has the added advantage of a few days break from the division bells, without the inconvenience of having their pay cheque docked.

Getting expelled from the Dáil is easy. The TD attempts to raise a matter of vital importance to their constituents during the Order of Business. The Ceann Comhairle rules that the TD is out of order as the contribution does not relate to promised legislation. The TD protests passionately, declaring that lives, livelihoods or children are at risk. The Ceann Comhairle points out that he is on his feet and that the deputy is therefore completely out of order and must resume his seat. The TD accuses the Ceann Comhairle of protecting the government. The outraged Ceann Comhairle demands that the deputy withdraws this scurrilous statement. The TD sulkily agrees to withdraw the statement but demands that he must be allowed raise this urgent matter. The Ceann Comhairle bangs the bell with his gavel and warns that unless the TD desists he will be asked to leave the House. With victory in sight, the TD bounces back to his feet in mock frustration, declaring that he will not be silenced on this vital matter. The Ceann Comhairle wearily announces that he is 'naming' the deputy. His colleagues will vote on it tomorrow but in the meantime he must leave the House forthwith. The TD slumps into his seat to a chorus of cynical guffaws from his colleagues.

In a bid to squeeze some added drama out of the incident, a TD will occasionally make a show of refusing to leave. In these instances, an usher is dispatched to stand discreetly at his side. A huff pulls up outside the chamber and they leave in it.

To be fair, some TDs fall foul of the Ceann Comhairle's gavel because they are genuinely concerned about an issue, and deeply frustrated by the standing orders that are employed to silence them.

On one memorable occasion in 1999, Róisín Shortall, having been named by the Ceann Comhairle refused to leave the chamber. As a female deputy, there was no question of her being manhandled out of her seat by a burly usher. In desperation, the Ceann Comhairle resorted to extreme measures. If she wouldn't leave the Dáil, the Dáil would have to leave her. He promptly adjourned the business of the Dáil for the entire day.

After the Order of Business is agreed – or the government wins the vote on it – the Dáil might finally get around to debating a bit of legislation. This stops abruptly at 7pm for Private Members'

Time, where the opposition can introduce some legislation of their own – which is almost always rejected by the government – or they may simply use the time to put down a motion calculated to cause maximum embarrassment to the government and score a few political points. (There have been a lot of debates on disability in recent years.) This grinds to a halt at 8.30pm to make way for Matters on the Adjournment where a minister is wheeled in to respond to four brief speeches on controversial issues by four opposition deputies.

In recent years a huge number of these have related to rat-infested schools. Rats are pretty much guaranteed to make the news. This slot can be of great benefit to a TD anxious to build his profile with a bit of exposure on local radio. The Ceann Comhairle calls a halt at 9.10pm.

Wednesday's business opens at 10.30am with Leaders' Questions, followed by Taoiseach's Questions, followed by the Order of Business and a brief stab at legislative debate. This is interrupted by lunch, before the Dáil resumes with Ministers' Question Time at 2.30pm. After that there is more debate on legislation, then the second leg of the Private Members' Time debate, followed by more Matters on the Adjournment. There is almost always a vote on the Private Members' motion at 8.30pm on a Wednesday night, and there is little mercy for the hapless deputy who misses it.

Because of a deal that Fianna Fáil cut with the Labour Party in 2002, the Taoiseach no longer has to be present in the Dáil on Thursdays. The Tánaiste usually takes the Order of Business in his place. After that there is more legislation followed by another minister taking his raft of parliamentary questions, followed by more Matters on the Adjournment. It's all wrapped up by 5.30pm to ensure that TDs can make it to the station for the evening train home.

Oireachtas members are aware of the sheer irrelevance of much of what passes for business in the Dáil and of the obsession with procedures and privileges to the detriment of debate.

John Deasy, who was first elected to the Dáil in 2002, is scathing about what he calls this 'pretty shoddy parliamentary system.'

'It's runs along antiquated rules which are made to protect the government. Backbenchers are just lobby fodder. It's no wonder that intelligent, ambitious people want to do other things – so you're left with a sub-standard level of people in national representation.'

CHAPTER 14

The Good Old Days

'I came into what I thought was the holy of holies and my illusions were shattered in less than a year' – Eamon O'Donohue

For twenty-two years, until his retirement in 2002, the Dáil was run with ruthless efficiency by the man they called 'the Super'.

Superintendent Eamon O'Donohue was not a man to be trifled with. He was a figure of fear for many who would dare breathe his name only if they were absolutely sure he was not within earshot. He patrolled the corridors relentlessly, always keeping a watchful eye out for breaches of protocol and lapses of decorum, marshalling his army of ushers to ensure that the houses of parliament were afforded the dignity they deserved. He liked to sit behind the railing in the Dáil chamber during the main set-pieces, casting about for note-takers in the public gallery (who would be told to desist or be ejected), or gossiping political correspondents on the press gallery (who would be taken aside and lectured on the dignity of the proceedings at the earliest opportunity).

His technical job specification was Head of Security, but he was much, much more than that. He likened his position to that of general manager of a big hotel.

'It didn't matter whether it was a waiter who spilled a cup of coffee on a guest in the restaurant, or a fuse that blew and knocked out the lights on the fourth floor, or the lift breaking down with someone stuck in it (a very regular occurrence back in the 1980s, apparently) it all came to me.'

He fought a brave, but ultimately doomed, war against the erosion of the Dáil's once strict dress code. He pounced on tie pins and lapel badges in a bid to keep the Dáil clean of even the most discreet political sloganeering. He decided when Charlie Bird could bring his camera crew on to the plinth, and when that privilege would not be granted. He treated the deputies with the utmost respect at all times – even when it was clear that they didn't deserve it.

It was only after he had retired, over tea in his native Castleknock, that 'the Super' confessed to his secret distaste for some members of the body politic.

He spoke of all the times he had to stand by in silence while TDs blamed him or his ushers to escape censure themselves: 'I've been at the receiving end of that so many times that you understand that it's the nature of their profession. They're so used to bad deadlines and impossible requests that they spoof and spoof and spoof. Sometimes they forget that the victim of their spoofing is standing beside them.'

He explained that he had come from a very conservative and institutionalised background, where authority and politicians would always have been held in high regard.

'I came into what I thought was the holy of holies and my illusions were shattered in less than a year. In the first eighteen months, if I had been on secondment, I would have gone back.

'I was disappointed to find that a lot of politicians were without honour. Dishonesty. You see I had no problems with someone coming up to me and saying "I'm over a barrel. I'm going to use you." I'd say fine, go ahead. Or I'd no problems with someone coming up to me and saying "you're a pain in the backside" or stronger. As long as they're honest and upfront. But what I find difficult is deviousness, or dishonesty, or lack of honour.

'I found that politicians and high-ranking civil servants could lose a moral at will. That's not to say that it doesn't happen elsewhere. But I expect high standards in the Dáil and it was very shattering to find that they weren't there. They'd have no compulsion about using you upfront with regard to any situation that was unpalatable.'

He recalls going to a senior civil servant to ask for guidance when 20,000 people were marching on the gates of Leinster House during the H-Block protests. Under the Constitution the sittings of the Dáil and Seanad must be held in public, and this was interpreted as requiring the gates of Leinster House to be kept open when the Oireachtas is in session.

They discussed the possibility of asking the gardai to close the gate under the circumstances. As he left the meeting he realised he had not been given a firm decision.

'I said "are you clear now on what we're going to do?" And he said "whatever you do, make sure you do the right thing."'

When he arrived in Leinster House, in 1980, it was a very sociable place.

'There was a drinking culture and a social culture. The bars and restaurants were where everybody mixed. That's gone now. It's a very lonely, kind of a sterile place in terms of the bar and restaurant now. In the old days fellas used to go off on a Wednesday evening to the pictures or for a meal or to a local hostelry. They were always back for the half-eight vote. They don't do that any more. They're locked in. They're cocooned in their own little offices. They're on the phone doing their constituency work. They're working much harder in terms of the input – whatever about the output to match the zealousness.

'I would have had a great reputation for calling a spade a spade and being very upfront with things. I dealt with them all the same way. I had my favourites but that was my own business.

'Any fella who acted the maggot... the occasion would come when you could level the score quite easily without going to too much trouble. But in general all you want is for people to be straight with you, to say "I'm in trouble. How do I get out of this?"'

Back in the early 1980s, Leinster House was packed to the rafters and TDs and senators were forced to share cramped offices and harassed secretaries. New TDs learned the ropes 'by the hard graft of watching the guys in your own party that you were close to, and learning from them and picking up titbits from the fellas in the opposition that you were pally with.

'T'was always interesting to walk around the place on a Wednesday night between seven o'clock and eight o'clock. If you dropped into Bill Loughnane's room – there'd be three or four fellas in there, the fiddle would be out, a tin whistle would be out. Someone might get up on the desk and do an ol' jig. There was that bit of camaraderie and revelry. It didn't have to be a mad drinking session. There was this craic and camaraderie and close friendships. Often cross-party friendships. A lot of golf was played on certain afternoons.

(There is still a thriving golf culture. It's not unknown for TDs to race from their constituencies for Dáil business at the crack of dawn on Tuesday mornings – in order to get in a round of golf with their colleagues in Birr before the Dáil resumes at 2.30pm.)

'They were laid back days. Europe wasn't a big thing. Life was a lot slower. The rat race wasn't as it is now. Now it's a cardinal sin to be seen in the bar. Whereas twenty years ago it was a cardinal sin not to be.'

When the new Visitors' Bar was built in the Dáil, Oireachtas staff were banned from entering it. Now, if it wasn't for the Dáil's secretarial and administrative staff, and the political correspondents, the Visitors' Bar need hardly bother to open its doors before lunch.

Back in the days when the bar in Leinster House was the most exclusive and popular watering hole in the city centre, the Superintendent's first job in the morning would be to ensure that all traces of the previous night's revelry would be dealt with. There would be puddles of vomit in the bar, in the toilets, and along the corridors. Sometimes revelers would filter up to the first floor offices or along the corridors beside the bar that leads to the Labour Party's quarters and leave their mark.

The most trying time for the Superintendent was the booze-sodden weeks leading up to the Christmas recess, and in particular the annual Fianna Fáil Christmas party which would traditionally be held in their fifth-floor party room.

'The Fianna Fáil parties were just desperate. Outrageous. It was like an office party gone mad. The place just wasn't designed for it.'

In the Eighties and Nineties, when Fianna Fáil was still on relatively good terms with the media in general, the party's press office would issue a general invitation to every newsroom in the city, inviting any journalist who wished to attend to roll up on the night. It gained a reputation as a drinkathon of mammoth proportions. If you only went to one Christmas party in the season, you had to go to this one.

The event drove the Superintendent demented. 'It's very hard to be going around on a Monday talking about the dignity and decorum of the House and then on Thursday to be turning it into a bit of a St Trinians.'

The political correspondents who work out of Leinster House were, until recently, a privileged few. This writer formally joined the

Dáil lobby in 1996, following the retirement of long-time *Evening Herald* correspondent Des Mullen. It was an intimidating affair. Three of the cohort had worked out of Leinster House for almost thirty years.

It seems quite daft now, but before the Visitors' Bar was extended, the political correspondents had their own private dining room. What are now the stationery stores was then an intimate restaurant seating about twenty that came complete with its own waiter. Only members of the political correspondents lobby were entitled to eat there, although occasionally a privileged few would be invited to join them. The construction of the new Visitors' Bar meant that the political correspondents were evicted. It was decided to put a table in the centre of the Members' Dining Room to accommodate them. They were warned that they were not to abuse the privilege of being allowed to break bread in the presence of Oireachtas members by reporting on what they saw as they ate.

As Eamon O'Donohue recalls it, 'there was a minor incident almost right away.' As he remembers it, the fact that one member had a Sinn Féin councillor at his table as his guest was reported. The menu was reproduced in glorious detail – along with the in-expensive prices. Much was made of the report that a socialist deputy had ordered the smoked salmon.

The experiment was abandoned and the political correspondents were ejected to take their lunch and tea in the less salubrious surroundings of the self-service restaurant.

'T'was sticking out something was going to give,' the retired Superintendent remarks in retrospect. 'You couldn't have your Christmas cake in front of you for a whole day and not be tempted to eat it. Bad feeling erupted at the time. I was in the front line because I was the messenger. There was no broadcasting committee or PRO at the time so I was sent out to bat.'

There are about three hundred staff in total in Leinster House. This includes fifty-two ushers and another twenty staff in similar uniforms performing similar duties, known as service officers. The ushers act like butlers with army training. Indeed, many of the older ushers were drawn from garda or army backgrounds. There was a time when one of a TD's many powers was getting a con-stituent fixed up with a gig as an usher. There was no criteria for the job, so long as they were aged between twenty-five and forty-five and had a clean security record. To this day TDs and senators can recommend a candidate for an usher's position. There is no basic educational requirement, but in more recent times there have been third-level graduates amongst their ranks.

Unswervingly polite and ever helpful, they stand guard at the entrances and exits of Leinster House and its chambers, run messages for the members, and generally ensure that the members are afforded the dignity and respect that they feel is their due. One of their prime responsibilities is to ensure the security of the Dáil. To this end an electric shaver sent to Oliver J Flanagan from London and Ben Briscoe's briefcase were both considered suspicious enough to be blown up in the basement of Leinster House.

However, long experience has taught them that they will not be thanked if they challenge an unfamiliar face who turns out to be a distinguished visitor or the guest of a sitting member. Leinster House is by its nature crawling with former and current members and hangers-on, with egos the size of Australia and a sense of self-importance that far outstrips their modest positions.

Some can take advantage of the ushers' reluctance to cause offence. Some years ago a well-known party hack set up a small but thriving consultancy business from an office used by three senators in Kildare House. Each senator innocently believed that the intruder must be working for one of his colleagues. No-one dared challenge him as he used their facilities and phone lines to set up meetings and organise public relations presentations under their noses. He was in business for at least six weeks before the Superintendent became suspicious. He was asked to pack up his things and be out of the office before five o'clock.

The official dress code in Leinster House is a jacket, collar and tie for men and business attire for women. The code was accepted without question for decades until what O'Donohue darkly refers to as 'the Tony Gregory episode'.

The various protagonists have different memories of this now infamous incident. Gregory remembers it all beginning with a bit of banter in the member's restaurant. Fine Gael TD Gay Mitchell joked with journalists that they should talk to Gregory because he didn't wear a tie and he wouldn't be allowed into the Dáil chamber for the vote to elect Charlie Haughey as the next Taoiseach.

Gregory now insists that he never had a problem wearing a tie. He was a teacher and had a brace of ties in his wardrobe at home. But the journalists present saw an opportunity for a story. Tony

Gregory was an instant Dáil celebrity, having just cut a deal with Charlie Haughey in which he bartered his vote for a generous package for his inner city constituency. His alleged stand off over the Dáil's strict dress code made headline news. The new TD for Dublin Central was inundated with letters and phone calls urging him to stand his ground and represent his working class constituents dressed as they would dress. He recalls being called in for a meeting by the then Ceann Comhairle, the Fianna Fáil deputy Dr John O'Connell.

'It was just for show. Imagine him telling Haughey "I didn't let Gregory in because he's not wearing a tie"! He said he was only going through the motions. He actually said: "I don't give a fuck if you come in the nude as long as you vote for Charlie." Then he signed a copy of the Standing Orders and gave it to me.'

Eamon O'Donohue remembers talking Gregory around to the notion of wearing a tie by pointing out to him that every seven-year-old boy in his constituency wears a tie when he makes his communion, every twelve-year-old boy wears a tie when he makes his confirmation, every man who gets married wears a tie, every man who buries his aunt or his uncle or his mother wears a tie. He remembers getting Gregory to the point where he was about to choose a tie from the Superintendent's desk drawer when two senior politicians arrived in and reassured him that he could wear whatever he wanted, as long as he voted the right way.

He took a small comfort from the fact that Gregory wore a scarf on his first day 'to cover up the fact that he wasn't wearing a tie.'

In any case, the dress code never recovered from that high profile breach. In the current Dáil there are at least five TDs who frequent the Dáil chamber in what used to be called casual attire.

'That put a dent in the armour,' O'Donohue says sadly.

CHAPTER 15

The Characters

'I didn't bring you up to be a politician' –
Moosajee Bhamjee's mother

Moosajee Bhamjee is wearing a check shirt with the wrong tie under a sports jacket. His eyes are hypnotic. Sleepy and long-lashed under unruly eyebrows.

We are in the Aisling Hotel across the river from Heuston Station, where country people make appointments to meet colleagues and friends in the big smoke. There was a small mix-up. He has been waiting for me for twenty-five minutes in the lobby while I killed time in the bar. But he's not bothered.

He wants a Coke and to tell me about his most recent excursions into the politics of the body. He had already garnered headlines for his dissertations on women's breasts. Now he tells me earnestly he has of late turned his attentions to bottoms. And lips.

Face to face with this diminutive, dishevelled, amiable Indian, one can only marvel at how he persuaded the citizenry of Clare that he was he was the man to represent them in the twenty-seventh Dáil.

Every Dáil, like every local pub, has its coterie of characters. They usually (although not always) hail from the further flung constituencies of this great little nation. They dress a little funny and do imaginative things with their hair. They speak in tongues. Or in a dialect familiar only in their home townland. They are regarded with amusement and affection in Leinster House. Except when it comes to the city slickers and the Young Turks, who roll their eyes and fret that they are making a show of the place. Cuter Dáil veterans suspect that their bumbling façade is a cover for a shrewd political brain. No-one knows better than they that winning a seat in Dáil Éireann is no mean feat. Anyone who manages it is treated with a certain caution and respect.

Moosajee Bhamjee was certainly a character. He came to the Dáil as a political innocent but wised up quickly. He had a well developed sense of mischief and a talent for self-promotion. In many ways, he remained an outsider. He ran only once. On the day he left Leinster House he packed a small holdall and walked out the gate, never to step inside it again.

Untarnished by sentimentality and unclouded by proximity to the game or loyalty to colleagues, his insights on modern political life are perhaps some of the most honest and unintentionally hilarious that you will find in these pages.

When Labour's general secretary Ray Kavanagh broke the news in party headquarters that they were going to run a South African psychiatrist called Moosajee Bhamjee in Clare, he was met with stunned silence. Barry Desmond asked if it was fair to assume that they were talking about a black man. He was told that in South Africa he'd be referred to as coloured. Desmond asked if the Clare constituency was really going to use the slogan 'A vote for Moosajee Bhamjee is a vote for change'. When he was told that it was, he concluded that they'd better agree 'if only so we can claim to have produced the understatement of the campaign'.

Bhamjee had been involved in community organisations in Clare for about ten years before he embarked on his political career. He also trained the local kids' soccer teams. He was invited to join the local Labour branch and elected chairman in his absence. When the general election was called in 1992, there was nobody willing to stand in Clare. Bhamjee stepped up to the plate.

The Labour constituency operation was poor in Clare. Bhamjee thought that if he could get about 4,000 votes on the back of Labour's national popularity, he would at least show that the party was alive and kicking in the constituency.

He was nominated on 10 November, just fifteen days before the election. Somehow the novelty of his campaign took off. His son's friends started asking for campaign stickers. When he went canvassing he was surprised at his high profile, partly from his work with local soccer clubs and partly from a radio programme he used to do on Clare FM. There was also a small but dedicated band of supporters with a real stake in a Bhamjee victory. Years later a man approached him in a pub and thanked him for winning the seat. The man identified himself as one of ten friends who had each put a tenner into the pot and placed a bet on a Bhamjee victory at odds of 33/1. Although none of the gamblers were Labour activists, the ten canvassed relentlessly for their man, as did their wives and friends.

Bhamjee backed himself, betting ten pounds that he would head the poll and another ten on his winning a seat. He got odds of 25/1.

He believes that the perceived hopelessness of the cause might have helped him. Several people confessed later that they gave him their number one preference because they were convinced that he would be eliminated at the first count. It also helped that he aligned himself to the lobby group campaigning against the interpretative centre at Mullaghmore and made a stand against the threatened closure of Ennis General Hospital.

His campaign machine was in a sorry state. 'There was nothing there. I had four women, what I called my four ladies, and we went canvassing two or three mornings. I took a week off work just before the election to go canvassing full-time, but before that I couldn't canvass until after five o'clock.'

No Labour TDs or former ministers bothered to come to the constituency. When Dick Spring was in Limerick, Bhamjee pleaded with him to come up to the neighbouring constituency; Dick ran in the opposite direction to Limerick West. The party leader did eventually agree to dawdle in Shannon for half an hour after a late flight from Cavan. But that was the sum of his support from the party leadership.

'I remember the chairman of the Labour Party in Clare asking somebody if they thought we'd get five hundred votes. "Will we lose our deposit?" That's all they were worried about. The embarrassment of losing the deposit. The previous time a Labour candidate had run in Clare they only got 1,200 votes.'

But as the campaign rolled on, people started to come out of the woodwork. On their biggest canvass, there were fifty canvassers knocking on doors. 'In the end we found that I was the only TD who had a vote in every box.'

On the day of the count he was dropping his daughter off at

school when he heard a radio report on the early tallies. It was the first public suggestion that he stood a chance.

'I thought "shite, what will I have to do now?" I thought "I'll have to change the clothes now". So I went home and put on the suit. And then went to the count.

'I'd never been to a count before. I hadn't a clue what went on. As time went on I remember one Fianna Fáil man walking behind me, a senior man in the executive in Clare, saying "who the feck voted for him in that village!"

'Later on he said to me "what the hell did you do for the people of this county for them to give you the vote?" By then they were getting annoyed. They realised the seat was going to go.'

Labour's general secretary Ray Kavanagh rang him at about three o'clock in the morning.

'My pals were telling me "look, people will ring tonight and annoy you just so that you won't sleep, and you'll be upset the next day. Don't worry about that". But he just rang at three in the morning and said "Bhamjee". Maybe I met him for about five minutes once about a year before. He said "you stand a good chance of winning a seat." I said "thanks" and put the phone down. I was very annoyed. For him to ring me at three in the morning just to tell me that!

'I did go to bed thinking "shite, how am I going to carry on these two jobs now, being a TD and a psychiatrist as well."'

When his election was eventually announced, he was surprised at how nervous he was when he had to make his acceptance speech. A man in a wheelchair shouted 'up Fianna Fáil' all the way through it.

He was whisked out to the RTÉ studios in Limerick and linked up with the main election coverage. Brian Farrell had been interviewing Labour's Joe Costello.

'Joe Costello says "how're you, Bhamjee!" I hadn't met Joe Costello. I didn't know what he looked like. I didn't know who he was. So I just decided to play along. I said "oh yeah Joe, fine". I'd never been to a party conference.'

Bono name-checked him on television on the night, declaring 'we have an Indian in the Dáil now!' News of his election spread all the way to the South African newspapers. His family were aghast.

'They said when I rang "what the hell are you doing standing for elections?"'

'My mother said: "I didn't bring you up to be a politician. I brought you up to be a doctor." She wasn't thrilled.'

When he went up for his first Labour Party meeting he just about knew that the Dáil was on Kildare Street. He decided to make his maiden speech on his second day in the Dáil. The only witnesses were the Ceann Comhairle, a junior minister and an usher.

'I knew that the only way to feel confident as a speaker was to make eye contact, so I kept looking at the usher. I spoke for ten minutes on constituency business. I told them about the smallest classroom in Ireland.'

Bhamjee held his first clinics in the private consulting rooms where he normally saw his psychiatric patients. Nobody had bothered to tell him that he was entitled to funding for a constituency office.

'I was very annoyed. It was three months before I realised that,' he recalls now.

It took him a little while to get the hang of things. At the start he used to refer his, no doubt, bemused constituents to the local citizens' advice bureau on the not unreasonable grounds that the problems they were bringing him would best be sorted out there. His handlers were quickly appraised of the situation and took the good doctor aside.

'And they said "hey Bhamjee, that's your job, that's what you're supposed to do!"'

'A guy I knew from soccer came up to me and said "Bhamjee, I haven't paid my TV licence. If I get a letter from you they won't send me to jail". He said once I appealed his case to the Minister for Justice he doesn't go to jail. I said "oh, a new trick. Okay, if you know the rules, there's your letter". So I was learning new tricks of the trade.

'Some patients would come to me for real problems, and they'd talk to me about their real problems and next thing from the other pocket they'd pull something out and say "doctor I have this other problem as well".

'It was the system. It struck me as crazy. Very crazy. But that was what you had to do.'

He knows much of the paper trails he generated from his clinic work were pointless, but insists simply that 'it's part of the job'.

'The important thing is that the constituent also gets a letter from the minister. These are the silly things, stupid things. It drove me crazy, but you had to do it. The public want you to do it.

No matter how small or irrelevant the query, they want the letter to show that you did something. The main thing is that you tried.'

Ultimately, he found political life frustrating. 'The system itself could be very frustrating. People think that you're a TD and you can ask for something and the ministers give it to you. In fact it was hard to meet some of the ministers.

'Gradually, the system eats you up as well. The different ways of talking. Of greeting people. Of behaving with people. You have to show your people that you're doing something. You have to shout the loudest. You also have to make sure that you get in the doughnut.'

The doughnut is the technical term for the group of wannabes who weld themselves to senior colleagues if there's a chance of a photo opportunity or a television shot. In more recent years party whips nominate TDs to strategically scatter themselves around whoever is speaking in the Dáil chamber to take the bare look off the place.

Bhamjee was not a regular attendee at the Dáil. Indeed he was caught on camera snoozing in his Dáil seat more than once.

He is unapologetic. 'There is no debate in the Dáil. You come and give your speech and go away. I used to enjoy Question Time. But even that got a bit boring because they were reading from these ready-made speeches. Plus, as a government backbencher, you couldn't question your own minister.

'I made sure I was there on Wednesday. When we had a majority of twenty-three I had an easy time. When the majority was tight I had to be there more often. I was getting bored. Most of the work I wanted to do in the constituency was done.'

It all came to a head when he missed a crucial vote on the Luas plan on a Tuesday night. He was in Ennis.

'After that the whip gave me a hard time. Up to then I was going for the seat again. But after I got caught out that time I didn't want to be caught out again. I had to take six months leave of absence from work then.'

He credits himself with saving Ennis General Hospital from closing, getting a sewage system for Sixmilebridge, a water system for Lisdoonvarna and £69m for new schools and school extensions. Like many of his fellow backbenchers, he believed that legislation was the ministers' job.

'We all think that politics is about legislation all the time. It's amazing how many people just bring constituency problems to the parliamentary party meetings.

'I always had politicians on a pedestal. And suddenly I was their equal. And the next thing they are giving out about me because I am in the papers all the time. I made friends with most of them. There are certain ones I didn't make friends with. Their personalities were not nice. I won't give you the names.'

As a psychiatrist he recognised the classic symptoms of addiction among many of his colleagues.

'It's a sort of psychological condition. When you're there you have to think politically, you have to make friends with politicians, it becomes an addiction.'

For Bhamjee, life after politics held no fear. 'I had a career to go back to. I felt sorry for a lot of the people who lost out the last time. Suddenly you're unemployed. Suddenly there's no phone calls. Suddenly no-one wants to know you. Suddenly there's no mail.

'Your mail was massive and a lot of it was rubbish. But you looked forward to it. You looked forward to people talking to you. People stopping you on the street. Some of it was intrusive, but it also showed that you were important. That you were needed.'

As the only non-national in the Dáil, he got a few unusual queries. Parents whose children were dating foreigners rang to ask if such marriages could work out. He was asked for a curry recipe. He obliged and later immortalised it in the *Ennis Cookbook*. Apart from the usual donkey rides and dressing up as Santy, he thinks the daftest thing he ever did to please people was to sing a song in public.

'It was at some local authority function. I can't sing. I never sing. I haven't a note in my head. I sang the song "We're off to Dublin in the Green, in the Green" in front of three hundred people. I learned that song in my drinking days. My wife couldn't believe it. I still can't believe that I sang a full song in public. Sober.'

But much of what he was expected to do bored him.

'It was boring to be in the Dáil. To be sitting there trying to ring government departments. There was tedious work involved as well. People have this impression that the life of a TD is always exciting. But ninety per cent of it is boring. There's only ten per cent of it that is stimulating.'

He walked away from it, he says, despite being asked by Dick

Spring to run again, because he 'wasn't getting the same buzz in the last year.'

'When I was a doctor people had respect for me. People needed me. But when I became a TD I became a very common man. You lost your status. Because you were now dependent on them. They had control over you. They could come and ring you, abuse you, they could stand outside your house, people could demand that you do something for them. Now you were the little man. "You need me, boy".

'Since I left the Dáil I haven't been back. I didn't have the time. I walked out with this black bag and never went back.'

Jackie Healy-Rae is another man who is comfortable in his own skin. Asked by the *Irish Examiner* which bit of himself he would change if he could have painless plastic surgery, he responded: 'absolutely nothing.' Asked if he could swap places with anyone in the world, who would he chose to be, he thought about it and plumped for: 'myself.' (He also admitted to a recurring dream of sleeping with Tina Turner, but that's another story.)

We met at a gymkhana in the heart of his constituency. I found him at the refreshments stand drinking strong tea from a polystyrene cup and turning down offers of apple tart and fruit cake.

He is a celebrity there among his own people. He was the special guest invited along to draw the ticket in the charity raffle. As he climbed over the railing into the showground I overheard him asking discreetly which charity was involved. He was told the draw was in aid of the Children's Hospital in Crumlin.

Seconds later he had the mike in his hand and was bellowing out a stream of consciousness collage of top-of-the-head thoughts about the Children's Hospital in Crumlin. Standing between the two show jumpers in riding jackets and jodhpurs, the squat becapped septuagenarian cut an unlikely figure. But he is a pro. Small children stopped squabbling and listened to him with something approaching awe.

Jackie was the eldest of six children who grew up in what he remembers as 'extremely tough' times. He used to run the mile-and-a-half through the bog to school but that all changed when he was just twelve and his father hurt his back so badly that he was bedridden. Jackie more or less gave up school shortly after that. There was no time for the books as he worked alongside his mother cutting and turning turf to sell by the horse-rail to their neighbours in

Kilgarvin. That and the money from the sale of a few calves every year was the young family's main source of income.

It was around that time that Jackie first helped out on the political campaign for Dr Patrick Lane from Sneem.

'I remember the night of the election crying tears down my face that my man didn't win.'

He can't say what it was exactly that drew him to politics.

'I don't know. There was a longing inside in my heart that I wanted to be involved in politics for some reason I can't explain to you.'

Jackie was co-opted into a seat in the county council in 1973 and headed the poll in his first local authority election in 1974. But his ultimate aim was always to represent his people and his party in Dáil Éireann. After over twenty years of slogging it out in the trenches, he thought his day was about to dawn in 1997.

Some months before the general election that year, Jackie Healy-Rae travelled to Dublin with his long-time supporter Maurice Galvin. Their meeting with Bertie Ahern lasted one hour and five minutes. He remembers vividly how it ended.

'He got up. I said one last thing of it. I said "Bertie, don't send me down the road on an Independent Fianna Fáil ticket. I've gone around the bend with ye." He stood up with me and he done that.'

Jackie reconstructed the moment by planting his hand firmly on my shoulder. 'He said "we're having a meeting with MacSharry's team on Monday morning at ten o'clock. And you can take my word you will not go down the road on an Independent Fianna Fáil ticket."

'That hand was there as firm as I have it on you now. And do you know the next time I heard from that man? It was when I was elected to the Dáil. He rang me personally to congratulate me, and he asked me to go to Dublin to talk to him about forming a government and about numbers. That's the next time the man got back to me.'

So Jackie ran on an Independent ticket and headed the poll.

'It was spectacular. A tour of the Ring of Kerry with cars and lorries and vans and motorcycles. With loudspeakers and sirens. We gave Cahirciveen (the home ground of his arch rival, Fianna Fáil minister John O'Donoghue) a desperate roasting altogether.'

The dice rolled his way and the man who didn't have the heart to tell him he would not be the Fianna Fáil candidate in Kerry South was forced to eat humble pie and ask for his support to prop up his razor-thin majority. Jackie became the unofficial leader of the band of four Independent TDs who agreed to back the government in return for packages of largesse for their constituencies.

'I was under mighty pressure. Nobody ever put down a tougher five years in there. Not one single vote did I miss.'

There were exciting times. 'I could tell you about the day I was coming down from the Dáil with another TD. We were coming into Monasterevin when the phone rang. They said "where are you?" I said I was going into Monasterevin. They said "pull in your car. You'll be picked up by a helicopter in two minutes." Here I am and I with a valuable car trying to get parking in Monasterevin. I've a son in Monasterevin and I'm trying to phone him to see would I get into his yard with the car, and Jesus before I'm as far as his place the phone rings again. The vote was cancelled.

'I never bought a razor in Dublin in those five years because I wasn't able to go to the shops. I was on call all the time. We were there for every single vote. And that went for the four of us. But I was under the worst pressure, because if the smallest thing in the world went wrong the others would tackle me about it. I did the donkey work for an awful lot of it.'

He reckons he got no thanks for it.

'I was highly blackguarded the last time by Fianna Fáil. They put out a rumour that's impossible to fight. You can do it once but you can't do it to the same person again. That he's dead safe. There's no reason of voting for him because he's there anyway.

'I know fierce friends of mine altogether that were going to give me five votes in the house and they said "sure we'll give two to Jackie and three to the other fella." That's the way they did me and that's the way a lot of fellas get done. But they can't do it to me again.

'Fianna Fáil have really let me down very badly. The last election was the most hurtful. After the performance I put up for five years and I saved their neck hundreds of time. And Jesus they really made an almighty attempt to get rid of me. I'd have it in my nose for them, of course I would. Don't have any doubt about it. I'd never again be the very same as I was with them. I mean, Jesus, they tried to hurt me to the very roots.'

He survived and was returned as the oldest member of the Dáil at seventy-one. Now tasting life as a powerless Independent back-bencher for the first time, Jackie Healy-Rae remains unbowed.

'I think I will run again. I don't think there's any reason in the world why I should not run at the present time anyway. I don't really know, but maybe I'd have a better chance than anyone else of getting elected. It's as simple as that.'

CHAPTER 16

The Greasy Pole

'You have to work the snakes and ladders' – Ivan Yates

Y ou can spot them almost immediately. The first-time TDs who arrive in the Dáil aching with ambition and desperate to make their mark.

There is always a tranche of TDs who are just relieved and grateful to have defied the odds and scraped back in. Once the exertions of the campaign are behind them, they settle back into a comfortable regime of constituency work and devote their energies to the care and maintenance of their first preference vote.

PJ Sheehan made his first attempt to be elected to the Dáil in 1969. Twelve years later he finally made it on his fourth attempt. In his twenty-one year Dáil career he was a Fine Gael front bench spokesperson on three occasions, and was a convener to the Select Committee on Enterprise and Economic Strategy for three years. And yet he went out of his way to talk down his interest in the business of legislation, and was careful to reassure his constituents that he would not be wasting his valuable time with that sort of tomfoolery.

'Jim O'Keeffe is the legislator,' he used to say of his Fine Gael constituency colleague, 'and I'm d'advocator!'

One of the best-loved TDs in the Dáil, PJ enjoyed himself hugely, trundling up from his home in West Cork every week with his wife in tow, collecting hefty expenses for the mammoth journey. He loved the banter of the Dáil chamber and occasionally delivered impassioned soliloquies on some issue of burning local interest. But he was always anxious to get home to minister to his constituents at the weekend.

PJ saw his role as a representative of his people in the big smoke. The business of ensuring that he would be repeatedly re-elected took up most of his time and almost all of his attention. He liked it like that.

But every new crew has a cohort with their eyes firmly fixed on bigger and better things. They draw attention to themselves by making impassioned speeches on policy initiatives at their parliamentary party meetings. Their support for the party leader of the day is overt and unswerving (unless of course the party leader is on the way out, when their support for the likely replacement is unshakable). They flatter senior ministers or party worthies with personal and public displays of affection. They suck up to the whips by making it clear that, however much it pains them, they can be relied on to show up and vote the right way. They are not above telling tales on less reliable colleagues which can be used as leverage down the line.

They fraternise with the Press and stalk the plinth on big news days hoping to snag an interview with a hard-up reporter that might make it on to the airwaves. They troop out to offer themselves up to the Vincent Browne radio show at 10pm to defend the indefensible or rabble-rouse for the opposition. They spend just enough time in the Members' Bar to keep their finger on the pulse of relevant gossip, but are careful that they are not mistaken for the lushes who are in there for the drink.

The Dublin North-Central TD Ivor Callely has meticulously plotted his political career from the first day he signed up for Ógra Fianna Fáil, indeed, probably since long before it.

A brutal workload, a startling memory for names and numbers and a razor-sharp political instinct saw his career progress apparently seamlessly from City Councillor to TD to Assistant Whip to Oireachtas Committee Chairman to Minister of State.

From this plateau the forty-four-year-old northsider, who combines a startlingly naked ambition with a penchant for flash chalk-stripe suits, has the first clear view of his ultimate goal. He casts about for a polite way to put it.

'Of course, like any politician, I'm looking forward to the next challenge.'

Once he has made that admission, his confidence grows.

'I've made quite a good mark with what I've done with my brief so far. I would like to think that when I complete my stint in my department those that will be in authority will say "well, he's done a good job there, he was innovative and creative" and give me the chance to do something even more challenging than what I'm doing as Minister of State, which would be a full ministerial position.'

'And that again, when I would take on a full Cabinet position, that I would again prove myself in that position.'

We are now locked into Ivor's fevered fantasy.

'And if the opportunity arose after proving myself in maybe a number of ministerial positions, that I would have other opportunities that might prevail as time goes on.'

Is he talking about becoming Taoiseach?

He offers a broad, even smile. 'Yes', he almost murmurs. 'Yes, yes.'

Or perhaps he'll settle for European Commissioner.

'We're also in a changing environment. Europe is becoming more challenging,' he muses. 'A lot of what you do needs a bit of the ball bouncing in your favour at the right time. When I look at my career to date, I have had luck. It is a vicious workload, but I absolutely love it.'

Tom Parlon is another junior minister with his eye on the big-time. He recalls an incident in a farmyard many years ago which gave him his first insight into how position and power can transform an ordinary man into a thing of awe.

'I remember going into a yard canvassing with Alan Gillis when he was going for the Presidency of the IFA. This guy was so honoured that Alan Gillis had come into his yard. In the course of the conversation Alan said he wanted to relieve himself and he went into a corner for a pee. I met this guy afterwards and he said "Jesus, Alan Gillis pissed in my yard!" He wasn't putting it on. It was a big deal to him.

'When you get up along the ladder you see what you can do. I feel now that I could work myself into a situation where I would have enough experience and know-how to work the system to be a leader.

'I haven't half enough influence where I am at the moment. I have to just make the best of it.

'Mary Harney is the biggest motivating factor in the PDs. I don't really see the PDs without her. I don't know what her plans are, but she is the biggest attraction in the PDs for me. Whoever would be the party leader after that would be a different story altogether.'

How about Michael McDowell?

Parlon's eyes flash and a little laugh escapes his lips.

'He'd bring his own attributes to the job,' is what he says.

He is not planning too far ahead, noting that he 'could get the biggest kick in the arse of all time next time around.'

The 'unbelievable' thrill of getting elected to the Dáil at the tender age of twenty-one wore off for Ivan Yates after about a month when he realised just how far down the food chain he was.

'You realised that as a government backbencher you are on the lowest rung of the ladder. So your sole motivation is to get re-elected.'

Yates was battling it out with Avril Doyle and Michael D'Arcy for one of two Fine Gael seats in Wexford in election after election in the early 1980s.

'The bottom line was it was a complete dogfight for five years. I was young and I basically just outran them. I did more clinics, more funerals, more functions, more branch meetings. I just ran everybody into the ground. I put out more letters, pumped out leaflets. I was just a workaholic with one agenda – to get re-elected.

'The farm was set. This was now my livelihood. I was getting married in 1985 and I was building a house. I had nothing to fall back on. At that stage I was very ambitious. I needed the rough corners knocked off me in a bad way. At times it (his ambition) was only barely concealed.

'Basically everything in my life – my relationships, my marriage, my parents, my family – everything was secondary. If I got a phone call I'd drop everything and go to this funeral or that meeting.

'I held six clinics every week. I was meticulous about them. I would not go on any foreign travel. I went on to the county council. I just realised that because I had the energy, the good health, the vigour, and the enthusiasm, that I could outrun them. And I enjoyed it. I had built up a team and they were battle-hardened. I was definitely pretty ruthless about it. I was there to win. I was not interested in second place. You see campaigning politicians now like those in the Green Party. I was a pure careerist. I could have joined any party.'

After twenty-two years in the Dáil, Yates understands that TDs fit into one or other of two pretty straightforward categories: 'There are people who do all the constituency work because they want to drive around the constituency and say "I am the TD, I am somebody. When I'm coming out of Mass or coming out of the mart, I'm a big fish in a small pond".

'Then there are people who say "right, just tell me the rules of the game. This is a means to an end. Politics is a national bloodsport. It's there to be played to win". You can quite easily suss out which TDs fit into which category.

'The guy who comes in and they have a bit of an auctioneering business, a bit of a pub business, a bit of an undertaking business, and they're fifty-five and they've been on the council for the last ten years. You can take it that this is it. They'll go on a couple of foreign trips a year. (They're thinking) when I speak to the county manager, he'll listen now. And that does for them. And maybe they have a son or daughter coming along. And there's no crime in that.

'The other class of TD could just as easily be in law or medicine. Politics is their piranha fish business and that's where they're coming from. The constituency clinics and the funerals and the branch meetings are purely a means to an end. You cannot win an All-Ireland medal without training through February, March and April. This is their winter training.'

He offers a pithy insight into how to get ahead in politics.

'The first thing you have to do is to secure your seat. That gives you the confidence to articulate where you're going. If you have a shaky seat you don't have credibility. You have to have a power base.

'After that you have to talk sense at the parliamentary party meetings. People have to see you as someone with courage, who is constructive and worth listening to. And then you have to develop a national profile. That goes down well in your constituency as well. Local boy makes good. They like that.'

He is frank about how one might go about developing a national profile.

'You have to attack somebody or something. You've got to go up to some sleeping dog and kick it good and hard. The more certain people squeal, the more publicity you'll get.

'I attacked building societies, dentists, opticians. I wasn't afraid to be vocal at parliamentary party meetings. That's part of it too. You've got to lay down the law. A bit of bottle is very important in politics.

'As we got to 1987 and I saw the government making mistakes, I was not happy to be a backbencher anymore. Having felt I had secured my base, I was determined when Garret was gone that I would be involved in the next leadership race in terms of backing the winner. It was about getting on to the front bench. And then working my way up the greasy pole.

'You have to be lucky. And you have to work the snakes and ladders. And if you attach your star to something that goes down you run the risk of retribution. That was my difficulty when (John) Bruton took over.'

Alan Dukes, Gay Mitchell, Alan Shatter and Ivan Yates were all from the Class of '81. After six years and four elections, they felt they'd served their time on the backbenches.

When Garret had run his race, the party's old guard moved to install Peter Barry, the Cork merchant prince, in his place. The hungry Young Turks saw a chance to mount a coup, and in an extraordinary turnabout, they succeeded in getting Alan Dukes elected leader.

'I went off to a rugby international that Saturday afternoon feeling that I had pulled off a mighty stroke. We had defeated all the power base in the party that was in Cabinet. So I went to the rugby international thinking "game on!" And it wasn't.

'Unbelievably, Dukes didn't put any of us on the front bench. He totally missed the point. He went and re-appointed all the others. These three people who had done everything to get him elected. It was absolutely... I couldn't believe it. I put it down to political naïvety on his part. I don't know what he thought, but he thought wrong anyway.

'No sooner had he made the appointments than he realised that I wasn't too happy, and that maybe this wasn't in his best interests. So he came to me and proposed I go for the chairmanship of the party. It was the only contest I was ever beaten in. All the old guard, the Barry people, they all had a knife in me. I was completely set up. I didn't even want to be chairman of the party.'

What does one do in a situation like this? Was there a screaming match with Dukes?

'I would try to be professional in my dealings. You don't get mad, you get even!'

Yates bided his time until Dukes started to flounder. And then, 'out of the clear blue sky I let him have an Exocet. I announced that Fine Gael should merge with the PDs.

'I got great publicity for it. As it happened, in a complete freak of coincidence, the very same day Austin Deasy resigned. Suddenly Dukes was dealing with a crisis in Fine Gael.'

Dukes summoned him.

'He said "What the fuck are you doing?" I was very bolshie about it. He was saying this was a matter for the leader. I was saying I'm just a humble backbencher. Basically, I was letting him know that I felt he had no authority over me.'

It worked.

'Within three months he got rid of half the front bench and did a complete reshuffle, and I was made spokesman on health. Which was my first big break.'

Yates' other top tip is that when you get thrown the ball, you run hell for leather for the touchline.

'I really wound up the health issue. I was in A&E wards, I was on trolleys, I produced people in Mullingar. One was a woman with her cat on her lap who was refused a heart operation. I sat down beside her and said what a disgrace this was. The whole election was fought on health. The haemophiliacs and everything. I was really in with them.

'I had a fantastic time. I was really out there. There were upper cuts all landing on (Health Minister) Dr Rory O'Hanlon's jaw. I produced a policy to say we should abolish the health boards. When it came to it, I could say where the cuts should be made. I was totally on top of the brief.'

It all begins on Oireachtas Committees. Of the 166 TDs in any Dáil, almost thirty will get a gig – and a few extra grand a year – out of the committee system. The first thing an ambitious TD must do is get well in with the whip and the party leader to ensure that they bag a seat on one of the more high profile Oireachtas Committees.

By far the best one is the Dáil Public Accounts Committee, which gets to harass civil servants and government agencies for wasting taxpayers' money. As this is guaranteed to put bums on seats in the press gallery, any TD who can count can build a profile with the use of a meaningfully-arched eyebrow and a good line in aggressive inquiry.

Then there are the thirteen joint committees shadowing the various government departments. Some of these offer more opportunities for sound bites and foreign travel than others so they must be targeted with care.

The Committee on Procedure and Privileges and the Select Committee on Members' Interests can mean that a deputy will have to censure one of their own. These members have considerable power over their fellow Leinster House inmates, but only the most strong of stomach will wield it.

Members of the Joint Committee on Broadcasting and Parliamentary Information get to periodically rail against the travesty that, as Rat Rabbitte once memorably put it, sees *Oireachtas Report* aired at a time when only drunks and insomniacs are tuned in.

There is the new Sub-Committee on EU Scrutiny and two other Sub-Committees on Dáil and Seanad Members' Services. The Joint House Services Committee looks after the library, restaurants, bars and shop in Leinster House.

From time to time there may also be a chance to sit on a Standing Joint Committee on Consolidation Bill or a Standing Joint Committee on Standing Orders.

The first step on the ladder to the top is a position as whip of one of these twenty or so committees. It comes with a handy €5,109 a year stipend for the legislative committees.

The committees will also have to have chairpersons and vice-chairpersons. Committee Chairs get the chance to generate a great deal of self-publicity and €16,030 a year for their trouble. Vice-chairpersons get an extra €8,198 per annum. The Committee Chairs get an annual budget of €12,832 which can be doled out to selected committee members to fund research for specific reports.

Outside the committee system, the crucial job is that of party whip. The term is borrowed from the Westminster system, which took it from the 'whippers-in' who keep the hounds in line during a fox hunt. The work can be tedious and is often resented, but the money isn't bad. Government whips are automatically made Ministers of State, with the requisite perks, while their assistants pick up a handy €12,832 a year on top of their TD's salary. Opposition whips get allowances ranging from €16,030 for Fine Gael to €5,109 for the smaller parties. But few do it for the money. The post is prized because the potential for networking and advancement is immense.

The Young Turk of the new generation of Fine Gael TDs, John Deasy, probably best captured the basic rules of engagement for any ambitious TD who wants to get a grip on that promotions pole:

'Avoid conflict at all costs. Play the game and mind your arse, and you might move up the ladder and get somewhere.'

Politicians constantly complain about the often arbitrary nature of political promotions. Sometimes they have a point.

Garret FitzGerald decided on the unusual course of nominating Professor James Dooge to the Seanad in order to facilitate his appointment as Minister for Foreign Affairs in 1981 on the advice of his wife, Joan. (One senior politician recalled this constitutional quirk when Mary O'Rourke lost her Dáil seat in the 2002 election and commentators were speculating on who might replace her at cabinet. No fan of O'Rourke's, he didn't dare breathe the name Dooge in political company for fear the precedent might be followed.)

The low regard with which taoisigh hold junior ministers' portfolios – frequently entrusting them to the care of hopelessly underqualified and inept deputies – was writ large when Stephen O'Byrnes wrote of the breathtakingly casual manner in which FitzGerald cobbled together his junior list in 1982.

In his book *Hiding Behind a Face*, O'Byrnes describes how a flustered FitzGerald decided he would appoint all his ministers of state together in the style of a political Moonie wedding to save time.

'Having checked they were all there, he charged on. First, Paddy Harte. Leas Ceann Comhairle. "Jesus Christ," muttered Harte. FitzGerald asked what was wrong. "Nobody has been thrown out of the House more often than me," Harte wailed. "Three times in one term," he added. The Taoiseach moved on.

'The others on the list were Eddie Collins, Fergus O'Brien, Donal Creed, Mary Flaherty, Michael Begley, Michael Keating, Michael D'Arcy, Ted Nealon and Jim O'Keeffe. Collins, Harte and Keating were sorely disappointed at not being made full members of the cabinet. Now the brusque doling out of junior posts was adding insult to injury. FitzGerald was behaving as if the whole thing was an irritant.

'"Eddie Collins, Overseas Development", he announced. "I don't want that," Collins interjected, "I want something in industry". FitzGerald just ignored him and ploughed on. When he announced that Jim O'Keeffe was to have Industry and Energy, O'Keeffe turned to his Waterford colleague.

'"Listen, Eddie, I'm willing to swap with you." Eddie Collins was unsure. He turned to the Taoiseach who was well down the list by now and galloping hard. "Excuse me, Garret, is it okay if I swap with Jim?" FitzGerald looked up. The penny dropped. "Oh yes. That's alright." And that was that. By this neat piece of barter, a small matter of state was settled to the satisfaction of all concerned.'

Dr Moosajee Bhamjee: dubbed the Indian among the cowboys.
(Photo: Eamonn Farrell/Photocall Ireland)

Embattled bus: tension on the Fine Gael election trail. (Photo: Leon Farrell/Photocall Ireland)

Political football: Michael Smith shows the boss how it's done. (Photo: Kenneth O'Halloran)

The sweetest feeling: getting the result. (Photo: Kenneth O'Halloran)

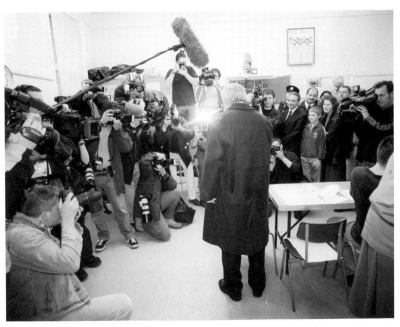

Tough at the top: alone again, naturally. (Photo: Kenneth O'Halloran)

On the line: Tom Parlon keeps his ear to the ground. (Photo: Paul Sharp/Photocall Ireland)

The political jungle: I'm the Taoiseach, get me out of here! (Photo: Photocall Ireland)

Winner alright: Mary Harney hits the jackpot. (Photo: Gareth Chaney/Photocall Ireland)

Ruairí Quinn: sealed with a kiss. (Photo: Leon Farrell/Photocall Ireland)

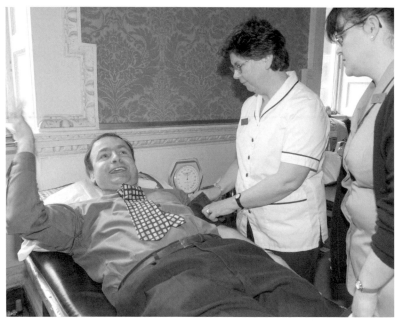

Blood sacrifice: Micheál Martin proves he has a heart. (Photo: Leon Farrell/Photocall Ireland)

*Arise and follow Charlie: Maureen Haughey stands by her man.
(Photo: Derek Speirs)*

*Going to the country: Dr James McDaid on tour. (Photo: Gareth
Chaney/Photocall Ireland)*

Beating the odds: Charlie McCreevy takes a gamble. (Photo: Eamonn Farrell/Photocall Ireland)

Power play: a young constituent gets a political baptism. (Photo: Kenneth O'Halloran)

Arresting development: Jackie Healy-Rae agrees to go quietly. (Photo: Leon Farrell/Photocall Ireland)

Martin Cullen: politics can be a dirty business. (Photo: Eamonn Farrell/Photocall Ireland)

In the name of the father: Brian Lenihan carries on the family tradition. (Photo: Gareth Chaney/Photocall Ireland)

One for the road: Bertie greets a voter. (Photo: Kenneth O'Halloran)

Getting in: Seamus Brennan finds a window of opportunity. (Photo: Gareth Chaney/Photocall Ireland)

Super trooper: Eamon O'Donohue lays down the law. (Photo: Derek Speirs)

Foot soldier: Padraig Flynn wipes the Boss's boots. (Photo: Derek Speirs)

Friendly rivals: Dublin Central's Bright Young Things. (Photo: Derek Speirs)

House call: Albert Reynolds is briefed by press secretary Sean Duignan. (Photo: Derek Speirs)

Doing the state some service: Austin Deasy behind the Dáil Visitors' Bar. (Photo: Derek Speirs)

In for the count: Bertie Ahern and right-hand man Chris Wall. (Photo: Derek Speirs)

Follow the leader: three taoisigh and a contender. (Photo: Derek Speirs)

Pole topper: Garret FitzGerald takes his campaign to new heights.
(Photo: Derek Speirs)

CHAPTER 17

Whipping Them In

'Is there anything better going?' – Seamus Brennan

It's no coincidence that a great many of our most senior politicians, including the current Taoiseach and the current leader of the opposition, have served their time as party whips. There is no better way to get to know your fellow deputies.

A good whip will know their personal habits and their lifestyle choices. If they drink, their whip will know where and in what company. They will know the dynamics of the little cabals and power centres that form in every parliamentary party. They will hear the ominous cracking of a fault line in the making. They will spot a leadership challenge before the stalking horse is saddled up and shod. They make it their business to know their deputies' family situations and their social and sexual indiscretions. Crucially, they know which deputies can be trusted and which deputies must be watched.

As former government whip Seamus Brennan revealed when he was still in the job: 'I know the ones that are likely to stay in bars on me. I know the ones who stay out late and probably won't be in for the first vote. I know the ones who sneak off because they have other little jobs they want to deal with and make a few bob. I have to know these things.'

This is invaluable information for anyone with ambitions to climb the greasy pole that is internal party politics. The position of whip also puts a deputy in close regular contact with the party leadership. Strong alliances can be forged. A well-whipped back bench is a great comfort to a party leader. They are likely to reward a job well done.

Just two years after he arrived in Leinster House, Charlie Haughey made Bertie Ahern his assistant whip with responsibility for the policy committees. The then Chief Whip Sean Moore became ill and much of the day-to-day running of the parliamentary party fell to the tousled young man from Drumcondra.

'What happened then was there was all the turmoil, all the hassle, all the things going on. If I had been there at any other time I may never have been heard of. But because I was there through all the heaves in '82/'83... ' Bertie Ahern breaks off as he muses upon the fickleness of fate.

He agrees that there is 'no doubt' but that being a whip enhances your political skills and, ergo, your promotional prospects.

'You learn the procedures of the House and the departments like nobody else understands other than whips. I watch it even now. You watch leaders. You watch the guys who haven't been whips. They don't really know the rules, they don't really know the structures. You have to be a whip. There's nothing like being a whip.

'I was blessed. I didn't like it at the time. We had a minority government when we had one of the toughest ever Finance Bills, the MacSharry Finance Bill, and MacSharry wouldn't give an inch. That was hell, but it was great experience. Now you could be fluthering around here forever and you wouldn't learn those things. And most TDs are. Most TDs who have been around here a long time still don't understand the rules.

'It made Seamus (Brennan). Seamus is a far better minister now than he was before he was whip. Being whip is a crucial part of the scene. But there's not many people want to be whip. Being whip is tough. Being whip is dealing with the problems at the weekends – it cuts the metal. Leaders spend a lot of time thinking about who'll be whip. They think more about who will be whip than about who will be some ministers. It's a crucial post.

'It gave me a national profile. I came from the end of '81 being just another guy knocking around the place with long hair who was generally seen as being a fairly ragged customer... I'd got a huge vote, I'd two quotas in three elections. That didn't make you anything, but being whip did. Being whip had me on TV every day for eighteen months.

'In all of those things, I never fell out with either side. I had a job to do, I was loyal to Haughey but I got on well with all of the people on the other side. I used to actually go and talk to George (Colley) and Des O'Malley and all the other people. I came through that period without ever losing a friend. And Haughey never said to me "don't be doing that". If Haughey had been beaten along the way I wouldn't have been an enemy of the others, I wouldn't have been written off by the others. I didn't think about it. I just got on with doing my job. At that time it was so mad there was no time to be plotting anything. (It was about) surviving.'

When Bertie Ahern asked Seamus Brennan if he would take on the job of Government Chief Whip in 1997, his initial reaction was to enquire if there was 'anything better going?'

Bertie replied: 'Not at the moment' and Brennan accepted his fate with the words: 'I'll take it so.'

It was to prove a gruelling five years, as the government's majority hung on the whim of the four Independent deputies who demanded constant attention. But it held together, and when Bertie Ahern chose his Cabinet in 2002, Brennan was rewarded with the plum Transport portfolio.

'I didn't want it. I wanted to be in the government. But I was only Chief Whip for about a week when I thought "this is much better than being in government." I thought it was great fun,' he says now. 'I met the Taoiseach two or three times a day. We were always working on political problems. I had to handle all that stuff when the Ray Burke thing happened, when the Liam Lawlor thing happened, when the Denis Foley thing happened. I was often the guy who went in the door and said "Taoiseach, this is coming at us next week."

'He'd say "where did you hear that?" I'd say "it's not official but it will probably burst in about two days." He'd say "jaysus, how will we handle that?" And then he'd say "you go and talk to this guy, and you sit your man down and find out the truth". And I ended up very often having to talk to some of those people I just mentioned and see how we could deal with the problem without damaging Fianna Fáil. Stop it from pulling the whole party asunder. There was a lot of that really raw politics.'

He says he 'loved' the four Independent TDs who were propping up their coalition arrangement.

'I instinctively knew that I had to be on their side. When I went to meetings, even in the privacy of the Cabinet, I was always on their side. I never took the government side against them. No matter what they were up for I took them in to see the Taoiseach, the ministers, different ministers of state and I would argue for them. I became an advocate for them.'

While this might appear to be a particularly advanced case of Stockholm Syndrome, where hostages begin to identify with their captors, there was method to Brennan's madness.

'They trusted me. So if I came back and said, "this is just not going to happen so stop crawling out the branch because you know where it's going to end up," they believed me.'

Brennan's account of a typical exchange with Jackie Healy-Rae when he was told he wasn't getting what he wanted is worthy of a run at the Abbey.

'Jackie was great. There would be an uneasy moment. He'd look at you. He'd say "do you tell me that?" I'd tell him it couldn't be done. He'd say: "Are you sure now?"

'I'd say "Jackie, I'm being level with you now. Some things can be done but this can't." "Right," he'd say, "you're a mighty man." There would be a pause. "You did your best?", he would enquire one last time. When assured that the Chief Whip had indeed done his best he would declare heartily: "Right, you're a mighty man so. We'll leave it alone so."

'They were very intelligent people who genuinely cared,' the former Chief Whip still insists, 'I never had a moment where they wanted something that was wrong for the country.'

A Chief Whip's prime responsibility is ensuring that the government always has enough bodies in the Dáil chamber when the division bells stop ringing for a vote. Brennan appears almost nostalgic for the times when he was organising Healy-Rae's travel schedule.

'I often had to ring him and haul him back. Once or twice my State car obliged him to pick him up off the train when we needed him.' And the helicopter? 'There was a time when they were sending a helicopter for him but it never happened in the end.'

He still laughs at his first meeting with the four TDs.

'The Taoiseach had told me that it was important that I explain to them about government policy. I made a big speech. I told them all about Northern Ireland, the Middle East, the UN, the Budget. Jackie was writing it all down. I stopped then and asked what was important to them. "The first thing now," says Jackie, "is there any chance of a photocopier? There's no place to put it in my room. And the secretary doesn't come in on Fridays. Could she come in on Thursday? We'll have a policy chat next week when I get me thoughts together on it." It brought me right down to earth.

'I was the first party whip who had previously been in the Cabinet and been party general secretary. I was arguably the most experienced party whip we ever had. That was useful, particularly in a coalition government with four Independents on top of it.

'I was able to watch what the PDs were up to, what Fianna Fáil was up to, what our own backbenchers were up to. I was able to tell the Taoiseach: "this is what they're at, this is the plan." He was very well informed too. He is a great man to pick things up.

'There are two kinds of party whips. There's the kind that goes around cracking the whip. In the modern world that doesn't work. My style was to sit down and sort out the problem. Firmly though. I got what I wanted.

'One of my TDs came to me one night and said he couldn't make the 8.30pm vote because his aunt had died. I asked him if that was the same aunt that died on the fourteenth of February last year. No, he said, that was the other aunt. I asked how many aunts he had. None now, he said. I told him he could go provided it was the second aunt and not the first.

'He came into me the next week and apologised. He said "I was chancing my arm. I only had one aunt and she did die. You had the month right. I didn't think you'd remember." To this day, when I see him I ask after his aunt.

'It's all about communication. One thing I would do regularly is ring certain backbenchers and Independents and the odd minister at 7am. I'd say "are you out of bed? Have you seen the paper? They'll be on to you within the hour wanting you to attack us. Here's the story... "

'Jackie would come on *Morning Ireland* saying "Seamus Brennan was on to me this morning and explained that the government were not going to do any such thing." Problem solved. If I didn't make that call he would have come out and said "this government is not staying in office a day longer." I used to write three four-letter words in my pad every day: Make That Call. It was the key to keeping everything together.

'I didn't stop them all. A whole lot of them got by me. That's one of the interesting things about that work. The things that didn't get by me will never be known. Fires that get put out don't make any stories. But it's a great job. I would recommend it to anybody in politics.'

The Chief Whip's spot was always the sixteenth position in the Cabinet. Over the years the role has developed and become more powerful within the party and government system.

Brennan saw this clearly: 'In day to day politicking, the Chief Whip is often much more powerful than most ministers in terms of the raw politics of what's going down. Now I don't now what's going on in the political world. In terms of what Mary (Hanafin) and Bertie have to get done, what's coming up in the Dáil next week, what's going to be on Leaders' Questions and the like. When I was Chief Whip I was on top of every single issue. I had to be. I could tell the Taoiseach "look, next Tuesday at Leaders' Questions there will be this, this and this. I'd have the notes organised. I could tell him what the (news)papers were going to go with at the weekend. He would know a lot of this. But it would confirm his own views. The fact that I was experienced and was able to give him a political read was useful.

'You don't get much thanks. I got thanks for holding it together. Mary (Hanafin) is working as hard as I worked and she's every bit as good, if not better, but she probably won't get the same thanks because she doesn't have a situation to handle. I was lucky that I had a situation to handle, but I did have to work extremely hard.'

CHAPTER 18

Getting the Call

'I just sort of felt I was going to faint.' – Nora Owen

A junior ministry is the first steady toe-hold on the steep climb to the political summit: becoming a senior minister with a serious portfolio, and onward to party leader and perhaps Tánaiste or Taoiseach.

It comes with a sizeable salary – €40,625 on top of the Dáil salary of up to €78,627 – and the requisite prestige and perks.

The decision on who gets the gig is determined by a number of factors, with ability being way down the list in terms of its relevance to the decision.

Junior portfolios are regarded as shiny baubles to be dangled before ambitious candidates at times of political difficulty and in the run-up to elections. A TD who stands by his leader at personal and political cost when the going gets tough may have his loyalty rewarded. A deputy who risks his own quota to bring in a running mate against long odds may also shoot up the preferment list.

But even these feats of courage and skill won't be enough if the geography is wrong. A map showing the spread of senior and junior ministers across safe and sensitive constituencies would leave our national spatial plan standing. No political talent is so outstanding that it can't be ignored in the name of getting the political geography right. No lack of talent is so debilitating that it can't be overlooked if the political map is looking a bit threadbare in places, or if passing a deputy over is going to cause more trouble that it is worth. In any case the civil servants are expected to take extra special care with junior ministers, and the madder and sadder ones are simply kept out of sight.

Of course, not all junior ministers are in need of constant hand-holding. Some are genuinely appointed because they have impressed. These will go on to become Cabinet ministers.

With 166 Dáil deputies, the odds of making the cut and being named one of the top fifteen deputies that will have the job of steering the ship of state are long. Some, like Willie O'Dea, wait for years with their noses pressed up against the Cabinet door to no avail. After over twenty years in the Dáil, O'Dea was devastated not to get the call up in 2002. He has served as minister of state in the departments of Justice, Health, and Education, making the junior team in every Fianna Fáil-led administration since 1992. But ten years' experience was not enough. The big job still eluded him. He was forced to accept another stint as minister of state with bad grace.

Others have high office thrust upon them. Alan Dukes, Noel Browne, Kevin Boland, Martin O'Donoghue and Niamh Breathnach were all made Cabinet members on their first day in the Dáil.

The long-time political spin doctor Fergus Finlay liked to observe the transformation that came over ordinary deputies when they got the call.

'They all start with this notion: "well, I'm wearing the blazer now. If you looked up to me with deference before, you can get down on your knees now". They all become a little haughty immediately and ninety per cent of them come down to earth with a bang fairly quickly. A couple of them never stop coming down.

'The first Cabinet meeting after a government is formed always takes place in the Áras. They always get a little pep talk from the Cabinet Secretary and then they discuss their own salaries. That is always on the agenda of first Cabinet meetings. It's about me. I'm suddenly a member of this elite club. I'm on the committee now. I get to wear the blazer.'

Gemma Hussey breathlessly noted in her political diaries that she felt 'numb, apprehensive, delighted, proud,' the day she was called into Garret FitzGerald's office and appointed Minister for Education.

Nuala Fennell was 'amazed' when she got the nod in 1983 and was made junior minister after just two years in the Dáil, ahead of a brace of much more experienced colleagues. 'It was unbelievable. I have no idea why he chose me. I never asked him.'

Albert Reynolds' initial elevation was more of a slow burner. The man who would go on to become Taoiseach recalls meeting Ray MacSharry at the gates of Leinster House on the day Charlie Haughey was appointing his first Cabinet. When MacSharry offered him his congratulations, Reynolds asked 'what for?' MacSharry said he had heard he was getting a job. Reynolds admitted that he had been asked to drop into Haughey's office but said he still didn't know why. He went to the new Taoiseach's office some time before midday. 'It being Haughey, there was some unparliamentary language,' he recalled, 'He said "I'm giving you the lousiest fuckin' job of all. We'll see how good you are now. Fix the fuckin' telephone system in this country!"'

Reynolds left the Taoiseach's office assuming that he had just been appointed Minister of State at the Department of Posts and Telegraphs. He rang his wife Kathleen and his children to tell them the good, if not altogether excellent, news.

As on all Dáil days when Cabinets are being assembled, speculation as to the identity of the lucky fifteen raged around the corridors.

Reynolds bumped into *Irish Independent* political correspondent Chris Glennon who asked him what he had got. Reynolds told him. Glennon asked him if he was sure. They had done the sums and there appeared to be one name missing from the senior line-up. 'We're short one and we thought it was you,' said the puzzled journalist. Reynolds assured him that he knew what he had been told.

But as it grew nearer to the time when the Cabinet would be announced in the Dáil, more people approached Reynolds asking if he was sure. He began to doubt his own ears. He was in a quandary. 'I couldn't go back and ask Haughey again. I'd be put out. I might lose the bloody job,' he thought.

He sought out MacSharry again and was told he was indeed to be in the Cabinet as the senior minister at the Department of Posts and Telegraphs.

'I rang Kathleen again to tell her. "Jesus", she said, "you'd better get a new suit." I had to send someone down to Grafton Street to buy one in a hurry. I then had to ring back all the children in their various places and tell them "it's not a minister of state job, it's the government". I was genuinely stunned.'

Micheál Martin took a more pro-active approach to ensure that he got the portfolio he desperately wanted. He rates his appointment as Minister for Education in 1997 as the high point of his career to date.

'That first moment, getting into the Cabinet, was a magic moment.'

In the euphoria after the massive vote for Fianna Fáil in the 1997 general election, the Taoiseach had visited his parents' home town and indicated that their loyalty would be rewarded with a minister.

'I was on the front bench so I was in pole position, but I still didn't know which one I'd get,' Martin recalls.

The longed-for phone call came through late one evening when he was staying with his family with friends in Dublin. 'He said, you're in. He didn't tell me what portfolio but kind of said "I know what you want". And bold as brass, I said "but you do know what I want, don't you?" Which looking back was a bit cheeky.'

Bertie Ahern left him hanging until he called his entire new Cabinet in to his office late the following evening and announced their portfolios.

After a triumphant period in Education, when Martin's star rose into the heavens, there was a reshuffle. Conspiracy theorists have often mused that the decision to hand the bright, young leadership contender the poisoned chalice that is the health portfolio was Bertie Ahern's attempt to clip his golden wings. Martin laughs at the notion.

'Sometimes there are conspiracies, but sometimes there are just theories. But the interesting commentary all the time is "what's behind that move?" And I think they attribute a greater degree of ingenuity and brilliance to us at times than we deserve.'

He says he genuinely believes that his Taoiseach had his best interests at heart.

'He actually said "this is going to be good for you". I believed that. And I think he was right ultimately. I did leave the room scratching my head saying "God, this guy has convinced me this is good for me!" That's a good achievement!

'When I went into Bertie Ahern he didn't have to do a hard sell. Some of my close friends who were advising me against it said "you're going to take it, aren't you?"'

He insists that remaining in the health portfolio after the 2002 general election was his idea.

'We had had a brief conversation before the election where I said "I'm going to play it again". There's a big issue here under the National Health Strategy. I think the simplest thing to say is "I want to be the next Health Minister". I said I'm not going to pre-empt you or pre-empt what you're going to do afterwards, but I'm going to be saying "I want to be the next Minister for Health."

'I went off and told a few people that and they said "are you mad?" Some of my close friends despaired to be honest with you and said "look, it's going to kill you" but I just had a sense of unfinished business. I didn't want to leave it.

'I had a meeting with him after the election for about an hour. We'd a great chat. We went through every constituency, where we lost out on seats we could have won. While he was happy with the result I think he really felt he could have pulled off the overall majority. It was there for the taking. We discussed Health. He said, I know you're exhausted at this stage. I wouldn't say I was the most enthusiastic at that point in time. The following day, he told me I was in Health again.'

Nora Owen was so sure that she would be appointed to the Cabinet by John Bruton in 1994 that she went shopping for suits and got her hair done the day before. She even got a friend who owned a shoe shop to send around a selection of shoes so that she could accessorise her power suits in the privacy of her own home. She was the deputy leader and she was a woman. 'There had to be a woman in the Cabinet and I was the most likely woman. It wasn't that you were big-headed about it but you had to be prepared.'

When the day arrived, an official called to her office and asked her to accompany him to the Taoiseach's office. The Taoiseach's office is in Government Buildings, which is accessed from Leinster House via a glass corridor. Before Leinster House 2000 was built, most TDs had a bird's eye view of this corridor from their own offices.

'I walked across and I knew that every eye in that building was looking at that corridor. I was walking with this official from the Taoiseach's department and I was just dying to turn around and catch them. My heart was just pounding.'

She recalls waiting in the ante-room outside the Taoiseach's office with a few other excited colleagues.

'You walk in and John is sitting at the table with papers around him and you just sit down and he said "I'm going to make you Minister for Justice". And I just sort of felt I was going to faint!'

She somehow managed to maintain her composure, thanking her Taoiseach and noting that it would be a great honour. He said it would be a very difficult portfolio and mentioned the many areas of responsibility that were included in her brief. She was particularly pleased that she was going to be involved in the Northern Ireland talks. It had, she said, a special resonance for the grand-niece of Michael Collins. And that was that. The entire operation took all of a minute-and-a-half.

She recalls emerging from the office to the whispered pleadings of her colleagues demanding to know: 'what did you get? what did you get?' And she remembers almost bursting to tell the world her news but being forced to restrict herself to sharing it with her husband, whom she warned to keep her confidence.

Before 2.30pm on the day a Cabinet is appointed, all the new ministers are called over to the Government Whip's office and lined up in order of Cabinet and Dáil experience so that they can enter the Dáil like a school-children's crocodile. This is to ensure that there are no unseemly squabbles about seating arrangements when they troop into the Dáil chamber.

Nora, used to sitting at John Bruton's right hand as deputy leader, was now way down the line behind colleagues who had already served in government. But she did get a few extra points for being deputy leader, a bonus that meant she just made it on to the last remaining seat in the front row.

'When you walk in you're suddenly conscious of what's happening. It's very, very momentous. You know everybody in the chamber is speculating about what you've got,' she notes.

Once the Dáil is informed about who got which portfolio, the opposition leaders get to their feet and congratulate them with uncharacteristic magnanimity.

In the same way that TDs do not interrupt a novice making their maiden speech, tradition dictates that speeches on days such as this are generally saccharin sweet. The new ministers are probably too excited to fully appreciate what are most likely the last kind words they'll hear about themselves across the floor of the House until the statements on their death.

The Fianna Fáil press office gleefully dredged up Dick Spring's kind words on the appointment of Ray Burke as Minister for Foreign Affairs to quell suggestions that Bertie Ahern should never have appointed him in the first place. The Dáil record did not record that Dick had spoken the words through gritted teeth.

After this bit of hypocritical nonsense, the new ministers sweep out of the chamber and march across the glass corridor to emerge from the front door of Government Buildings, where their cars are arranged in a semi-circle with their drivers already at the wheel.

A gig as a ministerial driver is a much-coveted position within the gardai and, as each appointment is entirely at each minister's discretion, the more likely candidates for preferment are subjected to intense lobbying in the run-up to the Cabinet announcement. Gardai who drive the new ministers to the Phoenix Park to pick up their seals of office hope that they will click with the elated minister and be kept on.

Once up at Áras an Uachtaráin, ministers are shown to a room where tea and coffee are served. One former minister recalls being tickled by the realisation over his cup of coffee that suddenly everyone was addressing him as 'Minister'. They are then given a briefing on the protocol for receiving their seals from the President. They are called up one by one and handed the precious little boxes while a bank of photographers preserve the moment for posterity from behind a red rope. Nora Owen was warned by Niamh Breathnach to open her box and take a peek at the seal. What few first-time ministers know is that the second the photos are taken, the seals are whipped away again. Many never even get a chance to see what they look like before they are snatched from their fists.

Once the seals of office have been locked away again, the ministers are led into another room where they have their first Cabinet meeting. They deal with whatever urgent matters may be on the agenda and are told what they can expect when they turn up at their various departments the following day.

'We all had a drink then. I think there was champagne. We were all chatting, very excited. It was lovely,' Nora Owen recalled.

When she arrived at her Department the following day, she was touched to find a letter on her desk from the previous incumbent, Máire Geoghegan-Quinn. It was a simple letter of welcome, assuring the new minister, whoever they may be, that they would enjoy working in the department and that the staff were great.

'That was a touch that probably would not have been done by a man. So I rang her and we had a chat. She marked my cards. That was very nice. I think I did the same for the next minister. I didn't know it was going to be John O'Donoghue. I think I did leave a little note as well. If I didn't, I meant to.'

Of course it can also all go horribly wrong. Jim McDaid still has the speeches from the Dáil debate on the formation of the Cabinet in 1991. He still has the tapes from the radio current affairs programmes that were broadcast that week.

He had been surprised when told at 9.55pm the night before the Cabinet was to be announced that he would be the Minister for Defence. But a photograph of him at a rally for an IRA member emerged and the opposition declared that he was a security risk and could not be in the Cabinet. He agreed to stand down.

'Haughey called me over four or five times. I had an instinct it wasn't going too well around four o'clock. I was headlines for the following four or five days. It didn't sink in on me until I sat down that Christmas.

'People had been taping the radio shows. I got presents of three tapes from three different people. By then it had all died down. You were nobody anymore. A month had passed. I think I felt very bitter at that stage. But if we had stuck by our guns at that time there would have been another election.

'I remember telling Charlie Bird on the plinth that I felt like I had been through an operation without an anaesthetic.'

It would be six more years before McDaid would get to see the inside of the Cabinet room, as Minister for Tourism and Sport.

'The appointment to Cabinet was then all the more sweet. Everybody who comes in here has Cabinet ambitions. They would all like that phone call.

'Geography plays a big part. But talent plays a part too. Any Cabinet could be divided into three. Those who are going to be permanent fixtures. Those who are in the lesser ministries who are probably going to go. And those in the middle who could go either way.'

In 2002, he was one of the middle-rankers who went the wrong way.

'I was very disappointed. But I had to be a realist as well. I had only two Bills. It can be hard to build a profile. You were always described in the media as being a lightweight at Cabinet when you actually never got a chance to prove yourself.

'I made the point that if I was Minister for Tourism and Sport there was no point in me going around with a sad face all day. My job was a good portfolio and I enjoyed it. You were always going to be in the relegation zone. But I thought we had done reasonably well.

'The previous time, which was a terrible thing because I had to resign, I had nothing to miss. This time I knew what it was like. This time it was hard to take.

'We had a breakfast Cabinet meeting at eight-thirty that morning. Nobody knew who was in or out. After that meeting we knew that people were being called over to the Taoiseach's office that morning. I was over in my office until 7.30pm. There was no call.' McDaid was relieved as he left Government Buildings. He understood that the Taoiseach had told all the Ministers he was dropping from Cabinet the bad news.

'The driver dropped me home. I ordered a Chinese and took off my suit and got into a pair of jeans. By now I was thinking "I'm in". The phone rang at eight o'clock. "The Taoiseach wants to talk to you." My driver had gone so I said I'd take the DART back in.

'I just knew then. I walked into the Taoiseach's office. We had a twenty-minute chat. He said he had a difficult job to do and unfortunately he didn't have a place for me this time. He explained the situation. I don't want to go into that part of it. So that was it. And I went home then. The Chinese take-out rang up angrily saying there was nobody there when they arrived.'

CHAPTER 19

Yes, Minister

'It was like we were dealing with such an arcane craft that it was bordering on mysticism' – Michael D Higgins

Mary Harney didn't get a full night's sleep during the winter of 1990. She would wake at 4am and stumble to the window of her Dublin 4 apartment to survey the skyline. She was a newly-promoted Minister of State, but it wasn't worries about her new responsibilities that were interfering with her sleep. At least not in the way that you might imagine.

When Mary Harney was appointed to the junior brief in the Department of the Environment in 1989 she knew she had limited powers. She quickly sifted through the files on her desk and decided to concentrate on three issues: establishing an independent environmental protection agency, recycling and smog.

Smog was a major issue in Dublin the late 1980s. Every winter the grimy mist would descend over the capital, filling casualty wards and respiratory units to capacity with its choking, spluttering victims.

Within weeks of her arrival into the Department, the coal distributors CDL, who had seventy per cent of the coal market in the city, invited her to a sumptuous lunch in Locks restaurant, one of the most expensive and exclusive eateries in Dublin. They hoped to convince her, as they had done with the previous government, of the merits of their latest innovation: the full-burning fire. They made their pitch. So fully did this full-burning fire burn that it burnt up all the smoke before it ever got up the chimney. Indeed, so fully did this full-burning fire burn that it could not be held responsible for the smog.

The previous government's approach to the smog plan involved imposing special area control orders around Dublin where homeowners would get grants to take out their fireplaces. It was estimated that it would take twenty years and £500 million in 1989 terms to complete the project.

Harney decided that the only solution was to ban smoky coal and prepared a memo to that effect. But her senior minister, Padraig Flynn, appeared to be reluctant to bring it to Cabinet.

'The way it works is that the junior minister reports to the senior minister who takes it to Cabinet,' Harney explained. 'If they want to leave something sitting there for weeks there's nothing you can do. You can't get into the Cabinet room.'

It sat on Flynn's desk for weeks until, in frustration, Harney phoned the Taoiseach Charlie Haughey, who called a meeting of all the relevant ministers. The controversial coal ban duly got Cabinet approval.

'If it wasn't for Charlie Haughey calling that meeting, it might not have happened, to be fair to him,' Harney now acknowledges.

There was a massive protest the day the government announced the smoky coal ban at the Burlington Hotel in Dublin. Coal workers carried placards bearing the legend 'Coal not Dole'.

Harney knew that she was walking a high wire with no net. She had taken full responsibility for the unpopular policy initiative with no cast iron proof that it would work. CDL would go to the wall in the wake of it. The citizenry of Dublin were not taking to the smokeless coal. It generated less heat and sparked dangerously. To this day people say to Mary Harney: 'you burnt my lovely carpet'.

So that winter she religiously set her alarm clock before retiring to bed in her apartment in Burlington Gardens.

'I used to hop up at four in the morning to see if there was any sign of smog. That's a fact. That winter I don't think I had a single night's full sleep.'

The skyline remained miraculously clear.

'I knew I had an element of luck. It might not have worked and it did. It would have finished me if it hadn't.'

The civil servants had not been supportive.

'A lot of the system thought it was naïve idealism, that I didn't know what I was talking about, and that they knew better. They said that you couldn't solve the problem in one winter, but we did.'

The official system 'really felt that you couldn't get people to change their burning habits without a grant,' Harney recalls. 'That was the culture. That was the way the system thought you solved problems. You must pay people to change behaviour.'

In this case the views of a strong-willed and determined minister won the day. But it is not always so. The interaction between transient ministers and the permanent government of the civil service is a complex affair. Most people will recall the sharply-written BBC comedy *Yes, Minister*, where a weak and malleable minister was putty in the hands of his self-assured and highly-political civil servant. It's not a million miles off the mark.

Ministers frequently arrive in their offices with little or no in-depth knowledge of their brief. Their senior civil servants, on the other hand, are armed with years of experience and enjoy an intimate relationship with all the relevant files. While the minister has all the responsibility, a canny civil servant can have much of the power.

Harney acknowledges: 'The system is more used to saying no to a new idea than yes. You'll get all the reasons why it should not happen. That's a fact.'

A minister must be up early in the morning to meet the challenge. 'You have to spend a fair amount of time reading the brief. When it comes to policies you need to know that you're going to be debating with people who know an awful lot more about it than you. And more importantly, they know all the players. Some of them have been at it for ten or twenty years. They may have a particular perspective. Or they may just have become accustomed to doing things in a certain way.'

Nuala Fennell presented a particular challenge to the status quo when she was appointed minister of state with responsibility for Women's Affairs and Family Law Reform by Garret FitzGerald in 1983. It was a new brief and it was decided that she would work within two departments, the Department of the Taoiseach and the Department of Justice. She recalls the 'wonderful and dedicated' civil servants who opted to go to work for her new division in the Department of the Taoiseach.

'They were warm, helpful and very loyal. And they worked very hard.'

However, her initial experience with the top brass in the Department of Justice was less encouraging. It was the tradition that the secretary general of their first port of call would drive the minister of state to their second department and make the introductions. So it was Padraig O'hUiginn who escorted Minister Fennell to her first meeting with the secretary general in the Department of Justice.

'We went in and sat down having tea. It was like I was a clerk they were thinking of employing and I was being interviewed. I remember this weird kind of across-the-table chat. He was a charming man and O'hUiginn and himself obviously had a good rapport. Then he turned around and said "well, that's nice now Minister, we'll send you over any post that comes here for you." I had just been appointed into his department and here he was dismissing me! I said "oh no, no, no. I need offices here". The secretary general then explained that this would be a problem as he didn't actually have any spare office space in the department.

'They didn't want me. I was a load of trouble. I would have been out on protests. They hadn't had to cope with a women's libber and all that went with that.'

The newly-minted junior minister dug her heels in. She told him that she didn't care if they put her into a broom closet as long as they put in a phone and a desk.

'So then he knew there was no way I was going to be dismissed over to the Taoiseach's Department. In truth I had a suite of offices over there. But I knew that I needed an office in the department if I was going to get anything done.'

Within a week they discovered a whole suite of offices that had once housed Dick Spring. Equipped with a superb private secretary, Fennell would fight many more battles to push ahead with her radical agenda of social reform.

'They didn't want to take on anything new, but once they saw that something was popular and they were going to get some kudos for it, they accepted it.'

It didn't take Fennell long to notice that her senior ministers developed a 'very strong antennae' about what their junior ministers were getting up to.

'It's in the secretary general's personal interest to make sure that his senior minister knows exactly what you're doing. Everything I was doing went up to the secretary's office, into the minister's office and back down to me again.

'As a junior minister you were never free to say "next week I'm going to launch this" or whatever. Everything had to be cleared. In case there was any kudos to be got out of anything, or in case the secretary thought you were doing something that was more suitable to the senior minister. It's civil service politics and they want to retain their control.'

Former Labour leader Ruairi Quinn admits that the common trait amongst all politicians is 'the idea of being able to do things, if the truth be known, for the sheer buzz of doing it.

'There is an incredible buzz in making executive decisions. In actually proposing something and seeing it happen. Of actually knowing how to make something happen.'

He honed his skills at local authority level, where city and county managers enjoy enormous autonomy and frequently treat the elected councillors as little more than annoyances to be mollified.

'Part of the thing about politics and exercising power is just knowing the route to push someone. There are no books around to tell you how to push something through. There are plenty of philo-sophical books about the theory of politics. But there is nothing that tells you how to get from A to B. It's entirely experimental.'

There is a marked difference between the cultures of civil servants in the various departments.

'A lot depends on the relationship of the secretary generals to the minister, and also on how involved the minister happens to be in the running of the department.

'Some ministers are just happy to be there. Are quite happy to be on the train and not very pushed as to where it's going. Some ministers want to make everything happen. Of course if you try to do everything, nothing happens.'

'Some make basic Faustian deals with the department whereby they say "I've got three priorities I want to go through and you can pretty much do what you like with everything else".'

Having held five different ministerial portfolios, Quinn reckons it takes 'an awful long time' to learn to be a minister.

'The first time around you feel that you're there and you're going to do everything. A lot depends on your training. Very few people who end up at ministerial level in politics have had any managerial experience. The nature of becoming an elected person is such that you really can't be a mainstream management type. Very few people have worked at a middle-management level in a big organisation. So learning management techniques and expertise on how big organisations work is something that you have to acquire on the hoof.'

The French poet Valéry suggested that 'Politics is the art of preventing people from taking part in affairs that properly concern them.'

Garret FitzGerald might not put it in so many words. But one senses that he'd be inclined to agree with the general sentiment. FitzGerald thinks we have been very lucky with our system of government – given the poor cloth from which it has to be cut. Or, as he put it, 'I mean, considering the electorate we have, the politicians are very good actually.'

It is, he says, a system under which an electorate who have no interest in legislation elect people for the wrong reasons. FitzGerald is deeply disappointed with the modern electorate, whose tolerance, even appreciation, of misbehaviour he blames for 'lowering the tone of politics'. He is adamant that the whole purpose of representative democracy is to have a system 'which doesn't give people what they want when they want the wrong thing'.

The former Taoiseach quakes at the current fad for referenda and the modish notion that public opinion should decide matters of public importance.

'Referenda were dangerous in Germany and that's why the Germans will never have them again. Public representatives have time, occasion and advice to act rationally rather than do the popular thing. With the civil service there behind it, the system is designed to block bad things being done in response to the wrong kind of popular pressure.'

But most serving and former ministers agree that civil servants also block positive initiatives in a knee-jerk response to the dangers of change.

FitzGerald accepts that ministers are at the mercy of the senior civil servants and notes diplomatically that there is 'a variation of quality there'.

FitzGerald's previous career meant that as minister and Taoiseach he had a more intimate knowledge of the civil service than of his own parliamentary party. 'I knew them all by their Christian names. I was very unusual in that way.'

FitzGerald's long experience has convinced him that departments have their own policies to which they are strongly committed.

'The idea that they're neutral is nonsense. They have developed policy positions over the years – like the protectionist policy in Industry and Commerce and the pro-farm policy in Agriculture. These were very strongly held. It isn't entirely a bad thing, but ministers would want to be aware of it and of what they're up against.

'If the Taoiseach appoints a minister who's going to be bullied by civil servants then it's his own bloody fault. And, on the whole, most politicians aren't easily bullied – most have sufficient self-confidence to hold their own. Not all of the time, but most of the time.'

He claims that he always had a very clear recognition that he was capable of making mistakes.

'I never saw myself as infallible. That would have been dangerous. What I wanted was civil servants and ministers who would not kow-tow to me.'

He claims he had exactly this difficulty with a particular civil servant.

'In the civil service I never dealt with this civil servant because I knew that he was a sycophant. I cut him out completely. Instead of telling me that (a policy initiative) wouldn't be wise he'd go off and do it. So, about once a year I would see him. I preferred people who would say "Taoiseach, have you considered the full implications of this...?" I knew I was safe with them.'

FitzGerald is quick to praise the professionalism of 'most' civil servants.

'The quality of what they do is high, their integrity is great. We never had any problems with corruption – it's a tradition that was established early on.'

There was one occasion, however, when a civil servant attempted to blackmail FitzGerald into appointing him to a job he was claiming did not actually exist.

'It was extraordinary. He came to me and said that the committee I had working on a particular issue had no authority and it would be very unfortunate if that got out. He wanted to be made chairman of it. He was threatening to talk to the press.'

The civil servant in question remained in his position, albeit with a less taxing in-tray.

'I never gave him any work to do after that.'

Michael D Higgins says that a minister's reluctance to agree to amending legislation can often be traced back to 'the irritation of their officials who are warning strongly against granting changes.'

Michael D enjoyed a blistering term as Minister for Arts, Culture and the Gaeltacht in the mid-1990s. He marched a raft of legislation through the Cabinet and the Dáil, abolishing Section 31, establishing an Irish language television station, kick-starting the film industry. In doing so he left a trail of bewildered civil servants in his wake. His relationship with his officials was, he says, 'a mixed experience'.

He noted very early on that the attitude of civil servants to their minister depended on how the minister was performing at Cabinet. Initially hostile civil servants would warm up once they saw that their minister was winning decisions at Cabinet. 'After that happened once or twice they began to treat you with a bit more respect.'

Senior civil servants would often use coded language to warn ministers off certain proposals that they considered to be too politically risky. Others tended towards the dramatic metaphor. One civil servant tried to talk the minister out of bringing one such proposal to Cabinet, warning darkly: 'Minister, you run the risk of being shot down in flames.'

When he told a senior advisor to the Government that he planned to proceed with the removal of Section 31, a provision that allowed the government to ban anyone with terrorist links from the public airwaves, the minister's bold move was unflatteringly likened to 'bungee-jumping'.

'I couldn't but be impressed with how dedicated they are to public service and to one administration as it succeeds another. But at the very top there is a resistance to change. They find change very difficult,' Higgins remarks.

Michael D's voracious demands for new legislation caused major headaches in a system accustomed to a more leisurely pace. He discovered that a piece of legislation could get stuck in the draftsman's office for nearly an entire government term. When he would inquire after a long-delayed piece of legislation at Cabinet he would be told that it takes seven years to train a draftsman.

'The Taoiseach would say this. It was like we were dealing with such an arcane craft that it was bordering on mysticism.'

There is a story that at one stage back in the 1980s the backlog in the drafting of legislation had become so acute that they hired a specialist. He was an elderly gentleman who hailed from one of the islands in the Caribbean.

Michael D remembers him slightly. 'You'd see him going in and out of here in my time with a bag. But the point was he was creating too much. He was producing so much that he was seriously undermining the seven-year preparation rule. His productivity was profoundly threatening.'

When he first became minister in 1993, the Labour TD frequently had a good laugh, in discussions with Noel Browne, at how ministers were given the run around by their civil servants.

'There are ways of defeating a minister. When you arrive at a minister's office for the first time, there will be this long sideboard of files. And they (the senior civil servants) will say to you "Minister, the files... "' He gives a little royal wave to demonstrate how it would be done. 'You must say to the secretary general at that stage: "which ones do you think won't wait until next week?" At which time you will notice that all the files will disappear.

'Civil servants love the ministers who know nothing about their brief. You could be completely at their mercy. You are at an immense disadvantage.'

Of course it depends on what you're after. 'If you're a career person... if you're watching your parish as it were, you can let them run you and they will.

'I think now, looking back, that I would have had a wonderful second term. You need to be very careful that your time isn't wasted. Some ministers are perfectly happy to be opening everything from ice-cream parlours to whatever.'

All ministers are deeply suspicious of potential moles in their departments and Michael D was no different.

'You're a minister and you have all these deferential people around you. You've your private secretary. Of course your private secretary really has a duty not only to you. They will also be reporting regularly to the secretary general of the department. On the minister and so on.

'I'm a constitutionalist. I put an enormous emphasis on the minister's role and on the TD's role.... What you need is fully-conscious, fully-viable transparent politicians who can take decisions. If you're doing it the other way, you're just drifting along with whatever is the departmental view.'

Before Tom Parlon was elected to the Dáil and became junior minister in the Office of Public Works, his previous experience as president of the IFA would have been with the Department of Agriculture.

'I would have known a major lot of the senior people in

Agriculture personally. Agriculture is quite a political department. I found the opposite in OPW. They are totally pragmatic in the OPW. Whereas (civil servants in) Agriculture would always be concerned about the government position and the minister's position, in the OPW there is a job to be done and they just do it. I found them very professional and pragmatic.'

And supportive. 'As soon as I was in there I was their guy right away. I don't have any airs and graces. I found the minute I was appointed I was their man.'

Martin Cullen, Parlon's predecessor in the OPW who went on to be Minister for the Environment and Local Government, describes his interaction with his civil servants as a sort of titanic struggle, requiring nerves of steel and buckets of grim determination, and the occasional throwing of tantrums and files.

'If you want a really major change of agenda, if there are key things you want to do that is not the safe and tried and well-tested path, you have to fight your corner. You have to force the pace, you have to challenge them, and you have to bring them with you, because if you can't get the stuff from them, or if they delay it or sit on it or whatever, it becomes very difficult for you to make those changes and do what you want to do.'

He reveals that his mandarins did not share his dream of purchasing Farmleigh House and converting the old Guinness mansion into a gracious guesthouse for visiting dignitaries.

'The civil servants weren't interested. They thought that we had other properties in the State that might have been equally suitable. So they wrote up proposals that suggested that you really couldn't go down this road. I found that very difficult. Arguing with that. It was very difficult politically to manage the project.

'*Yes, Minister* is not too far removed from the truth. Because when you say something you won't get anyone who will say "no, I'm not going to do that". You'll get "yes, Minister". But nothing will ever come of it. It will be buried in the bowels of the civil service structure in the department. I've seen it happen. That's why you have to keep your eye on the ball. You have to pull that piece of paper out again and again and deal with it.'

He describes another policy initiative that his mandarins tried to scupper by stealth. He wanted to make a policy change and asked his civil servants to prepare a briefing document. A thick file was eventually produced.

'It gave the impression that it was supporting what I wanted to do, but in fact when you read the detail, there was so much in it that it would never happen. I got very annoyed. It really frustrated me and I got mad and I said "don't ever send something like that out to me again. This is a lot simpler than this and this is what we're doing."'

About two weeks later a slimmed-down version of the file reappeared but its thrust had not altered. Cullen got even more annoyed and sent his official back to the drawing board again. The file was delivered for a third time, considerably shrunken but still not what the minister had ordered.

'At that stage I caught the file and fired it off the wall of the office and said "if anybody ever brings anything like this in to me again it will just not be tolerated". There was some very choice language used.'

He says it would be unfair to identify the policy in deference to the officials involved who, he says, 'probably laugh at it now'. I wouldn't bet the house on that probability.

Seamus Brennan, who was minister of state three times and a senior minister twice before he was appointed Transport Minister in 2002, has gained an enviable reputation as a can-do minister.

His secret, he says, is simple: put in the hours and pile on the pressure.

'If you tear off to the country on a Thursday afternoon and come back again on Wednesday morning and you don't spend a lot of time in your department, they will administer the country for you. They are very good at that. In terms of taking initiatives and breaking new ground, they will get around to them over a long period. But if a government wants to drive them through, the minister has to take it on himself – from nine in the morning until ten at night every day. And sit on it. And remember everything and remember who you told to do what and when you told them. A minister can't lose control of the policy. It's gotten to the stage where I'm in this office twelve hours a day and sometimes all of Saturday afternoons.

'There is a resistance in the system. I am blessed with a brilliant secretary general who believes in the same things I believe in. But you could have top civil servants who say "could we not study it? Could we not have a committee look at it?" If you're off travelling the world and you get a call saying "we want to appoint an independent person to study this", you'll agree to it if you're not up for pushing things through.

'If you're the kind of minister who wants to do that kind of work and are determined, it will happen. But if you're not, it will glide along on castors.'

Brennan, who boasts that he turns down foreign travel and has only been out of the country once since he was appointed to the Department of Transport, clearly feels that some globe-trotting colleagues get away with murder.

'You won't get into any trouble that way. You'll probably be seen as quite successful. The agencies will think you were great. We have about ten agencies under this department and we're fighting with all of their PR people at this stage. There is an alternative route and there is a quieter life. There are certainly two kinds of ministers.'

John Bruton found that while some civil servants were interested in solving problems, other mandarins 'regard ministers as ships that pass in the night' and are only interested in furthering the institutional agenda. The former Fine Gael leader's vast experience at the coal-face of some of the most challenging government departments didn't save him from being drawn into 'ridiculous jealousies between different departments' where rivalries over disputed territory curdled into institutionalised obstruction. But overall he admired the civil servants' dedication and was struck by their willingness to work extraordinarily long hours.

This will no doubt amuse those mandarins who dealt directly with Bruton, who as minister regarded it as his responsibility to question every file in the minutest detail, to routinely challenge recommendations and advice and send files back to officials for further consideration.

'I didn't make it easy,' he recalls with unmistakable pride.

CHAPTER 20

Promises and Compromises

'A lot of people start out with the best of intentions, but by the time you crawl your way up, you're beat' – Charlie McCreevy

Charlie McCreevy was once told by a senior journalist that he wasn't like a politician at all. He thought this was a great compliment.

McCreevy believes that his entry into politics 'by accident and a little design' and the lonely furrow he choose to plough as a voice of dissent on the backbenches saved him from the crushing compromises and craven compliance that taint so many in his profession.

'The one thing the multi-seat electoral system does is that it beats innovation out of you. Before you can get a nomination you must be a middle-of-the-road kind of fella because everyone knows that it is the transfers from the last seats that elect you. Then to keep the nomination and the party organisation behind you, you have to be careful not to take extreme views because they'll knife you at the selection convention, or they won't work for you against your colleague. So that by the time you get to the Dáil you can't be too extreme. Then you become a minister and you're warned don't be too extreme, to keep everyone happy.

'You see, I'm not like that. You'll never get anything done like that. However, you have to survive too. So you have to compromise on all sorts of things to get there. But in general, I don't like it.'

And there's another drawback. 'You do have to play the dumb eejit out there. It's a bad mistake in Irish political life to be someone who does too much thinking. That's a no no. Because then you're likely to come up with new ideas. And the system cannot cope with new ideas.'

McCreevy grew up in Kill, Co. Kildare, where he could play poker before he started school. He's not sure if the skills of a good card player are useful in politics.

'I'm a bad example. I don't think most people in politics think like me. They're very cautious. I honestly believe that if I had come up normally through politics – if I did ten years in the county council before getting elected to the Dáil, I think I would have been a totally different type of person as a politician. I mightn't be as interesting.'

'I didn't come into the Dáil thinking "I have to be a junior minister or a minister". It wasn't in my mind. I had no tradition like that. I wasn't at county council meetings. I didn't come to it with any pre-conceived notions. I came to it with a certain degree of political innocence. That you just did what you did. If I had come up through the normal route – manoeuvring and moving at county council level and then coming to the Dáil and working my way up along – I possibly would have been totally different. I took a different view as to how you could do it. All my life I've taken a different view. I believed then, as I believe now, that politics is not just about getting your arse in the back of a State car. That's what everyone thought you should be doing. And if you weren't getting on like that, you just weren't getting on. I just don't happen to believe that.'

Which was just as well. Because McCreevy's outspoken opposition to Charlie Haughey sentenced him to fourteen years on the backbenches. Instead of sulking at his lowly position, he revelled in it, playing a leading role in all three unsuccessful heaves against the party leader. He regards the more recent Fine Gael heaves as 'very gentlemanly, compared to ours.'

He obviously relished the high drama of those turbulent years.

'People were passing out and being brought off to hospital and everything. It all happened. If I came to politics the other way I would have been different. I would have had an easier life. But all the joking aside, some of them were dreadful times. It's like looking back on your school days and saying weren't they great times – well, some of them weren't that great.

'A pal of mine used to say to me back in Kildare during those years – "Jaysus, could you not give us an easy time. Could you not just be normal?" And then again, as a minister, I could have taken the easy way, and done the normal thing. But you won't achieve anything by doing that.

'I made a vow that if I ever got the chance I was going to do what I wanted to do. That's why I'd be very critical of other ministers in my own party and in other parties. You're in a very rare position. You can change things. So go about doing it. I've had to listen to ministers proclaiming about what they can't do. I say to them: "funnily enough, we are in the government. We can change the law."

'In each place I was I did an awful lot of what I wanted to do. Because when it's over, and it will be, I don't want to think "jaysus, I had the chance and I could have done certain things and I didn't do them." I approached the job with that view – that tomorrow could be my last day here – and I worked hard at it.'

He does not regard being appointed to the most senior economic ministry in the state as his greatest political triumph. That honour goes to his re-election against the odds in the 1987 general election. His marriage had broken up in 1985 and in the intensely conservative climate of the mid-Eighties, he knew that in-party rivals were spreading gossip about his changed circumstances to deny him the nomination. The PDs had also emerged in 1985, further complicating matters.

'I really didn't know if I'd survive. I remember contemplating stepping down in that period from '82 to '87. I thought about it. But then I said "feck them, I won't let them beat me." I didn't step down and I got the nomination and I survived it. It meant an awful lot. I felt I had beaten the rap. It was a personal thing. It gave me a great thrill. That was the biggest thrill I got politically.

'I got a kind of rejuvenation after '87. I was a born-again politician. I was more involved in politics after that. Not flitting in and out of it like I had been. And then I decided to give up the accountancy practice when I became a minister.

'For someone like me who was always interested in accounting and economics, being the Minister for Finance, that was it. And I've enjoyed every bloody minute of it. There have been dreadful times and I've been in unbelievable scrapes and will be again. This is only a temporary aberration.'

Mary Harney also considered leaving politics in the mid-1980s. By 1985 she was deeply unhappy and disillusioned with political life. She too had endured a fraught relationship with Charlie Haughey. One of its lowest ebbs came in 1982 when her party leader was considering who he would elevate to minister of state.

The date was 11 March 1982. The young backbencher was enjoying a convivial birthday lunch in the home of Haughey's mortal enemy, George Colley, when she received a message summoning her to the party leader's office. She rang and asked if it could wait until later in the afternoon and was told that it couldn't. Her colleagues naturally thought that Harney was being called in to be told of a promotion. She left the lunch with their congratulations ringing in her ears.

'Joe Walsh drove me in. I was saying I didn't want it. Joe Walsh was saying "don't be mad". Ray Burke was going out as I was coming in. He wished me luck.'

But Haughey didn't offer her the keys of a state car. He had called her away from her birthday lunch on the day he was handing out his appointments to dispense a humiliating dressing-down. Or, as she put it herself, 'a bollocking'.

But it wasn't just Haughey's flashes of political sadism that were threatening to break Harney's spirit. She profoundly disagreed with the party's stance on a raft of social policy issues and had grown weary of toeing a party line that was fundamentally opposed to her personal position.

In 1985, after Des O'Malley was ejected from Fianna Fáil, Harney spent a month in the US at the invitation of the US State Department. This extended period cut off from her Dáil colleagues gave her plenty of time to think. When the month was up she went to Cape Cod for a holiday with her sister, the journalist Geraldine Harney.

'During that period I made up my mind that the next thing that arrived that I didn't agree with, I wasn't going to just go along with it. It happened to be the Anglo-Irish Agreement, but it could have been anything.

'There was stuff on abortion and divorce and other things that I was very unhappy with. I voted with the party. There was the '82 referendum. I voted for the referendum in the Dáil. I was deeply unhappy around that time.

'I didn't know then that Des O'Malley was going to set up the PDs. It had blown hot and cold at various points and it eventually didn't happen until December of that year. Around that time I considered opting out. I was very seriously considering opting out. And if the PDs hadn't started I would have opted out. I'd made up my mind because I wouldn't have hung around as an Independent TD.'

Every politician who is a member of a party will know what it feels like to vote for a piece of legislation they believe to be ill-advised or simply wrong. In some cases it is an issue that directly affects their constituents. They will have made all manner of rash promises and pledges that they could not keep. They will know that they must return to their constituency on Thursday night marked out as a liar and a coward. In other cases, it is an issue they feel strongly about for personal reasons. They tell themselves small lies to soften the blow. That it doesn't really matter. That their vote wouldn't change the result. That they have to be team players. But, as Mary Harney discovered, the act of voting against your conscience and better judgment to keep a career on track chips away at the soul.

In recent years Fianna Fáil tightened up their internal party rules to ensure that any deputy who fails to vote with the party is auto-matically expelled from the parliamentary party. Expulsion is unpleasant but not terminal. It means that the deputy can no longer attend the weekly parliamentary party meetings and may lose their positions on Dáil committees as they are there at the pleasure of the party leader. In the intensely clubbable environment that is Leinster House, this isolation is seen as a cruel and unusual punishment.

But it lasts only as long as the next time the deputy is needed. When Beverley Cooper-Flynn put her family before the party and refused to vote on a Dáil motion censuring her father Padraig Flynn, she knew that she would be automatically out. But she also knew that it wouldn't be a life sentence. And, sure enough, as soon as the nominations for the 2002 general election had to be decided, Beverley was quietly shepherded back into the party fold.

Back when Mary Harney was wrestling with her social conscience, the idea of defying the party whip or speaking out against a party line was next to unthinkable. While expulsion was not automatic at that time, there were other slights and humiliations that would be meted out.

'You'd be completely isolated. You certainly wouldn't be on any Dáil committee. You wouldn't be going on a trip to Paris or wherever on a parliamentary delegation. The Taoiseach wouldn't be visiting your constituency or having you on the platform. There's more ways then one of skinning a cat.'

She believes that there is 'a greater maturity' in the Dáil now so that backbenchers are allowed little mini-revolts – on the plinth and in the media if not in the Dáil chamber.

But her memory of those hard early years of unpalatable compromises has left her deeply uneasy with the whip system.

'We still have a long way to go. And will have as long as we have the whip system. And that's not going to change in the foreseeable future. Essentially you should only be whipped on the fundamental things. On what I would call minor details relating to your constituency, does it really matter who votes which way? The sum total of the wisdom of the Dáil is more important in my view. That's invariably going to change. It's changed in most other countries.'

Garret FitzGerald admits that 'the pressures are such that politics does tend to bring out the worst in people. The constant tension between doing the right thing and the need to be re-elected can make it difficult for people to act as well as they should. There is a sense of public service. But over time it's very wearing. Over time it weakens people's resolve.

'There are always these choices between the popular and the right thing. You can't always do the right thing regardless or you'd never get re-elected. So there's compromise. What you have to do is not do wrong things, and do enough popular things that aren't wrong, to be able to do some of the good things.

'I think most people try to do the right thing, but the pressures on them of public opinion are such that they very frequently don't.'

Ruairí Quinn thinks that everybody copes with the inevitable compromises of political life differently.

'Everybody's different. In my case I run a kind of internal spiritual account. (I ask myself) am I ahead or behind? Can I afford to play it? Am I still in balance? How much of the idea is still there? Is now the time to do the deal? Can we still walk away and say this is acceptable in terms of where we started out and what we're left with?

'You have to say to yourself "these things are worth doing and if I get more than fifty per cent of it it's still worth doing". But if I have to trade to a certain point, then it's not worth doing. There's a bottom line below which you're not going to work.'

Does everyone work by these standards?

'It depends what you're there for. If you simply want to be on the pitch, there isn't a bottom line.

'What always offended me was people telling me that I should be in Fianna Fáil. In that I would have had better career prospects. And that there is no motivation other than power because that's what's they associate with so many people in Fianna Fáil, rightly or wrongly.'

Ruairi Quinn's brother Lochlann is a fabulously wealthy business-man. Ruairi admits that he did have fleeting moments when he wondered if he could have had a more comfortable life outside politics.

'You always get those thoughts when you get a bad day or a bad week. But you just go and attack the garden or go for a run or what-ever. There is a lot of things I would do differently if I was doing it again. But would I do the whole thing again? Yes I would. Without a moment's hesitation.'

Seamus Brennan thinks compromises get unfair press. Like Quinn, he says that 'in every compromise you have to feel that you got something out of it. That you got enough out of it to live with it.'

But, he protests: 'The alternative to politics is war. The reason they exchanged politics for war is that political people will compromise whereas in war there is no room for compromise. It's kill or be killed. And there is a difference between defeat and compromise.'

He can't recall a single instance where he felt forced to back a vote with which he fundamentally disagreed. And while he admits that he 'very often' entertained doubts about various political and policy strategies, he says he simply proceeded with a view that he would 'try to make it work.'

Brennan also insists that politicians so often get caught on the wrong side of a broken promise simply because of their overly-optimistic natures.

'Politicians are optimists. They are incurable optimists. They believe everything will be okay on the day. I have absolutely no doubt that when I say I am going to build a motorway to Cork, I actually mean it. If it turns out in two years time that it looks like a stupid thing to have said, and people are asking why was I promising that when we haven't got the money, and it's not going to happen and anyway some genius has now proven that it's the wrong thing to do... well.'

He offered the same explanation for the rash of ultimately empty promises that new schools and extensions would be built in the days before the 2003 general election. 'The intention was there to do that. They are optimists. They do exaggerate. It's all this wishing that things were better and hoping that things will be better. I believe that when politicians make promises to do something, that in their heart they believe that's really what they want to do. Where they get caught out is that when it comes to actually physically doing it, it gets very difficult. The system starts to take hold, arguments pop up, and suddenly the policy is in bits.'

He agrees with Charlie McCreevy that by the time they get into a position to do anything real, many politicians have had their energy and enthusiasm kicked out of them by the many compromises embraced and battles fought on their struggle up the greasy pole.

But, he argues, being battle-hardened doesn't necessarily mean that you are beaten into submission.

'That's one of the reasons I feel like I'm getting a fresh chance here. Because I've been through all that. I've been in all the scrums. I have all the scrapes and marks. And the slings and arrows of outrageous fortune – I have had them all. Now I feel that the battles I'm taking on are no bigger than the ones I had to fight before for negative reasons to protect myself. I now can fight them for positive reasons, because I want to get things done and leave them behind me.

'I think Charlie was right. But I think when you get to a certain stage of the game, you're past all that. He's now making decisions that the country needs and he's past caring whether it upsets individuals, or small groups of people, or even large groups of people.

'It's not actually arrogance. It's a sort of certainty that says "I'm through all of that and I've had thousands of people voting for me for years. I'm not going to do that pulling and dragging as much as I used to. Now I can do things".

'I'm into that area now too. So is the Taoiseach. But there's a whole lot of colleagues who are still at the far side of the wall. Who are still worried about missing the residents' meeting, or what will happen if they don't back the minister immediately even before his speech is finished. There is a great Americanism – "you care, but not as much".

'I had decided a whole lot of times in my life to get out of politics. I came closest about a week after I entered it. And a couple of times over the years I thought "I don't think I'll bother with the next election. I'll go away and do something else".

'But in a strange, paradoxical way, every time I started thinking that way I started to get better at the job. Then I couldn't go because

I was getting better at it. I was thinking "they're after promoting me here. I can't leave now".

'I have a second chance of delivering stuff. I'm right at the thick of it and I'm excited about what's happening. I think that if I get a couple of years here I can deliver nine or ten big policy initiatives that are essential to the country. I don't give a damn after that.'

CHAPTER 21

Changing Horses

'I felt like I was in a James Bond movie' – Martin Cullen

G arret FitzGerald referred to this business as 'one of the unattractive features of politics'. That is the fact that a politician who dares to change horses mid-stream is rarely a persona grata with the party they have left or, at least at first, with the party they have joined.

Party loyalty is a highly-valued commodity in Leinster House and those who choose to abandon it, for whatever reason, must expect to pay a high political and personal price for what will inevitably be regarded as their treachery.

Garret FitzGerald was referring particularly to one of the most celebrated cases of side switching in modern political history.

Michael O'Leary had resigned as leader of the Labour Party in October 1982 after his party's annual conference voted against involvement in a further coalition without prior approval by a special party conference. He decided instead to embark on a personal coalition arrangement of his own.

On the evening of O'Leary's successor Dick Spring's election as Labour leader, Garret FitzGerald answered a ring at his front door to find the former Labour leader on his doorstep. As FitzGerald recalled the happy occasion in his autobiography: 'He walked in and told me he wanted to join Fine Gael.'

And that, apparently, was that. FitzGerald knew that his entry to the party would cause some short-term problems with the Labour Party, but decided that this could hardly be grounds for refusing so senior a politician the Fine Gael whip.

But the sting was in the tail. It was soon made clear to FitzGerald, both by his own party and by Labour, that O'Leary 'would not be acceptable as a member of a coalition government'.

While the negotiations for O'Leary's shock move appear to have been limited, to say the least, orchestrating a clean walk across the floor of the Dáil in the gossip pit that is Leinster House can be a complicated business.

Martin Cullen says he realised very shortly after his election as a Progressive Democrat TD for his Waterford constituency that he 'just didn't fit' with the style of his party.

'That was very obvious from early days. It was an extraordinary sense of disappointment to me. The make-up of the party had a certain type of inbuilt perspective to it. It was formed for one reason and I believed that it had to become for a different reason if it was going to have a life beyond it.'

He lost the 1989 election and Charlie Haughey nominated him as one of the Taoiseach's nominees to the Seanad.

'I wasn't going to be given it but Fianna Fáil kicked up such a stink in Waterford when they presumed I was going to get it that they demanded that they would get a senatorship in Waterford as well.

'I didn't discourage the rumour. It wound up Fianna Fáil people locally and it backed people into corners. I wouldn't have said we initiated it, but if the truth be told we very much encouraged the notion and that made it such an issue that it had to happen.'

So he was back in the Oireachtas but still feeling uneasy.

'I became more and more disillusioned. I lost a lot of heart. I fought the local elections in Waterford in '91 for the county and city, and they nearly went horribly wrong.'

He scraped in on the last count to retain his Waterford City Council seat, and regained his Dáil seat for the Progressive Democrats in the 1992 general election, but only just.

'After that nothing much changed. There was a lot of upheavals going on at that stage and I didn't like a lot of it. I had kind of come to the conclusion that I had to either give up politics altogether or do what I always wanted to do. And what I always wanted to do was be in Fianna Fáil.'

And why was that?

'I always wanted to see if I could really cut it in a big party like Fianna Fáil. A lot of people said "he's a big fish in a small pond but he'll never make it in the real political kitchen". '

The word on the ground was that Fianna Fáil was rethinking its strategy for the constituency at national level and would not be averse to having Cullen in the party. There was a growing view that they needed a minister in the constituency. There followed much mutual ball-hopping and pointed banter, until finally Cullen was formally approached by a local Fianna Fáiler with, as he put it, 'the imprimatur from above'.

That was followed up by a chat with Tipperary minister Michael Smith, who wanted to confirm that he was serious. Cullen assured him that he was, but asked that their discussions be kept confidential.

Shortly afterwards he received a phone call from the Fianna Fáil general secretary Pat Farrell. He was told to go to the Berkeley Court Hotel in Ballsbridge and take the lift to a specified room. There would be no need to ask for a key at reception. The room door would be open. He was to step inside and wait.

Cullen picks up the breathless narrative: 'After about ten or fifteen minutes the door opened and in stepped the Taoiseach with a tray of tea and biscuits. He had come up the back elevator from the kitchen to meet me. He didn't want to be seen coming through the front door when I'd be coming in that way. If you remember that time, there was a lot of this cloak and dagger stuff. It was all very funny. I felt like I was in a James Bond movie.'

As well he might.

'I had never sat down and spoken with him personally and I'd never really engaged with him. This took me completely aback. You don't expect the Taoiseach of the country to be coming in the door and saying "Jaysus, do ya want a cup of tea?" Perhaps somebody brought them as far as the door and he didn't want them to see who was inside. We sat down and had a great conversation.'

He took to him instantly. 'He was one of the straightest guys I had ever met in politics, and I'll go to my grave with that view.'

There was a vacancy for a minister of state at the time and some suggestion that Cullen could expect to fill it should he make the leap. Reynolds made it clear that he would not.

'He said "get your head down and get on with the work, and if we're successful come the next election then (you will be appointed) at least into the minister of state ranks and who knows from there".

During this meeting and the two more that were to follow, Reynolds was also extraordinarily open about his secret moves to broker an IRA ceasefire.

'I was totally taken aback with this one thing. He was heavily engaged in the background talks with Gerry Adams on the whole original breakthrough. He told me all about it, I think trying to demonstrate to me that he trusted me, and he was taking me into his confidence.

'I was very grateful for that because it was a real trust and bridge-building exercise between two people. I think he was being up-front. I think he did want to demonstrate that he could be trusted and he was going to trust me.

'These talks went on over a couple of months. Always in secret. I met other people in different places. It was great fun. When you've never done it before, it is dramatic. Then I spoke to the general secretary. After that it was just a question of how the Waterford organisation would react. Would we get enough people in the Waterford organisation to bring me into the cumann and square everybody away and take the political heat out of everybody objecting?

'I had my mind made up from the first meeting. It had taken me ten years to prove that I was worthy of being in Fianna Fáil. That's the way I saw it. I hadn't had an easy route. I had to go out and prove myself before I was deemed good enough to get in.'

Then there was the little matter of dropping the bombshell. Like all defections to the enemy, absolute secrecy is paramount. No announcement can be made until the defector is safely over the border. Last minute leaks can scupper the most carefully laid plans.

Reynolds and Cullen picked a date. Every aspect of the day would be carefully choreographed. Cullen would arrive in Dublin at an appointed hour and he would be personally welcomed into the party by the Taoiseach amid a blaze of publicity. But events intervened.

Two days before it was to happen, the Taoiseach phoned a tense Cullen at home.

'It was a Saturday night. He said "Martin, we have a problem. We're going to announce the breakthrough with Gerry Adams".

'I thought that was an extraordinary compliment. I was one of the first people in the country to know about this. We had a discussion and I agreed that it would be almost disastrous to clash with this. I had learned to trust him by then. I liked him and I think he liked me.'

But Reynolds took one last precaution. Fearing that his new recruit might be got at while he was otherwise engaged, he suggested a quarantine arrangement.

'He asked if I had any relations anywhere. If I could get out of the country for a week. I said I had a brother in England. He said "leave tomorrow, get out, go away and disappear".

'At this stage there were a lot of people in the loop and it was going to be impossible to keep the lid on it. So I got out of the country for a week and had a holiday in England.

'I was on tenterhooks. The calls started early that week. The media noticed I wasn't in the Dáil. By the following weekend it had reached a crescendo. And I couldn't be found. And the fact that I wasn't found was giving credence to the speculation that there was something in the wind.'

The announcement was made the following week, immediately after he informed the Progressive Democrats that he was jumping ship and, as he recalls, 'it got the coverage it deserved.'

'It was tough at a personal level. I'm not sure who I called (in the Progressive Democrats). It's a blur because the pressure by the end of that week was just enormous. It was impossible on my family. There were so many phone calls. And some of them weren't pleasant either.

'It was very nasty but it's inevitable. It's not so difficult to cross the floor in other European countries or even in the US. It's no big deal. But in Ireland it was a very difficult move, and particularly with me going to Fianna Fáil.

'Overall, it went like a dream – but there are one or two people to this day who still don't speak to me. And I regret that. But you have to make decisions and sometimes you have to make tough decisions. Sometimes you have to make decisions at a personal level that do affect people, and when you do there are consequences. People take it very personally. But that's life.'

While he admits that fears for his seat and promotional prospects were 'an element' of the thinking behind his decision, he insists that his unease with what he terms the Progressive Democrats' 'elitist' political philosophy and the party's anti-Haughey obsession were just as relevant.

'I could have just fallen on my face and disappeared off the face of the earth. I was prepared to take that risk. But I instinctively and immediately began to enjoy politics again.'

There was one last pleasant surprise in store for Cullen.

'I was made very welcome. People had told me that Fianna Fáil is very insular and that I would never be accepted. I was warned that they would always hold it against me and I would be kept down. That once I went in and they'd had their day and a slap at the PDs, I'd be forgotten.

'The actual opposite was the experience and that was an extraordinary confidence-building boost from my point of view.'

It helped that party grandee Brian Lenihan proposed him. In politics, perhaps more than in any other sphere of life, what goes around comes around.

When a Sunday newspaper reported that the Progressive Democrats were backing Mary Robinson in the 1990 presidential election, Cullen went public with his intention to defy the party line and back Lenihan.

'He appreciated that and he never forgot. He hardly ever spoke to me about it but it was implicit between us. I thought it was one of the nicest things. He was decent to me. We'd sit out on the plinth and we'd have a chat and a cigarette. His imprimatur was a tremendous signal to the party and that was an enormous help to me.'

While Cullen paints a picture of a happy-clappy rebirth in Fianna Fáil, the truth is that there are jealous Fianna Fáil colleagues who have never forgotten his political past, while his former Progressive Democrats colleagues have never forgiven it. And even as his career soars and he strives to become the most loyal, the most dedicated soldier of destiny of them all, in certain circles and bitchy asides in Leinster House society he will forever remain a turncoat or a blow-in who may get their respect, but never their trust.

Sometimes you just can't win. Seamus Brennan refused to change horses – and was widely denounced as a coward and a tease for standing his ground.

When Des O'Malley formed the PDs in 1985, it was taken as read that Brennan would sign up. As a card-carrying member of the Club of 22 who moved against Charlie Haughey, he had opposed Haughey openly, and had resigned his post as Fianna Fáil general secretary because of him. And yet, when O'Malley jumped, Brennan stayed put.

'I never said I would go,' he protests now, and not for the first time. 'They just assumed it. And it was a wrong assumption even if it was logical.

'When I was finally asked I said no. I did think about it seriously. But my father was a big influence on me. It was assumed that I misled people, but nobody ever sat me down and said "if we start a new party will you go". It was just assumed that when somebody shouted charge, I'd be in the charging line because I had been charging for years at that stage.'

He says he has 'a lot of admiration' for Des O'Malley and Mary Harney. But, he says, 'they underestimated me. I had been general secretary of Fianna Fáil for seven years. That meant something to me. You can't be general secretary of a party, trying to build it through a general election, worry about it, work for it, care for the damn thing, travel the country for it, and walk away.

'For some group of people to assume I was going to walk away from that because I had a few rows with the man at the top – they greatly underestimated me.'

For whatever reason, many of the main players took it personally. In somewhat of an understatement, Brennan admits: 'Things were very strained at the time.'

Tom Parlon is luckier. Although he bought his party allegiance off-the-peg for reasons that have as much to do with his personal promotional prospects as any high-flying ideology, he took the precaution of doing so before he was elected to the Dáil. As the parties put together their election strategies in the run up to the general election in 2002, the affable Offalyman found himself at the centre of a bidding war between two party leaders.

While Fine Gael might have been considered a natural home for a former farm leader, he says that one incident in particular swung him in favour of the Progressive Democrats.

He had asked Mary Harney to act as mediator in a bitter dispute between the Irish Farmers Association and Irish Sugar. He got her on her mobile at the hairdressers. They spoke for fifteen minutes and she agreed to meet both sides at Dublin Castle the following day. It developed into a very acrimonious and highly abusive meeting. Finally, at 4.30pm, she said she had to go. She withdrew, declaring that both men were a disgrace.

Somehow, after she left, the two sides managed to come to an agreement.

On his way back into the city centre Parlon felt guilty about what they had put the Tánaiste through and decided to ring her.

'Her driver answered and I explained that I wanted a quick word with the Tánaiste to apologise. She came on the phone and said "I believe ye got a deal". I apologised and she said "no problem. And by the way, I've just got married".

'That left me very impressed with Mary Harney. Most people say politicians suit themselves. The last thing she needed was for some asshole to ring up and ask her to organise a last-ditch meeting on her wedding day.

'Whether she had any other ideas for me at that stage I don't know. Who am I to know what goes on in a woman's mind? I was moved by her commitment. When I heard she was married I was bowled over.'

But it took another four-hour meeting in the Tánaiste's home in Ballsbridge for Parlon to spurn Michael Noonan's advances and announce his betrothal to the Progressive Democrats.

How did she do it?

'She said "if you decide to go, you'll win. And if you win, the PDs will do well. And if the PDs do well we are very likely to be in government. In that scenario you will have been very influential in our success and clearly there will be some reward." She told me I would be one of the negotiators for the Programme for Government if it came to that.'

There were also a couple of potentially lucrative business offers on the table. But he found himself veering towards politics.

'I've always been borrowed all my life. Money doesn't really appeal to me in a big way as long as I can get by. Whereas political life did appeal to me. There is a madness to it but there is a lure as well.

'I consulted with nobody other than my wife. She thought either option was daft but told me to do what I wanted to do myself. I went with my hunch. I was impressed with Mary Harney. I felt that the influence that the PDs had previously had been very substantial. I could buy into that ethos in a big way.

'I found Michael Noonan extremely honourable, but I could only join one party. He was guesting on *This Week* on the radio the next day. Mary Harney said we should be decent about the way we announced it. I wanted that too. Also I didn't want him savaging me on the radio. So we delayed any announcement until three o'clock on Sunday.'

And the rest, as they say, is history. Parlon's move provided a major boost that helped lift the party's flagging morale. The party leader, reeling from the shock of returning with no less than eight TDs to the Dáil, honoured her promise and made Parlon one of the negotiators of the Programme for Government.

'I wouldn't have been happy on the backbench. To get two seniors and two juniors out of eight seats was a good deal. It took a lot of battling. I was under no illusion that Mary Harney and Michael McDowell were going to be the two senior ministers. I know my limitations. The two prime juniors are in Finance and Foreign Affairs. That was the choice I had. The complication with European Affairs was that my constituency colleague Brian Cowen was the senior minister.',

So he opted to take the role of Minister of State in the Department of Finance, with responsibility for the Office of Public Works. It came with its own substantial budget and an elegant office overlooking St Stephen's Green.

'I'm fascinated with the job,' he says now.

CHAPTER 22

That's Women For You

'All the secretaries were women, so ergo we were all secretaries' –
Nuala Fennell

Since the first Dáil sat in 1919, women have won just 196 of the 4,286 Dáil seats filled. Fifty-seven women have been senators out of a total of 624.

The first wave of women politicians were republican firebrands, women who grew up in a time when not having the Y chromosome meant that you did not have the right to vote, let alone sit in parliament. They were radicals, identifying themselves as either suffragettes, nationalists or socialists, and in many cases coming to politics from a background soaked in all of these political agendas.

But the initial surge fizzled and died. During the fifty years from 1922 to 1972, the average Dáil contained no more than four women. And most of those were widows or daughters of deceased Dáil members.

Pensions for widows and children of politicians were only introduced in 1968 by the Oireachtas Allowances to Members (Amendment) Act, so many of these may have been pressed into Dáil service by financial necessity rather than by any personal political ambitions.

While the Seanad has seen a greater percentage of women elected, the level of representation by women remains abysmally low.

Senior politicians have bleated about the dearth of women in the political arena for years, yet it's interesting to note that any

Taoiseach, who can nominate eleven senators to the Upper House, could have taken the opportunity to play a significant role in righting the gender imbalance. No Taoiseach since the new Seanad was created in 1937 has ever nominated more than three women senators to any Senate.

Women in Parliament, a study of women's role in the Oireachtas by Maedhbh McNamara and Paschal Mooney which was published in 2000, confirms that Ireland lags well behind other established democracies in terms of the number of women engaged in representative politics.

At the time, women held thirteen per cent of the Dáil seats. In Scandinavian countries women held between thirty-six per cent and forty-two per cent. In New Zealand, Australia, Canada and the UK, women held between eighteen and twenty-nine per cent. Between 1922 and 1977, twelve widows were elected to seats previously held by their husbands. The practice had died out by 1977, when Eileen Lemass, widow of Noel Lemass and daughter-in-law of former Taoiseach Seán Lemass, became the last of a breed, winning a seat in the new constituency of Dublin Ballyfermot.

Daughters began to step up to the plate from the 1970s, with ten becoming members of the Oireachtas between 1973 and 1997.

Sixty-one serving and retired women members of the Oireachtas (out of a possible seventy) co-operated with a survey on their contribution to politics in 1999. Over two-thirds of those surveyed rated family care responsibilities as their most significant barrier to a political career. It would be interesting to find out how many male politicians, the vast majority of whom are fathers, would even think of 'family care responsibilities' if presented with this question.

Another one-third rated husbands as the most important sources of difficulty for women in general – although many of them said they felt their own husbands were supportive. In fairness, we must suppose that Liz O'Donnell was joking when she stated: 'My husband said that if I became a politician, it would be grounds for annulment.'

Her party leader, Mary Harney, thinks it's no coincidence that women with children are reluctant to enter active politics. 'It's not family-friendly. Look at the women around: Mary Coughlan entered politics when her father and uncle died and before she was married. Cecilia Keaveney is single. Mary Hanafin has no children. I've no children. Síle de Valera has no children. Mary O'Rourke went into politics when her children were grown up. If you were to go through them all you'd find that there are relatively few women there with children, and when they have they've probably gone into politics before they were born.

'Fiona O'Malley is single, Mae Sexton's children are largely grown. I frequently hear women worried about not seeing a lot of their children. Mary Coughlan talks about it a lot. You rarely hear men say that. I'm not saying men don't concern themselves about it, but it is different.'

Harney is Ireland's most successful female Dáil politician, in terms of the offices she has held. She believes there are pluses and minuses to being a woman in politics.

'The pluses of being a woman are that you are more easily noticed so it can be easier to promote yourself.

'The downside was that you were completely raw and perceived to be such. You'd hear things back like "what the hell would she know about it?". There was a view that if you came from a political background you might know what it was about. But if, like me, you didn't, well... '

Nuala Fennell swept into the Dáil with the largest number of women deputies ever elected on a Fine Gael ticket in 1981. She thinks their male colleagues had some trouble coming to terms with this new political species: women who were TDs but who were not filling a seat vacated by a blood relative or a spouse.

'All the secretaries were women, so ergo we were all secretaries,' was the vibe.

'One of the interesting things I found was that when you were out at parties or functions all the men wanted to talk politics to me. It kind of distanced women from your orbit. There's a kind of an image that because you're an elected TD you know everything about everything. I had to make a point of talking to women. The women I knew, my friends, it kind of put a gap between us.'

Gemma Hussey, who was the only woman in her Cabinet, noted in her Cabinet diaries: 'Women in politics have all sorts of extra criteria to cope with, extra dimensions of comment: it did one no good, politically, to be found on a worst-dressed list (as I was once). If one looked tired or less than immaculate on television or in press photos, it was widely commented upon and seen as a black mark, or a sign of weakness.'

At another point, a glum Hussey mused: 'I often wondered if Garret's (FitzGerald) weight gain, like my own, was directly related to the stresses of the job.'

Weight gain is an occupational hazard of political life. In Gemma Hussey's time, ministers incarcerated in ten-hour Cabinet meetings would eventually crack and send their drivers for chips. The Dáil restaurants still serve up the hearty meat and two-veg fare beloved of the country TDs who, like Jackie Healy-Rae's plain people of Ireland, like to eat their dinner in the middle of the day. A fry-up is most often the order of the day in the lull before the adjournment debate and the late vote. The late sittings and the calories on the rubber chicken circuit all take their toll.

Male politicians simply make a trip to Louis Copeland to slip up a size and few pass any heed. But the waistlines of female politicians are the subject of relentless comment and speculation.

Mary Harney has noticed that much of this comes from a surprising quarter.

'You get used to it. You can't allow those things to get in on you or otherwise you wouldn't function. I suppose the surprising thing is that you get more of that from women journalists than you do from men. Women judge other women on the basis of image rather than substance a lot of the time. Not all women. But some do.

'I remember a female journalist commenting on Róisín Shortall when she was going for the leadership of the Labour Party. I heard it on the radio and I couldn't believe my ears. She said that she needed a make-over. None of the men were commented on in the same way.

'If you were to ask me now to give advice to somebody who is twenty-two years of age, I would say go for it if you really want it. I would definitely point out all the pitfalls. Given a choice you're better to have another career first. The best time to go into politics is probably in your thirties rather than in your twenties. If you have no other career, and you're not from a wealthy background, you're very vulnerable.'

When I met Labour Senator Kathleen O'Meara just over a year after she was defeated in the 2002 general election, she confided that she was seriously considering walking away from politics. She admitted that when she was informed, by text message, that she was not going to win the seat she had battled so hard for in Tipperary North, she cried. And cried and cried.

'I don't know how people can go at it again and again. I mean where's your soul? I don't think that men ask themselves the same questions. It's soul-destroying. How could you put yourself and your family through it?

'You're so publicly exposed. I wouldn't advise a true friend to do it. Unless I thought that they had the guts to withstand that kind of stuff. I know a woman who can, who somehow holds a little back for herself. But most people don't. You put everything into it. Everything.'

It's the often devastating disconnection between effort and outcome that O'Meara finds utterly soul-destroying.

'It's a spin of the wheel. It's like gambling on something that's going to happen in four years' time. You're stacking up those chips on the table and that wheel will spin and everything you did in the meantime won't make any difference.

'If the poll situation holds up there is a potential for the '92 situation (when the Spring tide swept thirty-three Labour TDs into the Dáil) to happen again. So sit back and wait for it again. But four years waiting for it to happen – what a waste of a life!

'You want to be very sure walking away from it that you don't mind what the outcome is. Because someone could walk into your shoes and they could get elected. But even if I was elected to the Dáil, the lifestyle issue would still be an issue. It's just not a life-enhancing thing to do with your life. It's a grind.'

She spoke of driving her son to do his Leaving Certificate exams the previous summer.

'If you give yourself completely to it they're the kind of things you're expected to give up. You're public property. No matter where you go. And there's very little appreciation that you have a private life.

'An election is definitely the most intrusive thing. You display yourself in such a public manner. And you never know when a door opens what you're going to meet on the other side of it. People can get abusive, they can heap personal abuse on you.

'The day of the count – and the public exposure of your vulnerability. It does get into you. On some level your soul is bared. It demolishes your confidence in your judgment.

'Men go to work and they forget they have children. They just forget. When you're a woman you never forget the child at home. There's that constant pull. And of course that translates into the bigger frame of worrying about the children in Iraq or wherever. It means you're not as tough. You're not as hard. But would you want to be?

'If you think about the women who've really succeeded… I was watching a documentary about Margaret Thatcher. She turned herself into a man. Is that what you're supposed to do? Turn yourself into a man to succeed? Sorry – I won't do that.

'Women care. And people who care get mangled by the thing. My husband reminded me that there's men with a feminine side who find it tough as well. Men like Ruairi Quinn and Pat Gallagher.

'I mean, Jesus, is it worth it? I ask myself that question. My daughter is ten. Is it worth not being there for the child growing up? What you miss as well as what they miss. Is it worth it? What do you get out of it at the end of it?

'As a rural TD you're absolutely imprisoned. I left home on Tuesday morning. I did the school run, got into my car and drove to Dublin and it will be Thursday night before I see home again. I don't think I'd be able to do it if I had a baby.

'It takes time to wind back from all that business and actually be a normal person at home. You can't just switch out of one and switch into the other and say I'll put on my apron now and I'll just be a normal mammy at home. Your head is still filled with all that stuff. You're waiting for phone calls. Checking the paper for funerals. You're not actually present there at all.'

She believes it is different for women.

'I wouldn't have said that a few years ago but I would now. A few years ago I would have trundled out all the stuff about how important it is for women to be involved, and that's true. It's just that it puts you in a particularly female-unfriendly location.

'Try a county council meeting for size. It's one big macho experience. It's all about power and one-upmanship. Much more than national politics, it's a bear pit.'

In 2002 there were three female councillors out of twenty-one members of North Tipperary County Council.

'I get on very well with my male colleagues on the Council at a personal level but politically it's down and dirty stuff. Don't let anyone away with anything, and fight your corner. It is serious confrontational stuff. Sharp, nasty and very, very competitive.

'Women are better at consensus, co-operation and getting things done. But it's never about that. It's about competing for attention, for credit, for who can get there first. It's highly competitive. It is a hurling county, I suppose.'

Six months later, O'Meara was a transformed woman. All thoughts of leaving politics were gone. She explained that she had taken the month of August off 'and all the layers of failure and disappointment just peeled away.

'And after all that, I realised that I want to do this. I love it. I'm doing what I want to do.'

She had made one promise to herself, though. 'This time I'm going to do it my way. If this is my last turn on the roundabout, I'm going to enjoy it!'

When Nora Owen was approached to stand for Fine Gael in the 1979 local elections, she laughed.

'I hardly knew there was an election coming up. There was a whole new ward and they were looking for new candidates. I would have gone to a few Fine Gael functions. But I wasn't an active branch member. I was married with three children under seven. I was a full-time housewife and mother.

'I rang my mother and said they've asked me to stand for the council and my mother, who had been a widow from when we were young, I thought she'd say "your children are young. Stay put". But she said she thought that would be a good idea. She knew I needed something.'

If Nora's mother thought it would stop at a little outside diversion for her bored daughter, she would have been sorely mistaken. Politics was to consume the best part of Nora's next twenty years. She won a seat in the Dáil for the first time against the odds in 1981. That year the number of women in the Dáil jumped from the four in the previous Dáil to thirteen. Most of the new women TDs had got in on their own merits, rather than having come in to fill their husband's or father's seats.

Nora is a grand-niece of Michael Collins and her constituency team had insisted that this fact was highlighted in her election literature. But she insists that that it was her high profile in the community, and not her famous grand-uncle, that won her the seat and counted herself among this new brand of female TD.

'It was quite an exciting time. Because we were new and novel, we probably got a bigger share of notoriety than the men, which I'm sure at times annoyed them.'

She recounts a 'funny' story that serves to illustrate just how the political establishment viewed women in 1981.

On the first day of the new Dáil, the TDs went to the traditional Mass in the Pro-Cathedral before heading on up en masse to Leinster House. As she entered the gates at the Kildare Street entrance, she fell into step with Sean Barrett, who was also a first-time TD. As they got to the front door, RTÉ's Brian Farrell took Sean Barrett by the arm and asked him to do a television interview. Polite to his fingertips, he then took it upon himself to follow Nora into the hall and apologise for his interruption.

'I hope it's alright,' he said. 'I'm just borrowing your husband for a minute to do an interview.'

Owen did not spare him. 'I said "first of all he's not my husband, secondly, my name is Nora Owen, and thirdly, I'm a new TD as well."

'Brian was absolutely overcome with embarrassment. With the result that he took me by the arm, pulled me out, put Sean to one side and interviewed me. It was very funny.

'That was telling of the assumption that any woman coming in there with a man was automatically the wife. And it was telling that they hadn't yet identified who these new women were. That's how it started.'

Labour advisor Fergus Finlay believes that constituents expect more of female politicians. 'I assume it's tougher for a woman in the Dáil. I think constituents approach women TDs differently. They expect more time in a clinic, they expect their emotional problems to be more readily absorbed and understood. It's a much more difficult job in terms of the relationship between the TD and the constituent.

'In terms of relationships between TDs in the Dáil, there isn't any difference. But the media are much harder on women TDs. Much more demanding of them. Because their appearance comes into play. Nobody's ever going to say that Willie Penrose spoke in the Dáil last night and by jaysus didn't he look a fright.

'When it comes to female TDs, everyone is so reluctant to say that she's put on a pile of weight that they say all the other things. They say that she's lacklustre or that she doesn't seem to care anymore. Whereas men can arrive in their crumpled suits with blood-shot eyes and smelling of drink. And nobody minds.'

Finlay notes that there is no such thing yet in Ireland as a woman's vote.

'The Fianna Fáil vote is still the Fianna Fáil vote. It won't transfer from woman to woman. The tribal vote is much more powerful than the woman's vote.'

He recalls the 1989 election in Dublin South when Eithne FitzGerald was the strongest of four remaining female candidates.

'You would think that the woman's vote would push her over the line. But the Fine Gael vote stayed within Fine Gael. The Fianna Fáil vote stayed within Fianna Fáil. And almost no votes transferred from woman to woman. Had there been even a tiny women's vote in that election, Eithne would have got elected.'

CHAPTER 23

Justice Denied

'They couldn't run a monkey's tea party' – Alan Shatter

H ell hath no fury like an ambitious politician scorned. Every Dáil will have its share of TDs who believe they have been unfairly passed over for promotion. Some accept their fate, apparently stoically, and dig in for the long haul. Others seethe with resentment on the backbenches, watching colleagues they regard as their political and intellectual inferiors basking in the glory of ministerial office.

As a brilliant law student who did ground-breaking work in the field of family law, Alan Shatter spent years trying to convince politicians of the need to reform family and children's law with little success. In the end he says he 'got fed up of being patted on the head' by TDs who were not progressing his agenda and decided to run for politics himself.

'I would have seen getting into Fine Gael and getting into politics as a mechanism to try and bring about from the inside some of the policy changes that I was genuinely interested in. I had no concept of "will this damage my career, will this prevent me accumulating property, will this affect my wealth?" It wasn't an issue for me. In those days it was simply where I was going.'

As a member of the Jewish community, joining Fine Gael meant leaping over a major cultural and historical chasm. The party's past association with the Blueshirts was viewed as a damning flirtation with fascism among the Jewish community. Oliver J Flanagan, who had made an infamous attack on Jewry in the Dáil in the 1940s, was still a member of the parliamentary party. But Shatter felt that Fine Gael was his political home. He hated Haughey and could not subscribe to the socialist agenda of Labour. And he admired Garret FitzGerald. From afar. That admiration waned somewhat after he became a Fine Gael representative.

'What I didn't know then was that, although he writes very well, and is an appealing speaker, and as a political debater he was very stimulating, he couldn't organise a monkey's tea party. This was something I discovered within a year of arriving in Leinster House.

'The manner in which Leinster House works – the incapacity to actually achieve things of value on the backbenches – would probably have driven me completely insane if I wasn't involved in my legal practice.

'What happened between 1982, when Fine Gael came in again, and 1987, nearly drove me out of politics. I was within an ace of not running again in '87. I had almost had enough of it at that point.

'I was a backbencher. I had come into politics with no illusions. But I had come into politics with a public identity, the nature of which was unusual. And with a recognised area of expertise. By 1981 I had written two definitive books on family law. As a young solicitor from 1978 onwards I did something no other solicitor had done. I was acting as advocate in my own cases in the High Court and the Supreme Court. I was recognised around the country as having a certain degree of expertise in this area. I suppose, to be quite frank, I would have expected that that would have got some recognition. And it got none at all.

'I didn't go around and knock on Garret's door and say if you don't make me minister I'm leaving. It wasn't until I got to about 1986 that I became utterly and completely pissed off.'

Instead, his constituency colleague Nuala Fennell was appointed Minister for Equality and Law Reform. His assessment of her performance in the ministry is less than flattering.

'I spent five years watching Nuala fustering around and it practically drove me insane,' he said.

Nuala Fennell remembers it somewhat differently. Despite stubborn opposition even among her own Cabinet colleagues to her reformist agenda, she nevertheless managed to bring forward the legislation that abolished the legal concept of illegitimacy, change citizenship laws so that men could not divorce their wives in other jurisdictions without their consent, set up a hugely successful women's enterprise scheme as well as driving ahead other initiatives.

She says she retains a respect for Alan Shatter's legislative work, but it is clear that there is no love lost.

'He brought in those private members' Bills – I wouldn't take it from him for a minute. But he couldn't get on with anyone. He was such a hate figure in the Dáil because he was personally nasty. You work with your party, you take advantage of the government's weakness, but you do it in a way that you're not personally wounding anybody. Alan couldn't do that.'

The focus of Shatter's still raw irritation oscillates between the minister who usurped him and the Taoiseach who failed to appreciate his brilliance.

'It was a personal thing. It wasn't "yeah, boo, she's a minister and I'm not". It was a case of here was an opportunity, a Fine Gael government with a leader with a reformist profile. I watched for five years not only a complete and total incapacity to implement anything he (FitzGerald) talked about, but the impossibility of playing any meaningful role of any description in it. And watching people fustering around not knowing their arse from their elbow. And it really drove me bananas. I don't think he had any notion of what my area of expertise was. I could have been the dustbin man as far as he was concerned.

'My view was that Garret talked very attractively and most journalists thought he was a great man because of this, but no-one has actually analysed what happened during this period.'

He fought a grim trench war against what he saw as the deeply flawed attempts to deal with the social agenda during this period. In 1983 he and Monica Barnes voted against the proposed abortion referendum – against party policy.

'I delivered a very long and tendentious Dáil speech on the '83 referendum debate, during which I predicted everything that subsequently happened over the next fifteen years.'

He was equally appalled by Barry Desmond's attempt to introduce a Children's Act.

'I had been talking about children's law throughout the 1970s. Barry Desmond as Minister for Health produced a Children's Bill which the first I saw of – which is the way backbenchers are treated – was the day it was published and distributed in Leinster House.

'It was absolutely appalling. It failed utterly to address the areas that needed to be addressed. In so far as it did address areas, it was utterly and completely clueless. There was no other way of referring to that Bill.

'Barry was a victim in this. He was relying on his advisors. I was the guy who had written about this in two bloody books where I had actually set out what needed to be done. I'm not the font of all wisdom. But here was this atrocious piece of legislation. That became the subject of another Dáil speech in which I took it apart line by line in second stage.'

He doesn't recall his insolence causing any political ripples.

'I was constructively contributing to debate. I don't think anybody cared or even noticed. I think the only people who would have noticed would be the department officials and whatever minister happened to be the victim sitting there at the time. I don't think anyone else gave a monkey's. I was filling Dáil time. Contributing to all sorts of debates. I was completely irrelevant. Providing you voted in the lobbies the way they wanted you to vote you were utterly irrelevant.'

In any case the Bill quietly went away. 'It disappeared. Never went beyond second stage. It was absolutely unamendable.'

He was appointed to the Oireachtas Committee on Marriage Breakdown. He reasoned that 'Garret had to do something with me at that stage.'

The Committee report, produced after eighteen-month consultations, bore, he can't help recalling with a satisfied smile, an uncanny resemblance to his own FLAC Report of 1971 and his recommendations for reform from his two family law books. The Committee concluded that there was much work to be done.

'There was no question of jumping into a divorce referendum overnight. You had to lay the basis for it by enacting major reforms in family law.'

Then, as he describes it, something astonishing happened. Wandering down a corridor in Leinster House of an evening, Garret called him over, saying that he had something to show him.

'He pulled a slip of paper out of an inside jacket pocket and said "we're going to announce a divorce referendum tomorrow and this is the wording". I looked at the wording which included a provision that divorce would only be granted if it was in the interests of the welfare of the children of the parties. I looked at him and asked if he was really serious about this. He said the AG had prepared the wording that morning. What did I think? I said "this is a disaster. Half the judiciary would be opposed in principle to divorce. Nearly all of them bar four are from a Roman Catholic background and education. The bar library is full of people who campaigned against the '83 abortion referendum. Some of them are now judges. How many divorces do you think would be granted on the basis that it would be in the interests of the children? This is complete insanity." I said "you could deal with it in such and such a way" and asked if I could take a note of the wording.

'He said Cabinet was meeting at nine o'clock. I said "can I take a note of this and meet you at eight o'clock and give you an alternative draft to consider?"'

FitzGerald declined, insisting that it was a confidential document, but agreed to meet Shatter at 8am.

'I walked straight into the Leinster House library trying to memorise the wording of this fragment of paper. I wrote it down as best I could.

'In the context of this and other contacts I'd had with him, it seemed to me that Garret was for the birds. Completely for the birds. I went home and told my wife. I made a whole series of notes and met Garret at 8am.'

FitzGerald had consulted with the Attorney General in the interim and had come up with a new draft.

According to Shatter: 'It took account of one thing I'd said. The court would no longer have to decide it was in the children's interest. We had a discussion about this. And then he handed me a document with all the other reforms they were going to bring in.

'I started reading them. It was very seriously defective. Things to do with inheritance rights, social welfare entitlements and pensions weren't even addressed, and there were some things in it that were just plain wrong.

'I said there were major problems with this document. He said "I don't have time to discuss it". At this stage he was getting phone calls telling him the Cabinet was sitting outside.

He said that he planned to circulate the document at that day's parliamentary party meeting and asked Shatter for a memo on his concerns saying 'I can't deal with that today'.

'He then let me out a side door. The Cabinet came in another door. And to this day I have no idea whether any of them know I had had this discussion with him.

'A few hours later at our parliamentary party meeting there was an announcement made that we were heading down the road to a divorce referendum. And this document I knew to be defective was distributed.'

Did he screech his concerns from the rooftops? Did he announce his fears from on high? No he did not.

'I stayed schtum at the meeting. If I had stood up and spoken it would have been leaked. There was enough people who were going to crucify the poor man – Oliver Flanagan, Alice Glenn – and he didn't need me doing it. And then I watched the divorce referendum campaign go right down the drain. They seemed to adopt the view that if they all keep their heads down it would all turn out right in the end. This may sound very arrogant but the only person who could have taken (the anti-divorce campaigner, William) Binchy on in 1986 on a legal level would have been me. I had absolutely no platform in FG to do that. I couldn't do it. I was just a gobshite backbencher. The media had no interest in me. With all respect to the political correspondents, they have no idea who is an expert on anything until they are told by the relevant press officer. They only wanted ministers. And very few ministers wanted to say anything. The reality was the referendum was premature anyway.'

He almost left in 1987.

'My wife and I discussed this. I was nearly going to do what David Maloney did and leave politics altogether. I had reached the conclusion that I was dealing with people who were extraordinarily incompetent.

'They couldn't run a monkey's tea party. It wasn't proving possible to get myself into a position where I'd have any real influence over events and I didn't want to have to defend the indefensible.

'We had the discussion and we decided that this was my first long term, I was still young, and I couldn't expect to be a minister overnight even though other people were.

'My only interest in politics was to be a minister. Not for the purpose of being a minister. But because it gave you the open sesame to actually implement reforms you wanted to see happen.' But it wasn't to be. When Fine Gael went back into government again in 1994, Shatter was overlooked again.

'I hung in, and I'm glad I hung in. For the simple reason that from 1987 to 2002, although always on the backbenches or on the front bench with Fine Gael in opposition, I got my private members' Bills through.'

One of his most important pieces of legislation is the Judicial Separation Act.

'If I had been a minister in the '83 government I could have produced that Bill within six months. I don't regret that I hung in there. It meant that I had an opportunity from '87 onwards to legislate. My only regret is that it would have been much easier to have done it if I had been minister.

'I produced twenty-four private members' Bills. I actually changed the ethos of Leinster House by doing that. At the time nobody was publishing them. 'There was, I think, one private members' Bill from '83 to '87. Now it happens so frequently that it's boring.'

Four of his Bills were accepted by the government. Many others were voted down and re-introduced as government Bills.

'If I regarded that as success, I would be able to say to you I managed to put through seventeen Bills.'

CHAPTER 24

Suffer Little Children

'They may not forgive me. That weighs very heavily on me' –
Martin Cullen

A
ny child with a workaholic parent knows the drill. The parent is an infrequent presence in their lives. And even when they are there in body, their mind tends to be otherwise occupied.

Any child with a famous parent must grow accustomed to having their intimate family business bandied about the newspapers. They often learn the hard way that they, too, are expected to dance in the media spotlight.

Minor incidents that would lead to another child's pocket money being docked can in their cases implode into calamitous events. Their teenage pranks can become national news. Their traumas and tragedies must be endured under the public gaze.

The children of high-profile politicians are doubly cursed – their parents are both workaholics and famous.

And few famous people would throw open their homes to their fans on a regular basis – or publicise their home and mobile phone numbers and actively encourage their fans to use them.

Worse still, their parents tend to spend so much of their lives deciding on how other people should live, that any failings in their own families are pounced on with barely disguised glee.

Being the child of a Justice Minister has been shown to be a particularly risky occupation. In recent years the teenage sons of two Justice Ministers found themselves the subject of national newspaper headlines.

Indeed Niamh Brennan, the wife of Justice Minister Michael McDowell, stated publicly that she would be reluctant to report another crime to the gardai after details of an assault on her son were splashed in a tabloid newspaper. She couldn't help noticing that while newspapers do not publish the names of minors who are convicted of criminal acts, no such protection is afforded to their young victims – especially if their victim's dad happens to be the guy in charge of tackling crime.

What is surprising is the number of politicians' children who go on to embrace this life themselves – and subject their children to it.

Brian Lenihan's father, Brian Snr was one of the best known faces in the land at the height of his career. And yet Brian's early memories of his father are scant.

'Because I was the eldest and he was a minister during most of my childhood and based in Dublin while I was in Athlone, I actually didn't see very much of my father as a child.

'My grandparents paid me a lot of attention. I saw a certain amount of my father but not a lot, I have to say.'

Brian was a conscientious son. He minded his Ps and Qs.

'As a student I was very conscious that my father was a politician. So, in a sense that was one time in my life that I didn't feel particularly free. He was in the government at the time. I was a member of the party in college, but I wasn't an active member. I was in the Hist debating society in Trinity. But mostly I concentrated on my studies.

'I certainly discussed public affairs a lot, but not in a public forum. I didn't feel I was free to participate in normal student activities like demos.'

In national school in Athlone everyone 'knew everyone's status in the town. There was a certain amount of ribbing at election time. It made me feel too prominent. I felt I was in the public gaze all the time. I was a sensitive child and I did find it hard to take. I felt I was being watched all the time. Obviously my father's occupation was a very unusual one.

'When I moved to Dublin I went to Belvedere College, which is a fee-paying school. That was a very different atmosphere. The children in that school were drawn mainly from the middle classes on the northside of Dublin. They weren't as political as the country people. They knew who you were but it wasn't as big a talking point. They were almost sensitive about it. There was some intellectual argument, but there was no ribbing.'

'I had no notion of becoming a politician when I was a child. I thought it was a very intrusive activity.'

As well he might.

'What I remember very vividly – between 1959, when I was born, and 1971 when we moved to Dublin – my father would do his clinic from home and hundreds of people would come to the house. It wasn't even called a clinic. You just visited Mr Lenihan at his house. There'd be traffic jams at our house on a Saturday morning as people thronged in from County Roscommon, where my father was a TD.

'A lot of them would sit around the house, so the whole house would fill up with people. They would wait in the bedrooms, on the landing, in the sitting room. There'd be lines of cars outside the house. He had a room in the house, an office where the telephone used to be, and they would pass through the office and talk to him. These petitioners used to arrive in great numbers.'

Did he resent this invasion of his home turf?

'It wasn't a matter of resentment. It was just the way things were. It's extraordinary that people don't call to politicians' houses any more. Since I was elected only a handful of people have called to my home.

'Of course I have clinics and people can come in and see you in the Dáil. But in the country there was this idea – rather like the Roman senators – the petitioners would all arrive at the senators' houses in the morning before they went into the Senate.'

His father lost his seat two years after they moved to Dublin.

'He decided to run for the county council. He was a senator. He had been a minister for twelve years at that stage, so that was quite a restart for him.

'That was the first real life experience I had of politics because he had a little Fiat car and I was sent off by my mother as the escort for good behaviour. This was June 1974. I was only just fifteen.'

He was sent to keep his father on the straight and narrow – and out of the pubs.

'Well he certainly wandered most days until one in the morning but he got home every night. It was very interesting. To see a politician who was down and out going about getting elected again to a local authority. I spent three weeks of my life doing that.

'He got elected and then he was elected to the Dáil in 1977 and he held his seat in Dublin West until he died. He continued the practice of using his house, but the Dublin people didn't occupy the bedrooms like in Roscommon. It was a lot more civilised in Dublin. He would often say to me that Dublin people are much kinder and much less demanding than country people and much more respectful of politicians.

'When I was a young boy in the garrison town of Athlone I wanted to be a soldier. In my teens I wasn't that strong in maths or science. I was interested in English and history. So I suppose that was the beginning of a political germ in a way. I decided to opt for law and right into my early twenties I wanted to be a professional lawyer. I thought the politics would be just something I had an interest in, in addition to law rather than instead of it.'

He can't quite place the moment when that changed.

'The problem with that question is that I never really didn't consider myself a politician. Not that I always wanted to be in the Dáil but I always considered myself a political person.'

Progressive Democrats TD Fiona O'Malley thinks that the word 'meeting' was one of the first words she ever learned.

'I used to think that meeting was somewhere you went where you got meat. I remember being very fixated with that word because Dad (Progressive Democrats founder Des O'Malley) was always going to meetings. He'd come home on a Friday and immediately have to go to a meeting. Mum would sometimes have to go too. You wouldn't see him until after his clinic on Saturday afternoon. And then they'd go to constituency dos on Saturday night.

'Sundays were easier. You'd be going to matches. We used to go to Shannon to watch the planes like everybody else in Limerick. Technically, it was Dad trying to spend quality time with the children. Dad is not a touchy-feely type at all. But I suppose part of it was that people couldn't be bothering you if you weren't at home.'

'I remember people would often call then on a Sunday night. And he'd be gone again on Monday morning. That's the difference when you're a country TD. That's when you're down in your constituency, so that's when people got to see you. He also had the pressure of being elevated quickly so that he didn't get the time to indulge his constituency.

'You didn't resent it because you didn't know any different. I remember when I was an obstreperous teenager I'd say things like "what would you know, you're not even here!" It was cruel. But then it was true at the same time. It must have hurt him. He's a lot softer than you think.'

If anything, Fiona now feels like the guilty party for making such a big deal about her father's absences and leave-taking.

'There was one time I remember really well. It was during one of those crisis times and Mum and Dad both had to go to Dublin. I remember the three of us standing at the edge of the footpath bawling our eyes out because they were going. It must have been heart-breaking for them.'

Fiona was just two months old when her father was first elected. One of her earliest inklings that her family was a little different from her friends' families dates back to when she was about four. There was a republican protest at their house in Corbally in Limerick. Red paint had been splashed across the lawn. She and her siblings were scooped up and deposited with their neighbours, the Reidy's.

'They were our surrogate parents. We loved it. They used to give us sweets and biscuits which we never got at home. I remember looking over the curtain and seeing people running up the street. And not really being aware what the problem was. But I remember looking under my bed when we came in that night. That's the first memory I had that our lives were slightly different. Why were these people coming to our house?

'The relationship with our next door neighbours was crucial. They were dyed-in-the-wool Fine Gaelers. Paddy always says at our family weddings "didn't I rear them well!"

'They were critical in our upbringing. Critical to our life infra-structure. When Mum would have to come up to Dublin for various things when we were younger we'd stay over in their house. When we were older we'd go in to them for our dinner and they'd just keep an eye on us.'

Most children of politicians recall the baubles from their parent's frequent trips abroad, often grabbed at airport shops on the way home. Some saw them as straight bribes or guilt gifts. Fiona just saw them as an added bonus. She still has a Chinese dress her father brought her back from the Orient twenty-one years ago.

'Nobody had anything like it. We got very exotic presents.'

As the offspring of a prominent public figure, children of polit-icians inevitably became targets in the schoolyard.

'I did get a bit of slagging. But because he was someone who was held in high regard, it wasn't that vicious. People would just be aware of it. They'd know your father's name. I'm not shy so I was able to cope with it.

'I remember when I was voting for the first time. It was the divorce referendum. I voted 'no' against the party line. We were going in to vote and because he was party leader they were taking photos. I was asked what I was doing. I said I was voting 'no' because I thought it was rushed. Immediately the journalists were all over to me.

'After that we were all happy families, smiling for the photos. Until we got into the car. Dad said: "Don't you ever do anything like that again!" I said what? He said "I don't mind what way you want to vote, but you can do it quietly!" God, he gave me such a talking to!

'I remember the *Limerick Leader* looking for me later, and I told my sister that I couldn't get into any more trouble and to say I wasn't there. I still have the little piece that appeared in the front of the *Limerick Leader*. "Fiona Votes No." I can see his point entirely. Of course I shouldn't have said anything. But, you know, it was my first vote and I was so excited.

'Back in the Eighties, it was a stressful time. He was strained and tired. He wouldn't be getting father of the year for it. He's a prickly guy anyway. The one time when he wasn't always on show was at home. He could be himself. And you could see the strain and tiredness.

'I remember looking at my Dad on the phone one day. It was in the middle of another one of those great crises. I remember understanding why he kept going. Why he continued to do it despite all the highs and lows. And I remember knowing then that I was going to get involved myself. Having a comprehension as to why he kept at it. Because it is rewarding.'

Each December Ivor Callely gets his wife and children to pose before some seasonal prop or other wearing winter woollies and wholesome smiles. The resulting sugary Christmas card gets a major print run. Some constituent somewhere must surely have saved the entire collection.

Ivor Callely is blessed with a stoutly supportive wife, Jennifer. Although even she balked at the announcement that their Sunday mornings would have to be interrupted for a regular meeting. He was serving on so many committees that Sunday morning was the only time he could find in his diary to squeeze the latest additional one in.

Ivor insists that his children, aged ten, fourteen and sixteen, are not bothered by the pressures of being the offspring of a politician. He says that he has no trouble persuading them to be a part of his official political entourage, having produced the family Christmas card every year since his election in 1989.

'They're so used to it now that it's just something we do. They don't get a kick out of it and they don't object to it. I'm very fortunate in that, even though they're still young, they understand the demands on me and on my time. They like being part of what I'm at.

'There's a lot of discussion at the kitchen table. They're now at a stage where they're questioning some of what I'm saying. They like the politics.'

When pressed, he acknowledges that his political commitments 'do have a huge impact on normal family life.'

'I'm not there for their evening meal. Maybe not as much now as in earlier years, but when I would see them was breakfast time. And I wouldn't see them until the following breakfast time. When I'd get home they'd be in bed.

'There are swings and roundabouts in every walk of life. Usually there are three quality weeks that we spend together in West Cork. I built a place in Bantry three years ago. You might squash in ten days at Christmas and a week at Easter. That is very much family time.'

Micheál Martin, who had four children under the age of nine when we spoke, describes his often thwarted efforts to make time for his wife and children as 'the constant nagging issue' in his life.

'I'm endeavouring to ring-fence time for the kids. It's very difficult for Mary (his wife) at home, particularly midweek. I haven't been at home now since last Monday morning (we were speaking on a Saturday afternoon). From mid-Sept onwards that's the scene. And in Cork, as a minister you're expected to attend at the dinners and functions at the weekend. It is difficult. You get increasingly jealous of your own time because you actually want to enjoy your kids.

'The young fella is getting older. He's playing soccer and Gaelic football, and he's had midweek matches. I am the one parent who's not at all the matches, although I've made a lot of them.

'Last year, I was one of only two parents missing from the final. Mary was there and I was ringing all through the match to get the score. I think he must feel that from time to time. You want your Dad there.

'It's a problem. But I suppose we won't always be a minister, that's the other side of the coin. Our jobs aren't going to last forever and that's what you keep saying to yourself. That you'll get time.

'Increasingly I have to be more ruthless with my own time. Maybe the Saturday clinics have to become fortnightly. The times you snatch are in the morning, before you leave home, and late at night. They wait up for me and I'm a good storyteller. Bedtime stories are my specialty.'

Nora Owen feels guilty 'to a degree' about the time she stole from her family and gave to politics while her children were still young.

'As soon as I got elected to the Dáil and I got a salary, I got a full-time housekeeper who came in every morning at 8.30am. I had her all the way up until '87. I got someone else in then. But when you look back you realise how much you missed. Any working mother will look back and say that. I was never home before midnight.

'A Dublin deputy has the disadvantage in that during the week they have to be at meetings. Whereas the rural deputies have to have a bit of a chill-out on Tuesdays and Wednesdays. In Dublin, you had to go to meetings.

'My husband really took over the child-rearing at that stage. He did all the bedtime stories and got the lunches ready the night before and unpacked the schoolbags. My housekeeper did all the washing and ironing and made sure they had their school uniforms. I did very little housekeeping during all those years.

'I was lucky I had a housekeeper. Almost all my salary went on her. What gave me the few extra bob was the daily allowance of £25 a day. I was getting about £800 a month and my housekeeper was costing about £600.'

She remembers one particular day when she asked her son Edward, who would have been about sixteen at the time, to make something for himself when he got home as they had some function to attend.

'He said, not nastily or anything, "Mom, I've been doing it since I was nine". It suddenly came home to me that they had been doing it, making their own sandwiches and putting on the chipper or whatever.

'I'm sure there were times that they haven't told me about where they got teased and ragged about their mother being useless and all that. But they got through it and I don't think they needed any psychological assessment.

'And then there were nice times too. Mother travelled a lot and they always got presents when I came home. Very often they were able to come to things with me. Receptions and things.

'The first years were tough. I'd be in a hassle. I'd get home for half an hour and I knew I'd have to go out again, and the phone would ring and I'd have to tell them to shut up. I'd get cross with them because there was a constituent on the phone. When I think back I probably did too much of that. I probably could have done less. I could have said to my constituent "look, I'm sorry, I'm dealing with my children now, could you ring me back in the morning". But you never felt you could do that. Because if I said that they would straight away go to someone else who wouldn't say that to them and I was conscious of that. That I was building my career and I had to build up more and more support.

'There are times when I regret. Maybe on a Saturday I'd agree to do something. Really I should have stayed at home on Saturdays but you really didn't feel you had a choice. I nearly always made a rule that Sunday was sacrosanct. The only things I might do would be a garden fete where I could bring the kids.

'I remember this time when we were in government and we were going to have a meeting of the Fine Gael ministers. John (Bruton) said we'll have it on Sunday at twelve thirty. I said "no, we won't. It's all very well for all of you. You can go home then at two o'clock and somebody will have cooked your lunch. I do the lunch in our house." We had the meeting at five o'clock. Sometimes you just had to put your foot down and ask them to be conscious of the fact that some of us had slightly different responsibilities.

'My husband was very supportive. He worked nearby. He was home by five o'clock. He'd say "there's no need for you to do that". I'd say there was. I'd come home wrecked and he'd say "just stay in". Now I found it very hard to just stay in. In some ways now I realise that it wouldn't have mattered if I'd stayed in.

'It made me feel I was doing what I was elected to do, and maybe I was. But when I look at some of the people who weren't making the same effort and still managed to get elected... there are times now when I say to myself I was a fool. I shouldn't have burnt myself out as much.'

Her former colleague Alan Shatter admits now: 'If I look back on it I wasn't as available at all as I believe a father should be to my young children. I would come home weekdays at maybe ten or eleven at night or one in the morning. But because I was in Dublin I would get home for tea at around 7pm.

'One of the things I used to do when my children were young – I never told the whips this, they'd have gone bananas – was I used to leave the Dáil during private members' time from seven to eight thirty. The early 1980s traffic meant that I could get home to Rathfarnham in fifteen minutes. If I wasn't involved (in private members' time) I'd be in my car at 7pm. I'd leave home at 8.15pm and I was always in time for the vote.'

But there are few politicians who have the luxury of being able to nip out to grab some quality time with the kids in the lull between division bells – even if they had the inclination.

Mary Coughlan couldn't manage it even if she had a helicopter at her disposal. Torn between her responsibilities as a mother of two young children in Donegal and the challenges of running the Department of Social and Family Affairs, she says she 'kills' herself with 6am starts after late nights at the office in Dublin in order to spend three nights a week in the family home at Frosses, near Donegal town. And even so, with constituency work to be dealt with, only Sundays are available for family time with her husband David Charlton, her six-year-old son Cathal, who is hearing-impaired, and her four-year-old daughter Maeve.

She tries not to think about the extent of her sacrifice. She told the *Sunday Times* newspaper in August 2003: 'If you started to think about those wee things, you know yourself, it would start to eat at you. It is difficult. I'm lost when I go home. I don't know how Cathal is doing at school. I don't know how he's doing at speech therapy.'

Most poignantly she admits: 'It does put you outside the loop a little, especially when he (Cathal) has new words or something. I mightn't quite understand what he says.'

Martin Cullen separated from his wife and the mother of his four children while he was minister of state with responsibility for the Office of Public Works. He blames the pressures of political life.

'It led to it. It was a huge contributory factor. I have no doubt in my mind but that it was.

'It is a very heavy price to pay. I'm not alone in paying that price and it is becoming an even more common price that is being paid.'

He admits that he sees his children, the youngest of which is nine, 'very rarely', but adds that he tries to talk to them on the phone on a daily basis. He's not sure if they will forgive him his frequent absences.

'They may not forgive me. That weighs very heavily on me. The eldest guy and I have spoken about it and he has resented that I wasn't there at the school for the soccer or rugby or hurling matches like other fathers. That's the sacrifice. And it's an enormous sacrifice and it's a life I wouldn't wish on anybody.'

But no-one forced him into it.

'I chose it and I don't mean to be crying or complaining about it. But that is the factual position.

'You weigh that up in that you hope your life has a broader meaning. You actually do hope that the fact that you were there made a difference for a lot of people. That you did something significant nationally that shaped Ireland in some way or got an issue dealt with, and it was the right thing to do and you've left that legacy. And then you look to your own city and county and hope you've left your mark on it in some way. But that is the life of service.'

It seemed hardly necessary to point out at this juncture that his children had not chosen a life of service.

'No, they didn't. But on the other hand I can't live their lives for them. I can try to give them all I can. I suppose because of my ability to look after them they can do things other kids can't do in other ways.

'You do feel guilty. You wouldn't be human if you didn't. The love between a parent and a child is an unbreakable bond and any politicians who would say they don't (feel guilty) would be either foolish or extremely lucky. But you hope that over the course of their lives you will be able to balance it out and at the end of everything it will have meaning for them. And what they've lost, they have gained.'

John Bruton is not as forthcoming when asked about his children's response to his career choices. While he acknowledges that he missed out on his four children's best years 'to a degree', he says he is busy making up for it now that the pressures of high office are behind him. Indeed, on the morning we met he was late for our appointment because he was doing the school run. But when asked if he felt it was tough on his children, he looks puzzled.

'You'll have to ask them that,' he says, apparently taken aback by the question, before adding quietly: 'I think they were proud of what I did and am doing.'

While many politicians pay lip service to their worries about the impact of their career on their families, their political life inevitably takes precedence. Indeed, when Máire Geoghegan-Quinn announced in 1997 that she was withdrawing from politics in disgust at media intrusion into her family life after a minor incident involving her son was reported in a Sunday newspaper, few within political and media circles took her protests seriously. Political players knowingly whispered that the 'real' reason the former Justice Minister was bailing out was her realisation that she could not hope to hold on to her shaky seat in another election. The idea that a senior politician and mother could put her family ahead of her political career was considered preposterous.

Yet that is precisely what the former Labour TD Pat Gallagher did. Gallagher listened to the reports from the count centres on the *Pat Kenny Show* from beneath his duvet in 1992. When he heard reporter Aileen O'Meara announce that early tallies showed there was going to be an upset in Laois-Offaly with the election of Pat Gallagher, the community worker ran to the bathroom and threw up.

Once he was over the shock of getting elected to the Dáil, Gallagher settled in quickly and enjoyed his new life enormously. He lost his seat in 1997 and threw himself into the Seanad campaign. Once safely installed in the Seanad, he set about shoring up his vote with the full intention of running for the Dáil come the next election.

By then he was married with a young daughter. A second child, Ciara, was born in 1998. But losing his seat in 1997 had rattled him. He realised he had a family to support and nothing to fall back on. With the quieter pace of life in the Seanad, he had time to think about how out of touch he was with the jobs market. He got some part-time work lecturing in Maynooth.

Then, out of the blue, he spotted an advert for the post of Director of Community and Enterprise for each local authority.

'I remember seeing the advert in the paper and thinking if I wasn't in politics I'd love that job. I don't know what made me do it, but at the last minute I applied for it just to see if I'd get an interview. I wanted to see what my currency was like on the jobs market after all those years in full-time politics.'

He did his first interview in April 1999, just before the local elections. He topped the poll for the Offaly County Council but decided to go back and do the second interview to see if he would get it.

'I got a letter in July offering me the job of Director of Community and Enterprise in Westmeath. I said to myself "shit! What am I going to do now?" It was only a theoretical thing, an exercise up to that. I had a month to answer that. And I put in probably one of the most difficult months of my life.

'I tossed it up and down. We went on our holidays in Fermanagh. Then one day my mother and my wife went into Enniskillen shopping and I had the kids. And it suddenly struck me that it was the first time that I had spent more than two hours with Ciara since she was born. Ciara was eleven months old by then. That did hit me. It was a road to Damascus moment.'

But he was still torn. 'The decision didn't make itself though. I had given so much of my time to this very demanding but very rewarding business of politics which had huge risks attached to it. I found it very difficult to make a decision.

'In the last week I went to a beach in Mayo. I walked it for two days on my own. Bernie (his wife) was there and I know afterwards what she wanted me to do. But she said at the time that it was my call. I weighed up the options. And made the decision to take the job.'

His organisation was stunned when he went to tell them that he was walking away from politics.

'They were very good about it. Most of them were genuinely very good. Some were only good to my face. But nobody turned around and said 'you f-in' bastard'. I think they understood that I had been single when I got into politics and now had a wife and two kids.   I had lost my job in 1997. They understood the context of the decision. I started the job four years ago and I haven't regretted it.'

CHAPTER 25

Married to the Mob

'We all have trouble with our wives' – Éamon de Valera

When Éamon de Valera first offered Jack Lynch a place at the Cabinet table, the future Taoiseach was uncertain. 'My wife wouldn't like it,' he remarked. Dev is said to have responded: 'We all have trouble with our wives.'

Elsewhere in Bruce Arnold's biography of Jack Lynch we hear that his wife Máirín 'was naturally quite shy. She dreaded what she believed would be the loneliness of public life; the separations that were an inescapable part of men being successful in a man's world from which women were traditionally excluded.'

The average Dáil deputy is a married man in his fifties who has sired 3.5 children. The twenty-ninth Dáil elected in May 2002 has the largest proportion of single TDs since the foundation of the State. But there are still just twenty-nine of them.

A spouse is a major bonus to any aspiring politician. For starters, there's the question of the optics. A personable, supportive wife (or husband) and a gaggle of well-behaved kiddies does wonders for a politician's image. A partner may also come with a vital dowry – a long-tailed family sprinkled liberally throughout the constituency.

But the husbands and wives of politicians get a raw deal. They get little of the glamour and all of the grief.

Kathleen Lemass must have known what she was getting into when she married Seán Lemass. Their courtship lasted eight years while her fiancé busied himself with the republican activities which would be the forerunner of an extraordinary political career.

But she could hardly have imagined the toll it would go on to take on their family life. Years later, when her daughter Peggy was in school, a nun asked her to intervene with her father for the granting of some favour. Peggy responded earnestly that she was unable to do so because 'she didn't really know' her father.

Michael O'Sullivan, biographer of Seán Lemass, wrote that Kathleen 'learned early in her marriage to Lemass that she and the children had to be prepared to make personal sacrifices in order to help him fulfil his sense of public duty.' There were no bonuses for the wife and kids from Daddy's exalted status. No guilty gifts to make up for his lengthy absences from the family home. Indeed when a diplomat presented Seán Lemass with a large chest of tea at a time when it was still being rationed, the then Minister for Supplies returned the lot, explaining that if the people of Ireland had to go without tea, so too would the Lemass family.

Forged in this austere, dutiful background, Maureen Lemass was destined to follow in her mother's footsteps, albeit married to a different kettle of political fish. In agreeing to marry the ambitious aspirant Charles J Haughey in 1951, she gave her husband the social and political credibility he craved.

In 1987, in a very rare newspaper interview, Maureen Haughey said baldly: 'I am a very private person. Joan FitzGerald is very much to the fore. I prefer the background.'

She touched on the gross intrusions into her personal family life, and in particular of her horror that her children would become the target of an avaricious media.

'At one time, I think it was during the Arms Trial, a photographer came into Eimear's class at school and took a photograph of her. I thought that was really terrible.'

But she laughed at another memory which might have made other less-hardened mothers fret.

'I remember one time when we were going to the St Patrick's Day parade and Charlie must have been taking the salute or something and we had a motorcycle escort. I remember Eimear and Ciaran lying down on the floor at the back of the car in case anybody saw them.'

At a time when Terry Keane was boasting in print of her trysts with Haughey in their 'beloved' South of France, when the illicit couple were booking private dining rooms in Le Coq Hardi, there is something especially poignant in Maureen's wifely remark: 'well, of course Charlie won't go anywhere. He doesn't like the sun. I might go with a friend to the Canaries.'

Or: 'He's very easygoing at home. But if he was out of politics or out of a job he might drive us all mad... nowadays we only go out to what we have to go to.'

Arranging to have her photograph taken, she balked at being its main attraction. 'Oh no, I'm always at the back. At the races in the Phoenix Park when JR – Larry Hagman – was there, his wife and I were both behind the crowd. I turned to her and said "you must be like me, always at the back."'

A guest of Charlie Haughey's recalls having lunch at their Gandon mansion in north Dublin in the Seventies. When Maureen arrived in to serve up the food, Haughey introduced her with a smile as 'my staff'. This source is adamant that Maureen did not take offence. This was her role and she did not appear to mind it.

When Phyllis Browne, wife of the most controversial Health Minister in the history of the State, was casting about for a title for her autobiography she settled on: *Thanks for the Tea, Mrs Browne: My Life with Noel*.

It's a reference to how she imagines all the important people who came to visit her husband at their numerous homes must have perceived her. She too was forced to make innumerable sacrifices because of her husband's strongly-held political beliefs. But she, at least, shared them wholeheartedly. Her memoir exposed the penury behind the outwardly glamorous life of being a minister's wife.

'I am quite sure that many people believe that politicians, and indeed doctors, can make a lot of money – and indeed they can, most of them. In our case, it was during Noel's period as minister that we got into serious debt. As a minister, Noel actually earned less than his departmental secretary, and to help keep (down) the expenses of the party offices he was expected to forfeit half of his salary to it. Added to these was the purchase of a reliable car, which we had never owned, and the expenses of running it.

'Then we had to rent a house, one after another, for somehow it proved impossible to rent for longer than six months, possibly because few people believed that the government would last any longer than that length of time.'

Her neighbours were agog.

'A girl who lived next door to us in Howth said once: "Phyllis, I can't believe you're the wife of the Minister for Health. One minute you're in the coal shed with a bucket, the next you're stepping into a gleaming limousine – and in between you've made your own evening dress".'

Indeed, Phyllis used to reserve the drives to Leinster House for taking the tacks out of the ball gowns she sewed herself.

Because of his clash with the Church authorities over his Mother and Child Scheme, Noel's career after politics was severely curtailed. Blacklisted by the bishops, he could not get a job in a medical establishment cowering under the shadow of the crozier. The family moved twenty-six times, at one point living in a condemned two-roomed schoolhouse, without water, electricity or sanitary facilities of any kind.

But these hardships were nothing beside the serial discrimination visited upon their children, Ruth and Susan. They were repeatedly refused admission to a number of schools, both Catholic and Protestant. On one occasion Ruth was asked to leave the National College of Art. The official excuse – her alleged lack of artistic talent – appeared suspicious as just weeks before her rejection she had won first prize in the National Caltex Art Competition, ahead of 22,000 other artists.

Anne Devine grew up in an apolitical family in Athlone, the daughter of a garda superintendent and a GP. She married Brian Lenihan at twenty-one and became subsumed in what she would describe as 'the terrific highs and terrible lows' of political life.

The story of Brian Lenihan's political life reads like a damning parable to warn other travellers of the dangers of taking the political road. A former minister who lost his seat in a shock defeat, only to claw his way back to the lowly position of councillor before making it back into the Dáil and another seat at Cabinet. A man whose extraordinary popularity was enhanced by his battle with life-threatening liver disease. A veteran politician who was elected to Dáil Éireann in his absence as he recovered from a liver transplant in the Mayo Clinic in Minnesota. A shoo-in for the presidency whose 'mature recollection' of a political indiscretion became a national joke. A loyal servant who was dismissed by the master he had served so loyally when his presence became a liability.

'It was not the life I would have chosen for myself,' his wife admitted thirty-two years later, 'but I loved Brian and therefore I was interested in his interests.'

But she acknowledged that her husband's lengthy absences made her the head of what she described without rancour as a 'one-parent family'.

After the humiliation of the presidential election campaign, and his subsequent forced resignation, Lenihan's son Conor spoke with bitter eloquence of the public hypocrisy and bogus morality inherent in the political game.

'It's not nice to see somebody publicly mugged,' he said, 'You'd have to be a pain freak to want to go through that.'

Conor was elected to the Dáil in the Dublin South-West constituency in 1997. His eldest brother Brian had already taken his late father's seat in Dublin West in a by-election the previous year.

When Des O'Malley's uncle Donogh O'Malley died in 1968 it was the young solicitor's wife, Pat, who encouraged him to contest the seat in Limerick East. Sitting at her dining room table in their comfortable Ballsbridge apartment thirty-five years later, she laughs now at the madness of it. They had three children under two-and-a-half and very little money, but Pat knew that politics was her husband's passion. Indeed, in other circumstances, it might have been Pat who took the plunge. As a student she used to carry a hat around in her bag because ladies were required to wear hats in the Dáil public gallery. Pat and her friends used to go to Leinster House and sit listening to the likes of James Dillon for entertainment in those days 'because it was free and warm'.

Once Des was elected, Pat quickly discovered that life as a politician's wife was no cake walk. With Des in Dublin from Monday to Friday, she too often felt like a single mother, juggling the child-rearing with her unpaid work as a supportive spouse, surrogate TD, constituency secretary, dinner dance escort, and semi-professional mourner.

'I don't think I considered the reality of what it would be like. When Des went into the Dáil the salary was just £2,500. When he was made parliamentary secretary we thought we were made up!'

In those days the TDs used to share secretaries, a situation that could only work because their wives picked up the slack at home.

'All the wives did the letters. But the rural TDs' wives had a much harder time of it, because as soon as Thursday evening would come, their house would be full of people looking to have their problems solved.

'Funerals were the big thing. People would ring me up and say so-and-so is a great supporter. I got into a very handy way of doing it. The removals were the best. You could get in and out and just meet the people. It wasn't even so much for the benefit of the bereaved, but for your supporter who had told you about it. It kept their status up. When you showed up it showed that they had an entrée with the minister.

'There are some that went to every funeral whether they knew people or not. Des tells a story of being away with Paddy Ger O'Sullivan of West Cork and Paddy coming off the phone to his wife and saying "great, she's done six funerals this week!"'

'Des wasn't great for trekking down during the week. A lot of TDs only went up for the Wednesday, but Des loved the parliamentary work as well as all the other stuff. And he was a minister from early on.

'He hardly ever missed his constituency clinic on a Saturday. We could never go away for weekends and we could never go to rugby matches or anything because Des always had to be in Limerick for the Saturday clinic. That's what I find great freedom from now.

'It's funny what you get used to. You just did it. You would be resentful of having no time together. And if you went out and the two of us were sitting having a drink together you were an immediate magnet. People would say "God, you're sitting there on your own!" There were times when you resented all of that. Having people controlling you. Saying what he should and shouldn't be doing and you having very little input into it.

'I did feel like a single parent. I used to be listening to Rodney Rice and John Bowman. They were always on about single mothers. I used to very much feel like it. Or like a truck driver's wife. I used to say that at least when their husband comes home at the weekend he'd be there.

'On Friday evening the phone calls started. When would he be down and where he had to be. People had this idea that it was a glamorous life. I remember listening to a radio programme about this glamorous life we were supposed to have and there I was down on my knees with a leaking fridge. You hear this thing about how a TD couldn't know about ordinary people's lives. Well, their wives know.

'I think there was one time he thought of pulling out. It was before the second-last election. He thought he wouldn't stand but he was prevailed upon to stand because things weren't going too good for the PDs.

But mostly they just soldiered on.

'He'd come home on a Friday evening. There would be branch meetings. That time there were dinner dances for everything. That was something I got to hate. You never sat down to eat before eleven o'clock. You were at these things week after week. For the most part you didn't know anyone. They'd no longer any interest in you once the photos were taken.'

Pat is grateful for the small mercy of usually managing to keep Sundays free 'unless something extraordinary happened'.

But then, lots of extraordinary things started to happen after Des was made Minister for Justice. In what has to be taken as a major understatement, she recalls this period of their lives as being 'fairly traumatic'. It was at the height of the Troubles in the North, and tensions were running high. The O'Malleys became the first political family in the history of the State to have full-time security assigned to their home.

Pat recalls two times in particular when, as she puts it herself, she "didn't feel secure".

'One was a Christmas Eve when a car came for Des. There was a phone call and Des said there's a car coming down in the morning, I may have to go to Dublin. These two men came in and he went off with them. Then one of the gardai that were outside the house said "God, I wonder should we have left him off with them." I said "what"? They said they thought it was the Commissioner's car. That made me uneasy. It was Christmas Eve. I didn't know where he was or whether he'd come back. You didn't really use phones much in those days. It was a guard that was arrested for leaking information to the IRA. He came back at one o'clock on Christmas morning.

'There was another occasion when he went suddenly. We were down in Kerry. I just had this feeling that I might never see him again.

'You knew there were definite threats against him. The gardai drove the children to school even though it was only five hundred yards from home. Luckily, the kids were too young to realise what was going on. There was one particular time when the guards had to stay outside the school. There were obviously particular threats. They thought they might have been kidnapped.

'I don't remember if I was terrorised. I was pregnant with Owen at the stage when it got to its worst with the IRA. I just had this habit of managing to keep calm and it was good that I was like that. If the children had been older it would have been much worse.

'There were a few occasions that you would be nervous. After Bloody Sunday I remember we were told we had to get out of the house, but it was too late and we only made it next door. There were protesters marching on the house with a coffin.

'There were a few times like that that we had to get out. We used to have to go to Dublin for weekends where nobody would know where we were. We used to stay in Buswell's then. That's why he bought a house in Dublin in 1977. The guards wanted him to have a place that they could secure. Prior to that there was a period where they wouldn't allow him to stay more than two or three nights in the one place. You forget all that now actually.

'It wasn't great going to friends. There'd be a special branch car as well as the local gardai. Our friends would say "God, you ask the O'Malleys and you end up with eight people!"'

What is extraordinary about Pat's story is that these years of living on the edge and coping with IRA death threats pale in her mind in comparison with the fear and loathing unleashed by Des's political battles with Charlie Haughey. She only ever really started to challenge their life's path when 'politics got really vicious and nasty'.

'It became very unpleasant for a while. People were afraid to talk to you in case they'd be seen or that it would be interpreted that they were on your side. I found that very hard. It was more internal and it was more real. And you couldn't really open up about it either.'

When he was expelled from Fianna Fáil in 1985 and went on to form the Progressive Democrats, Pat was 'very nervous'.

'It wasn't the happiest time. I was very nervous during all that time. I thought, "what are you putting your head up for with everyone ready to knock you."

'The best thing about it was that you were there when important things were happening. And you knew about them. You were part of history happening. And also you were meeting loads of different people, both here and abroad. Jack Lynch and George Colley were your friends. We'd often go to Colley's house and sit talking. That's where I would hear what was going on. Rather than Des coming home and telling me.

'The worst thing was that time when you knew Fianna Fáil was trying to get rid of him. It was very hard. People thought he was trying to be leader for the sake of being leader and it was all being misinterpreted because it suited them. The sooner they got rid of him the better. I would consider that the most hurtful time.'

And yet, she would do it all again.

'I don't think I'd have changed anything. Once you've gone into it you sort of go along with it.'

CHAPTER 26

The Media Hounds

'I still don't trust them, the bastards' – Tom Parlon

Even as fewer and fewer issues of national importance are settled in Leinster House, the number of journalists who base
themselves there has grown exponentially. At the time of
writing there are about thirty journalists based in Leinster House.
That is to say that their membership of the Oireachtas Press Gallery
entitles them to the use of a desk, a phone and an Internet link in
Leinster House.

Their offices are located behind the Press Gallery on the second
floor and under the eaves in what were once the Lord Kildare's
servants' quarters on the third floor. They work in the kind of
crowded, overly-intimate conditions that the deputies and senators
used to complain about before they were given extra accommodation
in recent years.

As most political correspondents sit within spitting distance of
their colleagues from rival media outlets, there are a great many
whispered phone conversations and shouts of 'could you just hold
on one minute... ' as reporters dash out to the corridor to probe
their sources by the entrance of the men's loo with something
approaching privacy.

About two-thirds of these journalists are members of the Dáil
Lobby, the inner sanctum of the Oireachtas Press Gallery.
When the Dáil is in session, lobby members are invited to attend

daily briefings by the Government Press Secretary and the Head of the Government Information Service. Many myths have grown up around these briefings. Journalists who are denied access bitch that the lobby journalists are spoon-fed propaganda which, for reasons of laziness or ignorance, they unquestioningly reproduce.

The truth is that the lobby briefings are treated as a sort of mild diversion by its members, where more often than not banal information is trotted out to keep up the appearances of transparent government.

Each press secretary in successive administrations has a different style. Some have been pally and chatty, arguing the toss amicably, offering off-the-record insights and trading apparently indiscreet anecdotes. Others have adopted a more high-handed approach, regarding journalists as a class of dangerous and unpredictable junkie, and information as the methadone to be doled out with caution to keep them mollified and dependent.

Of course, if a political correspondent has a sniff of a really serious story the last place they will think about raising it is at the lobby briefing. Most business is done with the press secretary or the various press advisors and officers attached to the ministers by phone. Or in casual chats and privately-arranged briefings with the ministers and their aides.

Working cheek-by-jowl with each other in Leinster House, journalists and politicians enjoy an uneasy kinship. They eat joint-of-the-day or chicken supreme with each other in the self-service restaurant when the Dáil breaks for lunch. They buy each other pints and small ones while they wait for the division bell in the Visitors' Bar on Wednesday nights. They feed off each other, they need each other to survive professionally, but they can never really be friends. Any member of either party would do well to remember the tale of the scorpion and the turtle from *Aesop's Fables*.

Every politician should know that sooner or later the journalist will shaft them. It's not personal. It's in his nature. Just as every journalist knows that sooner or later the politician will give him reason to. It's in his nature.

Nuala Fennell didn't have to wait long to get stung. Shortly after she was appointed junior minister for Women's Affairs and Family Law Reform, the former journalist and women's rights campaigner decided to invite all her former colleagues from the women's pages of the national press into the Dáil.

'It was something I thought was going to be friendly and interesting,' she says. 'I had never been in the Dáil before I was elected
and I thought they would enjoy it.'

Her former colleagues didn't share her enthusiasm.

'They came in their droves. There must have been about forty of
them. And they went out and they were so bitchy and vicious. They
absolutely castigated me. Not all of them, but a lot of them. They
thought this was twee. They totally misinterpreted it.

'The interesting thing was that subsequently some of the stuff that
was written about things I was doing showed incredible ignorance
about how the Dáil worked. It's very easy to criticise something.
When you're on the inside you know there are reasons that some
things take so long. I suppose they thought I was patronising them.
Maybe I was. It didn't seem like that to me.'

Nuala Fennell didn't have a press officer. 'I used the government
press office. I probably could have gotten better press but it didn't
seem that important to me. People know how important it is now,
but they still don't get good press.'

Politicians do indeed know how important it is now. As a group,
they are hypersensitive about media coverage. All the senior ones
have a press cuttings service, provided by the likes of Terry Prone in
Carr Communications, where all stories of relevance are presented
to them with their morning post.

If there is a major running story, and they have enlisted the
services of Carr Communications, all of them will get a note saying
'this is why this is happening and this is where it will go unless... '
Or, according to Prone, sometimes just: 'what the hell are you at?'

Carr Communications also runs media training courses for
aspiring – and sometimes expiring – politicians.

'This is available to people off-the-peg,' Prone's partner Tom
Savage explains. 'Then if we have a contractual arrangement with a
particular political party or parties we will look after different
people appearing in the predictable slots. It involves sitting down
and talking about the issues.'

After years of coaching politicians on their dealings with the
media, Savage knows more than most about how it works.

'Politicians begin by seeing the media as just something that is
out there. The ones who are good at it very quickly discover that
the media needs them. They develop a link system to journalists, so
the reporters can reach them without having to go through press

officers. That link system is two-way in its productivity – it's useful to both the politician and the journalist. But it's also two-way in its capacity to corrupt. Once a journalist knows a politician, likes a politician and gets good leads from a politician, that journalist isn't going to be as fearless a seeker of negative truth about that politician as they might have been before the relationship got going.

'At the same time, politicians develop a mental panel of favourite people to send stuff to. Which in turn means that journalists who get material in advance, say, of official publications, are in fact getting scoops without significance. They're not actually competing on the merits of the stories. Advisors, whether within the public service or – like Carr Communications – outside it, get to know very quickly that when a minister says, about some issue, "don't worry, I'll sort it out", what they mean by that – without ever saying it – is that they have a tame journalist who'll do something on the angle the minister wants. The journalist will do it because they'll get the inside track on something else down the line.

'Of course, if you're a struggling backbencher and you want to know how does media work, you're thinking: "how can I be interesting, what can I get in?" But of course nobody gives a flute about backbenchers unless they are in revolt.'

Terry Prone confides that 'some politicians work the system to their best advantage in ways that we'd disapprove of. For example, leak and counter-leak between partners in a coalition can destroy trust – not only between the parties in government, but trust on the part of the public in the political system.

'Some politicians spend more time chasing headlines than can be objectively justified. And as we saw in the case of Mo Mowlam, background briefing against an individual who has fallen out of favour is destructive and almost impossible to counter, although it's less effective in Ireland than in Britain.'

The fragmentation of media over the last thirty years has meant that politicians have to spend an ever-greater chunk of their time placating an ever-increasing number of media outlets. According to one media handler, the relationship between the media and the body politic has changed 'violently' over that period. The advent of the television age, perhaps more than anything else, rocked the political establishment to its core.

According to Prone: 'When the dominant medium was print, when people got most of their information and impressions from the newspaper, there was a distance. That very distance, that sense of seeing someone in formal black and white still photographs, created a respect and a formality. It's not quite the same as seeing someone on a really closeup shot on TV. Television tore away some of the formality. It was the media equivalent of knocking down the Lenin statue. It just sheared away all of the mystique. Once you create that sitting-room thing where you're commenting on people's appearance and watching a bead of sweat gather on their nose, the relationship is never the same.'

Bunny Carr has confided that the political programme he presented, which led to the launch of Carr Communications, almost drove him to drink. He was heartsick to discover that, at most, twenty per cent of the politicians he interviewed believed in something and were going somewhere. The other eighty per cent would say to him over an after-show drink in the Merrion Inn 'now, you didn't get much out of me!'

'The grim thing is that we've almost completed a circle on this one,' Bunny Carr's fellow Carr Communications director Prone comments. 'First, there was a great eagerness on the part of politicians to come to terms with TV and radio. Partly pushed by individuals like failed presidential candidate Walter Mondale who, post-election, said the most important thing he'd do differently if he had his life to live over was come to terms with media.

'But, more recently, there's been a trend towards political aspirants who don't even want to hide the fact that they don't believe in anything. They want a few tips on what to wear, how to do their hair, what frames to have on their glasses. They want tricks: how not to answer a question. Fewer of them arrive with a hunger to influence people, to change lives. In some cases, you get the feeling that they'd happily pay for a few focus groups to find out what are the issues it would be safest to stand for. But that's partly due to the fact that the media is now almost completely focused on celebrity, personality and contention rather than policy.'

According to both Prone and Savage, the need to be liked is a major disadvantage to any politician in media terms, forcing them towards a banal centrist safety position on most issues and edging them away from risk-taking.

'That's reinforced when a rare politician runs hard on something he or she really believes in and fails to achieve it: suddenly all the commentators are kicking them for "poor political judgment",' says

Prone. 'So we're perilously close to the situation Bunny talked of, where politicians regarded themselves as having won, in a TV encounter, if they said shag all and looked reasonably good. Which is profoundly dispiriting. And makes for rotten television and radio.'

Most expert and amateur media analysts would class Charlie McCreevy as that rare beast – a politician who doesn't give a fiddlers about the media and all who sail in her. They would be very wrong.

Asked if he took media criticism personally, he responds curtly: 'Oh, I do. But I cover it up a bit better. Would you like to have nasty things written about you? No.'

I point out that I haven't had his years of experience to dull the blade.

'Years of experience won't take away the hurt of having something nasty written about you. I can understand fellas getting very upset about it. Maybe I don't let it show. I'll have to psychoanalyse myself. Perhaps it's that there has been so much of it over my lifetime. It comes in waves. It's hard to see over one bit of the water when the next wave comes at you. Some people have definitely gone over the top on occasion.'

He explodes at the suggestion that his natural affability has afforded him quite an easy ride.

'Are you serious? Are you living in the real world? You look back over the last couple of years and read all the stuff in all the papers about me. Yeah? Was it fair? Go back and analyse it. I've had more than anybody else. Except maybe Bertie. I understand that it has become part of our roles. Some of the time anyway. But that's some compensation!'

He traces what he considers to be the rot in the relationship between journalists and the media back to the 1960s.

'I always like to go back to the roots of a problem – maybe it's the mathematician in me. I think the root of this problem goes back to the Sixties. I put it down to John Healy, the most gifted writer of his day. Healy developed a technique in his *Backbencher* column of analysing what politicians said and suggesting what they really meant.

'Comment and analysis became the thing. So the politicians began to think "if I say it like this, this is what it will mean." Until the Healy era, what you said was what you said, then it got to the stage that you couldn't find what the politicians said, only someone else's opinion about what they meant when they said it.

'We started to live in each others' pockets. Then we started to have a quiet word in a journalist's ear. Journalists started using the politicians and vice versa. It has been, in my view, an unhealthy relationship.

'Now we have the radial mile of Leinster House where we all talk to each other, we tell each other the same stories, we go to the same dinner parties, and it's no wonder that we all get it wrong together. Independent thinking suffers. Because most people in life don't like to be fingered out.

'I'd like to think that I wasn't just like that. That I wasn't thinking all the time about what they're going to say about me or what they're going to read about me. I just do what I want to do and that's it. I take the grief.

'I coined a phrase well over twenty years ago: There's one thing you can do in Irish politics. You can tell the truth because no-one is going to believe that. Most people are followers. Most journalists are followers. They think they're leading but in fact they're following. They seem to go out of their way sometimes to be more vitriolic than the next fella. I don't think there's much skill in writing vitriol.'

Fergus Finlay also believes that the approach of John Healy and colleagues like Dick Walsh fundamentally changed the way politics was filtered through the media.

'They were players and they saw themselves as players. The watershed was the Arms Crisis. The three national papers decided that Charlie Haughey wore the black hat and that the national interest demanded that we stand by Jack Lynch. From that moment on, those very senior respected journalists whom I admire enormously stopped being impartial. They were partisan and they were players.

'On one level, I've no problem with that because they chose the right side. But they shouldn't have done it. They should have been more neutral. Different things happened after that. Television forced Irish politics to be much more presidential. Party leaders became the only people who mattered.

'Television also introduced the sound bites. I know spin doctors have been accused of introducing sound bites. But sound bites were the only way you could get your man on television.'

'It also forced the print media to change, it tabloidised them. So now personality is equally as important as vision. The doubling in size of the political media meant a doubling in competition.

'The easiest place to start a rumour used to be the Law Library. Now it's Leinster House. I have heard many a thing come back to me in gilded form. It's also a very easy place and a very tempting place to plant a story. Much easier than it used to be.'

Obviously stories have to be leaked. 'It's part of the process,' Finlay acknowledges, but he insists: 'I've never given a journalist a piece of paper in my life. I wouldn't do it.

'I would frequently go to a journalist and say "if you're writing anything about such a thing, this is our point of view". I would frequently go to a journalist and say "have you heard that… " After that it's up to the journalist.'

When is a leak not a leak? 'We're publishing two documents next week. I will give those to any journalist that wants them in advance of publication. I don't regard that as a leak.

'In my experience, most leaks are done to damage somebody. Most leaks are done out of spite. And usually done spontaneously. While some are done to curry favour, the ones I remember best were done for spiteful reasons.'

'Yes. When we were in government, I frequently told journalists what was coming up. What was going to be on the agenda.'

Finlay has always been blamed for one of the most spectacular media leaks in recent history, where the high-profile political journalist Emily O'Reilly was given a draft text of the Framework Document which was to pave the way for the peace process that followed. He has always denied any involvement.

'If the garda file on that is ever published it will point very strongly in a particular direction.'

'The garda report, which was never published, exonerates Albert Reynolds, Martin Mansergh and myself, but said there were three other people with access to the document that they can't exonerate. Some day it will come out. But until then I will always be the one.'

Alan Shatter believes that what he calls a 'user relationship' exists between politicians and the media.

'A lot of the people in the media regard a lot of politicians as complete gobshites. As pliable and as usable as the leaders may see the foot soldiers in politics. Because when you have to write a story, you will first of all identify what kind of story you want to write. You then identify what politician you're going to phone to get an appropriate quote out of them so the story has the spin you want to put on it.

'So there's a symbiotic and exploitative relationship between the media and politics. We need each other. On occasion we despise each other. And the relationships are no more real than the other relationships in politics.

'But, for the naïve politician the pretence of closeness is made to get information for writing stories. It's an exploitative relationship. It means that if you're in politics you have a whole variety of unreal relationships, which take over your entire life. This is why I would be regarded as one of the most cynical people in politics. Because I understood this from day one. This isn't saying "poor old Alan Shatter wasn't written about lovingly". I did pretty well actually, by and large, from the media coverage I got. Bearing in mind the fact I was never a minister I probably got more media coverage than I deserved.

'Also there is the cynical journalist aspect in politics that equally drives me insane. There are some journalists who write considered articles that are based on some kind of serious and intelligent analysis. And then there's the type of journalist that we have far more of now than we had in the 1980s – the type of journalist that takes the view that all politicians in every party are complete and utter gobshites. Their only purpose in the world is to use them and portray them as utter gobshites while portraying themselves as heroes.

'I think that that element of journalism in Ireland is helping to undermine the credibility of Irish politics, and must take some responsibility for the degree to which ordinary people are cynical of politics and unwilling to regard anyone in politics as anything more than some sort of self-serving individual prostituting themselves for their own financial benefit. I do think journalism has contributed to that. I think Charlie Haughey has as well.'

Some of the more recent comers to the game are less cynical. After just over a year in national politics, Tom Parlon maintains that he never refuses an interview.

'I always say too much rather than too little. Thanks be to God, I've gotten over that with all the practice. Over the years with the IFA stuff there were really hairy moments when you had to think on your feet. I'm able to concentrate now on what I want to say rather than be concerned about the fear of it. And that's a help.'

He pauses before adding with a glint in his eye:

'I still don't trust them, the bastards.'

CHAPTER 27

Sex and the Single Transferable Vote

'You can't let your erogenous zones go mad' – Fine Gael TD

In a Dublin newspaper office in October 1999 a group of newspaper executives hovered around a flickering computer screen. On the screen was a file of photographs starring a former high-profile married politician. The setting was a family saloon with steamed-up windows parked near the Sally Gap in the Dublin Mountains. The series of salacious shots were taken over the course of a three-hour stakeout by two photographers and one journalist. The journalist recalls one frame where the politician was captured nipping from the front seat to the back seat of the car. He was naked from the waist down.

The newspaper in question planned to run the pictures along with a story detailing an enthusiastic liaison with a young woman. But they had a problem. Despite an extensive trawl of the cuttings files, they could not unearth a single incident when this politician had defended family values. Unable to justify running the story on the grounds of exposing the politician's hypocrisy, an editorial decision was taken to pull the sensational spread.

A story about a married politician having sexual relations with a twenty-nine-year-old 'auburn-haired' administrator subsequently ran in the *Sunday People* newspaper. The newspaper was never sued.

For rural politicians, national politics offers a lifestyle tailor-made for what used to be called 'playing offside'. They are away from home and living in the relative anonymity of a hotel or apartment for three days a week during the political season. On the downside, Dublin is far too small a town to hope to keep extramarital affairs secret.

And there is now the added fear of national exposure. The media, which just three years ago balked at printing photographs of a politician in a compromising position, is getting more aggressively intrusive by the day.

Politicians do, of course, sometimes risk all. Most journalists who are privy to the political world could name a number of senior politicians who have had, or are having, sexual relations with women who are not their wives.

But we have moved some way from the hedonistic 1970s and 1980s. And while a presentable woman might still expect a brace of indecent proposals at a party conference, on a day-to-day level politicians have belatedly, if reluctantly, embraced political correctness.

The number of married TDs has fallen over the last twenty years, from a high of 148 in 1982 to just 131 in the Dáil that was elected in 2002. Marriage break-up first showed up in the political statistics in 1989 when two deputies listed their marital status as 'separated'. In the current Dáil, seven TDs are listed as separated, including the current Taoiseach. Two TDs, Ruairí Quinn and Charlie McCreevy, have divorced and remarried. A number of others are, in fact, living apart from their wives but have not officially acknowledged their changed status.

The new social realities sit uneasily with a political class used to playing by the old conservative rules.

Perhaps the single politician who has had to cope with the most intrusive media attention is Dr James McDaid. His attempts to be philosophical about it curdle in the face of the memories of the worst of it.

When his estranged wife's memoir about their turbulent life together was serialised in a Sunday newspaper, he kept his counsel.

'I found it very hard but I didn't speak about it. When I read what she wrote I felt that a lot of them (the stories) didn't need to be said. They were untrue.

'But I felt that coming out and responding wasn't right. So I just had to take all that. All the things I was accused of. Basically, myself and Marguerite weren't living together since 1988. I was supposed to be having affairs all over the place. I never said I was celibate. What I did do was I made my own tape about how things were at the time. I'm keeping it for the time being. I didn't read the book.

'I accept that if you're in public life, anything that you do is up for grabs but some of the things that happened to me...'

He shakes his head when he recalls his highly-publicised relationship with a major media figure. He refers to it as 'the Anne Doyle thing'.

'Somebody was actually across from my place in an old derelict building taking photographs and following us.'

The media interest in his personal life was relentless.

'On another day I was having lunch with a journalist. She told me later that there was a photographer there and that she had had to go to him afterwards and tell him who she was.

'I suppose people didn't understand the situation with Marguerite. It looked like I was a married person flirting with high-profile women. So you could say I brought it on myself. I mean it didn't dawn on me for ages. I thought "why can't I go out? Why can't I have a date? If I was going out with anybody it had to be a private thing or else a lunch".'

He also found that women were reluctant to be seen with him. They didn't want to come out in the open. 'They felt that having dinner with me started tongues wagging. I probably handled it wrongly by not coming out and going on dates, but the fact of the matter is that I had this unsolved situation at home.'

He doesn't believe being a politician makes him more attractive to women – 'I don't think women are attracted to it, no' – but he acknowledges that there is some glamour attached to the life of a minister.

'I suppose it's being in the public eye. There is a celebrity thing about it.

'There are people who detest politics and think everyone in it is crooked. But you do have others who think you are a celebrity. It does curtail you socially. Twice I've gone into a pub in Dun Laoghaire (where he lives while in Dublin) just to watch a match. But even at that people know you.'

While McDaid now rarely takes a drink, he remains nostalgic for the time when the Dáil bars were 'a hive of activity' on Wednesday nights.

'You'd go down and have a drink. A lot of people would be drunk including myself. You hardly see anybody in there now apart from a few hardcore ones. The craic is gone out of it.

'I'm here fifteen years and I can see the change. Some kind of a social change occurred and it was a fairly dramatic change. Around the mid-90s. It probably has something to do with the changing faces in here – the huge turnover at election time.'

He believes that the infamous altercation between Ned O'Keeffe and then journalist Una Claffey in the Visitors' Bar sparked an attitude change.

'You don't know now if you touch people on the knee or the shoulder what will be made of it.'

I wondered how another long-serving TD who enjoyed an enthusiastic social life through the Eighties and Nineties, managed it. He confided that as a politician, one has to take precautions. Or, as he put it, 'you have to travel in threes if you're meeting company. You can't let your erogenous zones go mad.'

John Deasy, the Fine Gael justice spokesman who entered the Dáil for the first time in 2002, believes that TDs might actually get their rocks off on the competitiveness of the business. And that this appears to suffice.

'I have not been regaled by tales of sexual exploits,' he says.

Although handsome and eligible, he claimed that since becoming a TD he had received exactly the same number of Valentine cards he got for the previous ten years – 'zero'. He wasn't ruling out the possibility that his growing profile as a national political figure would impress the opposite sex.

'It could work – but I don't use it to get laid,' he stated frankly.

'This business is so all-consuming that you tend to become self-obsessed. You end up having a few pints at the end of the night.'

But he knows he can't go on this way. 'You need emotional back-up. Politicians have a lot of emotional baggage. I've been advised to get a wife.'

Less then six months after we spoke, John Deasy announced his engagement to TV3 news reporter Maura Derrane.

In an age when it's accepted that about ten per cent of the population is gay, where most straight adults, at least in urban Ireland, have gay friends, it appears that Leinster House is the last refuge of the sexual ostrich. Of the hundreds of TDs and senators who have passed through Leinster House in the decades since independence, just one has been out and proud.

David Norris, the flamboyant senator and lecturer, revels in his camp-as-Christmas persona. His sexual preference stopped being an issue a long time ago.

But that breath of fresh air did little to blow open any more closets in the Houses of the Oireachtas. It remains resolutely firm-wristed. On the face of it, a heterosexuals-only house.

A TD's sexual preference has hit the headlines in this country on just two occasions.

In the run-up to the Labour leadership contest in September 2002, Brendan Howlin stunned the nation by telling the *Star* news-paper that he wasn't gay. A photograph of the leadership contender supping a manly pint of porter accompanied the story.

Rumours about Howlin's alleged sexual preference for men had raged intermittently in political and media circles for some years.

The most persistent rumour linked the former minister with a prominent Dublin businessman. A much-embroidered urban myth about the pair being caught in flagrante delicto did the rounds and entered the public domain when hundreds of handmade posters detailing the allegations were slapped up on kiosks and poles across leafy Dublin 4.

As Labour activists worked through the night to scrape them down, the businessman hired an investigator to find out who was behind it. According to one source, the finger pointed to a business associate with a grudge against him. While there was absolutely no substance to the outrageous allegations, the innuendo lingered and the rumours grew ever more lurid.

Sources close to Howlin's leadership campaign said they felt they had to nail them – or risk a whispering campaign scuppering his chances in the leadership race. In the event, he lost the race anyway.

The only other occasion when a TD's ambiguous sexuality hit the headlines was in March 1994, when a newspaper reported that that the then junior minister Emmet Stagg had been questioned by gardai in the Phoenix Park. The devastated politician confirmed that he had been sitting in a car with a man he had just met 'in a part of the park known to me as a place where gay men met'. The fact that the media had crossed a new line in breaking this story sent waves of fear and loathing reverberating around Leinster House.

The incident was treated as a personal crisis that need never be referred to again in political circles. When Labour's national vote plunged in the following general election in 1997, Stagg's vote held up better than most.

Perhaps the times they are a-changing. In January 2004, a Fine Gael councillor called for same sex unions to be recognised under Irish law in the wake of his marriage to his gay partner in Canada.

Peter Kelly, a Fine Gael councillor in Cork County Council, married his long-term boyfriend Nick Dunphy in a civil ceremony in Vancouver in December 2003.

They stayed in The Counting Sheep Inn in Mission, near Vancouver. 'It was advertised as a little sheep farm but there were only five sheep, so it sounded more romantic than it was,' Councillor Kelly revealed.

'It was quite simple really and very emotional for both of us. Afterwards we had a few bottles of champagne,' he said.

He is pragmatic about the impact his decision to speak publicly about his homosexuality may have on his political career: 'I am what I am and I'm not changing that. I don't expect everyone to agree with me, but my approach is that I have never hidden anything. People can take me or leave me.'

But, of course, it is the personal lives of two of the most senior figures in Irish politics that have been the subject of the greatest media and public intrigue.

Charlie Haughey's affair with the gossip columnist Terry Keane kept those in the know agog for years. Keane, who would mark the end of the affair with a spectacular kiss-and-tell in the *Sunday Times* newspaper, recalled her first meeting with Haughey in Iveagh House in 1964.

'He was Fianna Fáil's Young Turk and he had a reputation for being loud and dangerous. After the dinner and his speech I was among a crowd he invited upstairs for a drink. He was surrounded with cronies, fawning reporters and pretty girls.' She was not impressed. 'Along with everyone else, I viewed Charlie as a bit of a wild boy with a terrible reputation as a womaniser... he was considered so wild that no woman would even consider an affair with him.'

She was to change her mind, of course, and embark on a well-documented romance with him that spanned more than two decades.

Most recently it is Bertie Ahern's personal life that has the chattering classes in its thrall. When it first emerged that he had separated from his wife, Miriam, he denied reports that he was involved with another woman. Even five years after the separation, he was still giving newspaper interviews bemoaning the breakdown of his marriage and making no reference to his then long-standing partner, Celia Larkin. In the run-up to the leadership campaign to replace Charlie Haughey, the then Minister for the Environment Michael Smith – a backer of Ahern's rival Albert Reynolds – was quoted in his local newspaper, the *Tipperary Star*, as saying there were question marks over Ahern's suitability for the Taoiseach's office because of his unclear marriage situation.

Reynolds himself was quoted as saying 'people do like to know where the Taoiseach of the day is living.' Both men later claimed they were misquoted.

Eventually, Ahern couldn't keep his second relationship a secret any longer. By the time he was elected Taoiseach everyone was very clear that he was separated and openly living with a another woman. And few seemed to care.

Since the relationship with Larkin ended in the summer of 2003, Ahern has been linked with three named women in the tabloid press. All denied any close relationship, and few in the media seriously believe that he has been involved with any of them.

He says himself that politics plays havoc with any politician's family life.

'It just makes it hard. I remember when I said that, somebody said it depends on how you organise it. That's fair enough. I think it's Alan Shatter said that. He's out of the House now.

'But it's a hard thing to do for anybody. And I think anyone who goes right through it without a problem has done very well. But it does make it hard. It does genuinely make it very hard.'

Another politician who was separated and single when we spoke wondered how he was ever going to get involved in another relationship.

'How do I organise a date? I can tell you that I never intended to live as a monk. But it's really only striking me now that I'm in this situation. It's really very, very difficult.'

How much more difficult that must be if you happen to be Taoiseach.

CHAPTER 28

Leading the Party

'You feel responsible for others in a unique way' – Mary Harney

The election of a party leader, perhaps more so than in any other part of the democratic process, is an essentially selfish business, driven by fear and favours.

Ask not what you can do for the leadership candidates, but what the leadership candidates can do for you.

Ambitious and influential TDs will vote for the candidate most likely to put them on their front bench or in their Cabinet. Ever-paranoid backbenchers will vote for the candidate whose face on the lamp posts is most likely to boost their own vote and secure their seat.

The preferred candidate of the outgoing regime is rarely the candidate that gets the gig. A new broom carries the promise of a new front bench order, and there are always more people on the outside hoping and wishing than there are available on the inside to batten down the hatches. And so it was that Garret FitzGerald's departure saw his anointed successor Peter Barry swept aside in favour of Alan Dukes. And so it was that Jack Lynch's flag-bearer George Colley failed to secure the leadership despite having – or most likely because he had – the backing of thirteen members of the outgoing Cabinet. And so it was that Charlie Haughey's crown prince Bertie Ahern lost out to Albert Reynolds.

Ivan Yates described how he explained this numbers game to John Bruton in 1994 as the then Fine Gael leader teetered under the weight of poor opinion polls and media coverage highlighting his 'charisma deficit' which, as Yates colourfully recalls, had plotters in his own party 'coming at him in shoals.'

'It was starting to get John down. I said "John, this is politics. This is just a game". In all the battles I would say to him "look, this isn't about John Bruton, this is about six jobs. If you get into government, there are only six cabinet positions. This is what this is all about now. They're out and you're in at the moment".

'Politics always boils down to mathematics. If there is a coalition formed between Fine Gael and Labour, there are only six Fine Gael Cabinet ministers. That's the only game in town.'

Enda Kenny's best day so far has been 'the day I was elected by my own peers as the leader of my party. It's a wonderful honour and a privilege.

'To be recognised a leader of the party, you're treated differently. They recognise the challenges that you face and they also recognise that this is the person that could become Taoiseach if there's a change of government. That's a pretty daunting prospect in its own right. I think you're expected to behave accordingly. Wherever you are now, people cross the street now to shake hands with you.'

Kenny learned a hard lesson shortly after he was made party leader when a joke he told at a Fine Gael gathering was branded racist and inappropriate.

'I was actually sick for two days when I saw the reaction to that. It was a salutary lesson and obviously a pretty steep learning experience. It made me realise that I'm in a different place now. People expect different things. In so far as changing my nature or personality, I don't think it has done that. I still hope I'm the same person.

'It's about Cabinet governance. You are in there to make decisions. Do the leadership thing. Make decisions and stand by them. And if you don't like that, get out. The ultimate sanction is that people can throw you out. You get a run at this, do it as best you can, and if they don't like it, they'll throw you out. And people should be able to exercise that right.

'People are ambitious. I think it takes a number of years before you appreciate that if you sit at the Cabinet table, you do have a serious impact on people's lives. It sort of dawns on you after a number of years that you know what to do. Whether you present yourself as a credible person to take on that responsibility is for others to judge.'

Mary Harney, the only woman to lead an Irish political party, insists that becoming party leader 'wasn't something that I sought for myself.'

'I didn't think Des would stand down so soon. I thought there was a lot more years left in him. When it happened a number of people said "go for it!" and it was one of those things that if you didn't you might always regret it.'

She is dismissive of suggestions that the other leadership hopeful, Pat Cox, had been shafted.

'There were ten people to canvass. There wasn't exactly a large constituency. And we each spoke to all of them.

'Anyway, leadership elections in parties, whether they are big or small, always leave their wounds. I know of none that's smooth. Even ones that are smooth on the surface, you'll find that under the surface there is often a lot of annoyance.

'I had come from a group where there was a lot of antagonism and internal strife, where there was two, and sometimes more, distinct camps, and you almost felt like a traitor in your own organisation – so the last thing I wanted was to have that replicated in a smaller group. It did bother me and I tried to mend bridges but it wasn't possible.'

In the triumph of becoming the first female party leader in Irish political history Harney could not have envisaged all that lay in store for her. She rates her worst day as the day the votes were counted in the 1997 general election and her party colleagues fell like skittles.

'As party leader you feel responsible for others in a very unique way. The 1997 election was a nightmare, it was like a bad dream.

'I always remember a very nice gesture. The doorbell rang and it was Jonathan Philbin Bowman with a beautiful bunch of flowers – lilies – and a bottle of wine or something. I thought it was a lovely gesture. He wasn't even looking for a story. Those are the things you remember.

'The big challenge for me after '97 was to try and keep the party together. We'd a huge debt. How was I going to raise the money to keep the show on the road, to keep the headquarters open, to keep staff? If we hadn't been in government I would say it would have been impossible.

'I was also conscious that Bobby (Molloy) didn't want to run. And Des (O'Malley) certainly wasn't going to run. So you were in a scenario where there might have been only Liz O'Donnell and I running. And after Liz's bad health experience – she had a virus that lasted a year – there were times when I thought to myself "she's going to come to me one day and say she isn't running". So you're trying to build up an organisation and keep people on board. Keeping the show on the road and trying to do it all very quietly. Every small thing that goes wrong is a big issue when things aren't going well.'

Dick Spring believes one of his greatest contributions to politics was 'uniting the Labour Party and making it into a serious political force, as opposed to the mess of a party that I became leader of in 1982.

'I was always annoyed with Dev's "Labour must wait" and wanted us to be a serious force in Irish politics.'

He rates the election of 1997 when many Labour TDs lost out as the worst day of his political life.

'I believe our record in government was exemplary and the floating voters were harsh on us.'

He says that, looking back, the pluses outweigh the minuses in his long political career 'although enormous sacrifices had to be made to juggle being TD for a very demanding rural constituency, a Minister and party leader. Oh, to be a Senator at the Cabinet table with no constituency duties! The multi-seat constituency brought extra pressure as well as some TDs in opposition who wouldn't spend too much time in Dáil Éireann. And coalition partners wouldn't ever defend tough decisions which left "the Minister" – me – being attacked on all fronts.'

After twenty-one years at the coal-face of Irish politics, Spring, now in the throes of a new career in financial services and business consultancy, says he is 'enjoying his new-found freedom'.

'It's a great relief to be free from the constituency pressure, the chicken supper circuit, et cetera, and being free to make decisions without political considerations – most of the time.'

Ruairi Quinn doesn't accept the infamous Enoch Powell claim that all political careers end in failure. However, he says 'you can overreach yourself in that your last level is deemed to be failure because you're fired or defeated or whatever.

'An awful lot of that is knowing when to move on. Because knowing when to go is nearly as important as knowing when to make a push to rise.

'If the motivation is to have power for the sheer sake of it, if it's the biggest buzz you can possibly get and if you associate your identity and your being with it and your centre of gravity as inextricably linked with the exercise of power, then if that's taken away from you, a part of you is taken away.

'I always go back to my republican ideology. The idea that you would be capable of walking away as well as walking into was always important to me.'

He was 'grateful' to have the space and time to decide it was his time to walk away.

'I had worked extremely hard over the previous five years: the merger of the two parties, the policy platform. I felt we'd won the argument but we'd lost the war.

'I just said to myself "can you really do this again for the next six years?" I just felt I couldn't do it with the same degree of passionate commitment it required.

'Myself and Liz (his wife) had agreed that I would retire at sixty anyhow. That would have been mid-term. I think there is a lesson in looking at other people not being able to move on. That's the way I felt then and I feel extremely comfortable with the decision now.'

CHAPTER 29

Leading the Nation

'Uneasy lies the head that wears the crown' –
William Shakespeare

On 11 December 1979, Charles J Haughey rose to his feet in Leinster House after a tempestuous debate in which reference was made to his 'flawed pedigree', his supporters were dubbed 'sectarian nationalists, crypto-Provos' and his political success was attributed to his 'total lack of scruples'.

The debate had concluded with a vote that elected him Taoiseach.

'I am deeply conscious of the great honour just conferred upon me, and I extend my most sincere gratitude to Dáil Éireann,' is what he said.

Since the foundation of the State, this great honour has been the preserve of TDs from the two main parties.

Of the eleven taoisigh who have served to date, six have been leaders of Fianna Fáil. In senior Fianna Fáil circles, the aching ambition to one day be elected Taoiseach is the truth that dare not speak its name.

Micheál Martin was dubbed the former future Taoiseach around Leinster House when the inevitable difficulties of his Health brief threatened to thwart his path to the top. But shrewd observers warn that the angel-faced Cork politico is far from being a beaten docket in the Fianna Fáil leadership stakes.

Of course, in time-honoured fashion, Martin himself insists that he is not gagging for the gig.

'Well I'm not one of those, strangely enough. I know I'm touted all over the place, people say you're going to be this, that and the other, particularly in Cork. I'm not saying that any person wouldn't like to be Taoiseach but I have watched the Taoiseach at the moment in terms of his workload, in terms of the pressures now on the job, pressures that weren't there five or ten years ago. I'd think about it and I'd have to reflect on it.'

So he'd turn it down if it was handed to him?

'No-one comes to you and hands it to you. Taoiseach is something you have to go for. I'm not running here, there and everywhere at the moment thinking "when am I going to be Taoiseach?" or that I need to be Taoiseach next week. I think you can make a huge contribution as a minister. There's a lot of satisfaction and reward in that.'

'Of course, I'd be a liar if I told you that I haven't thought about being Taoiseach at some stage into the future. But in reality, at the moment I'm not pressing or running around saying I want to be Taoiseach in a couple of years' time.'

I point out that he has time on his side.

'That's possibly true, yeah, but I've a life to get on with too.'

Charlie McCreevy is generally overlooked when commentators are casting about for future leadership contenders. But he should not be discounted. While he hid the white light of his burning ambition under a bushel of bluff bon homie during his years wandering in the political wilderness, he can now reveal that he always had a plan.

'I always said that if I ever became a minister that I'd like before I finished to become a minister for finance. It'd be the zenith of my ambition.'

Now that he's been there and done that, would he consider going for the top job?

'If some people asked me to become Taoiseach I'd take it. But I'm not going to go out knocking on doors asking for it. Or I never asked anyone to make me a minister either. I'd never put myself in the way of lobbying for it. In previous times if I'd have bended the knee I might have got it. But I didn't.'

Seamus Brennan insists that he wouldn't be gone on the job of Taoiseach. Not that he'd refuse, mind you.

'I'm not personally ambitious. I was. About twenty years ago I probably wanted to be Taoiseach. I wouldn't turn it down, of course. But I'm not going after it.

'I watched four taoisigh. There is a great quotation from Mr Shakespeare: "Uneasy lies the head that wears the crown." It's a lousy job. And I personally wouldn't particularly like it. But then I didn't like the idea of being Chief Whip either. For as long as I'm in politics, whatever they offer me I'll take it. But I don't know how long more I'll be in politics.

'I'm fifty-five. I'd like to do other things. The serious people in politics know one thing. You have to know yourself when it's time to go. All great political careers end in disaster because people don't make their mind up themselves. I would like to decide the day I am going to go. To pick it and stick to it whatever is going on. That's what I'll do.

'I genuinely don't have any ambitions to jump up the final rung of the ladder. I've seen it and I don't want it. I'm not going looking for it. I don't think it will be offered to me anyway.'

And yet, when the moment is upon them, there are usually more than a few contenders for this supposedly lousy job. And not one of them has relinquished the reins of power easily. Haughey famously hung on through a relentless series of heaves. His successor, Albert Reynolds, insists now that the heave that was launched on the day that he was sacked as Finance Minister by Haughey in October 1991 was not of his making.

'If I was part of it you can be damn sure I wouldn't have put it down at that time. Timing is everything and the timing was totally wrong. The homework hadn't been done. That's why it failed.'

When Haughey finally stepped down in January 1992, Reynolds was back in the frame. As was Haughey's most loyal lieutenant, Bertie Ahern. Reynolds described how he dashed his rival's hopes at a crucial meeting in the Berkeley Court Hotel on the eve of the leadership vote.

'They were telling him that he had bigger numbers than he had. I said that one of us is wrong because there isn't that number of votes out there.'

How did he know his numbers were solid?

'You'll never get it spot on, no matter what contacts you use and how often you double or treble check it. But you would get damn close.'

Ahern withdrew from a leadership race he had never formally entered. Curiously, Bertie Ahern now insists that he actually had no interest in the job at the time.

'I liked Albert and I reckoned Albert was going to be the next Taoiseach. Everyone was saying I was dithering but I was trying to do me first Budget. I came into Finance in mid-November and the Budget was the end of January. And then this bloody hassle starts.

'And when the fellas were all out lobbying in January, I just wanted to do me Budget. This was a huge thing. I wanted to be Minister for Finance and this was Budget Day and I couldn't care a monkey's about what happened. I couldn't care if there were fifty-five leaders of the party elected during January. I just wanted to do me Budget.

'I had guys coming to me. That is true. But I just wanted to do me Budget. I was saying "listen, I'm not interested. I want to do me bloody Budget. I've been Minister for Finance a few weeks. I'm not ready for this. I'm just in here and I'm not going to win a vote any-way, and I'm not going to canvass for a vote". And I never did. I never canvassed anybody in that leadership campaign.

'To be frank, it came about from two sets of things. There were people who didn't want Albert to get it. Who saw that I was the only one who could get a good vote against him. That was their reason. It wasn't my reason. The other thing is that they were just trying to pressure me to get on with it. But I just didn't want to do that.

'We made a pact. The pact was that I'd support him for Taoiseach and I'd be Minister for Finance.

'He did say "I'm only here for a short period". He didn't mean for the period to end up like it did. And, by the way, I didn't want it to be that period either.

It was assumed he would be a one-term Taoiseach? 'Yeah. He never wanted to stay a long time and he made that clear. It was absolutely fine. I wanted to be Minister for Finance. I was more than happy.

'Albert and I were good buddies. We went to the Galway Races and all that stuff together so there was no hassle. It was just the media pressure. The media wanted a contest. And there was no contest with Mary O'Rourke and Michael Woods because they knew they were only going to get a handful of votes. I would have got a good vote. I wouldn't have won. I didn't want to get into that. I had the job I wanted. And I had the job for only a few weeks. So all the bullshit that was written at that time was bullshit.'

The last twenty years have seen five men rise to the highest office in government. It would be difficult to detect a pattern. Garret

FitzGerald and John Bruton both enjoyed the kind of background and education that moulds leaders.

Garret FitzGerald's tale of their family penury when his father lost his Dáil seat in 1937 speaks volumes about his style and class.

'My mother said "of course we'll still have parties but we won't really have staff or anything like that so we'll have to do the cooking ourselves". So one brother did baking, one did roasting, and I did puddings.'

He says his specialty was homemade strawberry ice cream – he can still tell you the recipe.

John Bruton came from wealthy farming stock, and was dispatched to boarding school in Dublin at the tender age of five, and on to Clongowes Wood College when he was twelve.

He remembers the pictures of the college's past pupils lining the walls – from Daniel O'Connell's sons to John Redmond and Kevin O'Higgins – but he claims he was never conscious of being groomed for greatness.

'The leaders of society tended to come from people who could afford to go to second level school. It wasn't so much the second level school that made them leaders, it was that they were the people who could afford to get the education. That's the pool from which one drew the leaders,' he says in retrospect.

Charlie Haughey had no such natural advantages. He affected the manners and attitude of a medieval prince – utterly disdainful of the little people and their middle class hang-ups. But scratch the surface, and he was still a rough-hewn Joey's boy, a street fighter in a beautifully-cut suit. He struggled to shrug off his lower middle class roots by mixing with the political elite in his college days in UCD. Garret FitzGerald believes that he was plotting his path to the top even then.

'Everybody knew about him. I have a diary of the summer of '44 in college. I could tell you where he was and with whom he was with in the great hall. He was always with the sons of three Fianna Fáil ministers. In second year then he took up with the daughter of another. So everyone knew exactly where he was going.'

Albert Reynolds never heard politics discussed in his home in Roosky, Co. Longford. His formal education ended with the Leaving Certificate at the Summerhill diocesan college in Sligo, which specialised in moulding young minds for the priesthood. He says his parents couldn't afford to send him to college so he launched himself enthusiastically into the university of life. While having no intellectual pretensions (he confided to this author 'I'm not a great reader of books'), and no political pedigree, he nevertheless had one trait that set him apart from his peers from an early age – an eye for the main chance and a talent for making money.

He sent tens of thousands of punters home sweating from his dance halls and brought gambling to the masses with his gala bingo nights. And he did it his way. There can be few Prime Ministers in the world who could boast of their early business venture: 'I took the money at the door, went up and called the numbers, sold them tea and minerals at the breaks, finished calling the numbers, paid out the money and brought the rest of it home.'

At forty-four, he was a latecomer to politics, but he applied the skills he had learned in business and quickly leap-frogged over his colleagues to win a place at Cabinet in less than three years.

Bertie Ahern hailed from a working class terrace in the heart of old Dublin and put himself through an accountancy course at night while working in the Mater Hospital by day. While his four predecessors all had some character trait that set them apart, the power of Ahern's political persona lies in his sheer ordinariness. Few could have predicted that his unremarkable childhood, with its humble Christian Brothers' education and modest academic achievement, dominated by alley soccer and GAA, steeped in traditional Catholicism, would produce one of the most successful political leaders in the western world.

Much has been made of the fact that he wrote an essay on 'Why I want to be Taoiseach' when he was a boy of eleven.

'That was a joke,' the man himself insists now, 'That was to win a fountain pen which I hadn't got at the time. Bord Bainne was doing these things about what would you like to be. So I wrote a thing about how I would like to be Taoiseach and I won a pen.' He had been introduced to the thrills and spills of electoral politics by a music teacher in his school. Stan O'Brien stood for Fianna Fáil in the 1963 by-election and had an army of pupils delivering leaflets bearing the catchy slogan 'Stan is Our Man'.

'If you ask me when did I think I would like to be involved in politics, I'd say when I was sixteen or seventeen. I liked the idea of the local stuff, of being involved in the local stuff. I wasn't really involved but I was conscious there was a local cumann. I was conscious of the local TDs and because in our home area there was a very strong cumann in Drumcondra. Haughey and Colley used to regularly come there and you would be hearing people talking about them at that time. I put up posters in the '65 election when I was fourteen. Haughey gave a party for the kids after that election so I would have met him then.'

Was that a big thrill?

'Not really, because I would have met George (Colley) at around then too.'

He remembers being fascinated by the pageant organised to mark the fiftieth anniversary of the Easter Rising in 1966. 'I went to that on my own at fourteen or fifteen years of age. I went on my own because no-one else was going.

'My mother and father were republican and Fianna Fáil. My father hadn't been that active. He would always have helped Fianna Fáil at election time but he wasn't involved on a day-to-day basis. He was a Cork republican. And very proud of that. Easter Sunday was very special in our house.

'There was a girl called Lorraine Booth who was a neighbour from three doors down who got me to go to a cumann meeting.'

Was there a romance?

'Not a hope. She was a bit older than me and I think she was actually with her fella that she subsequently married. She was recruiting and she brought four of us on that night.'

Garret FitzGerald was tagged for the top job from a young age. When still just fifteen, a priest told him he should enter politics 'and try to be Taoiseach'. The teenage FitzGerald wasn't daunted at the prospect.

'It seemed rather a worthwhile thing to have a go at,' he remembers thinking.

He also recalls a conversation with his friend Maurice Kennedy and his future wife Joan while 'fooling around' the grounds of UCD in the summer of 1945.

'Maurice said to Joan "if you get further along with this guy you'll end up in (what he described satirically as) the royal box in Croke Park, explaining the finer points of the game to the British Ambassador".'

'So he warned her. I could always use that ever after. "Maurice told you! You married me knowing that, for God's sake".

'It wasn't a serious thing. But it was a case of "let's have a go at this and see how far we get. If I hadn't become leader of the party or Taoiseach it wouldn't bother me. I would have worked happily under Tom O'Higgins or Declan Costello. I wasn't hung up about it. But it was always on my mind. Well, if you get into politics what else would you want to be?'

But while he revelled in his role as Minister for Foreign Affairs, he came to view his tenure in the Taoiseach's office more as a duty than a pleasure.

'I don't think I can say that I enjoyed being Taoiseach. I felt there was a job to do and it was better that I should be there to do it than not.'

FitzGerald felt 'delighted' to be elected Taoiseach 'until I got my seal of office and was told the country's bankrupt. That wasn't a good moment.

'I didn't realise quite how difficult it would be. I was confident that we could solve the problems which we only partly did.

'I wouldn't say I'm a clever tactician at all. Not at all. I make mistakes. But I've always had long-term strategy. I tended to be more strategic and occasionally made mistakes on tactics. Bertie is great at tactics but I'm not sure what the strategy is. I got thrown out and he'll get thrown out too eventually.'

He believes it helped that he wasn't egotistical about his position. 'I don't get too upset about things. I don't worry about me particularly. If you're doing what you think is the right thing, acting reasonably sensibly... If you did something you shouldn't do or did something really stupid unnecessarily, which caused immense damage, you'd be upset about it. But I did nothing perhaps totally disastrous on the whole. I never worry.'

His secret? 'You see politics was a phase. I didn't want to be there forever. There were other things in life to do. I was quite happy to move out of it in the end. It wasn't a life ambition to end up in politics.'

He was 'totally exhausted' after his final stint in government ended in 1986.

'As was most of the government. It was the most wearing government since the war. Apart from the period from 1922 to 1927, it was the toughest government ever.

'The big thing was "don't leave Haughey in with an overall majority", which was a view shared by over two-thirds of the Dáil. It wasn't just a party thing. But an overall majority seemed to me to be a dangerous thing. That's why I asked Des O'Malley to join me in government, and if not, to form a new party. Which he did.

'Unfortunately it turned out to be a right-wing party. I didn't expect that. I didn't know he was right-wing when I said it to him. It was a surprise that he was a right-winger. He was probably going to form the party anyway, even if I hadn't said it to him. Pat (O'Malley) said to me once "never tell anybody that. It would ruin you in Fine Gael!" I'm responsible for the PDs, God help me!'

John Bruton, the only party leader to become Taoiseach without a general election, remembers the moment of his surprise elevation as 'astonishing.' He swears he has already forgotten much of the detail of the negotiations that tacked together a new coalition arrangement that brought him to power in unique circumstances in 1994.

'I think leaving Leinster House that night I had a pretty good idea. Proinsias (de Rossa, the then leader of the Democratic Left party) was driving out ahead of me in his little Fiat and I said to myself: "that man has my future in his hands!"'

His trademark laughter gushes forth at the memory of it all.

'Ah, t'was great. It was terrific.'

He can't remember who called him to seal the deal and neither can he remember who he called first to relay the good news.

'I don't remember any of that. It's all gone out of my head. Honestly. You see you had so much to do that day. You just had to get on with it and select a government.'

Coming just months after an attempted coup, he remarks dryly of this task of picking a Cabinet that 'some of my colleagues had made it easy for me by ruling themselves out a few months earlier.

'I only had a limited number of positions. I think of all of the positions – and this would be probably normal for taoisigh and PMs – four-fifths of them would suggest themselves and be obvious, and the last two or three positions, you'd have a few line calls to make.

'You have to look at a number of considerations. Obviously ability, and then geography and loyalty. Each one is valid in its own way. You can't reward disloyalty. You can't ignore geography. And you certainly won't have a good government if you ignore ability.'

'I would have done lists. I would have been doing those lists for a few days before. In fact I have them. Lists of names and places in government.'

He will, he acknowledges, have 'a massive archive'.

For Reynolds, his best day 'had to be the day you were elected Taoiseach. No question about it.'

Asked why he thought he made the grade, the former Taoiseach reeled off a lengthy list of his achievements in each government department in which he had served before noting: 'I suppose I'm not the best man to say it but there were a lot of people in the party who liked the way I went about things. If I told them I would do it, it would get done.'

He says he enjoyed the ride thoroughly. 'I kept myself busy. I never had a dull moment. The X case arrived on my desk on my first day as Taoiseach and it was all go until the day it ended.' He says he never let the pressure get to him. But then he says he has two character traits that are vital for the role of Taoiseach. 'I don't mind hard work and I don't mind abuse.'

Bertie Ahern can confirm that being Taoiseach is everything it's cracked up to be.

'The hours are long. It's tough on me and tough on the staff and everyone else. But it's enjoyable. You do really feel that you're making a difference and that you're dealing with the crises of the day and the week.

'In any job there are times when you say "God, can it get any more difficult, can it get any tougher?" But I genuinely like it.

'If somebody said would you like to be Taoiseach for twenty years, that would be a different thing. When I get up in the morning I relish the thought of getting on with it rather than saying "yeach". Some days are harder than others, but I genuinely enjoy it, so far.

'A lot of it has to do with your age. If you were to come in at sixty and you were to be trying to do it between sixty and seventy I don't think you could do it. If you're fit enough and able enough you certainly can do it for ten years. It's a job that's like a lot of jobs. You can do it as long as you feel you can do it, that you have the energy to do it. If you weren't enjoying it you just couldn't do it. Most of the guys doing it now work a seventy- or eighty-hour week. You just couldn't do that. And the trouble is that's every week. It's not just this week. But I'm happy. I'm enjoying it.'

Despite setting out why he wanted to be Taoiseach in an essay at age eleven, Ahern claims that his ambition did not stretch quite that far.

'I wanted to be Minister for Finance. If you had asked me in 1980 what would be your pinnacle of your career, I would have said to be Minister for Finance. I would love to be Minister for Finance.'

He rates the brokering of the Good Friday Agreement as the most satisfying moment of his career to date.

'Even though it was a hard week for me, a sad week for me, (it is) the Good Friday Agreement in '98. It was a rotten week for me. It was a real tough week. But you had to pick yourself up.'

Once he begins it, the story pours out in an almost stream of consciousness monologue.

'The terrible thing about that week was that I was to meet Gerry Adams and Martin McGuinness at nine o'clock on the Sunday morning. I came back from London late and there was a Mass on in Cabra. I was to drop up to my mother and I didn't drop up to my mother.

'I was to meet Adams and McGuinness from nine to ten o'clock the following morning. I was to go up to her and I didn't and she had a heart attack at half-ten and I never met her and that killed me. So I was killing myself all week. But I had to keep going. I felt terrible, terrible, terrible.

'It was great at the end of it. I didn't sleep all week and it wasn't all work. I was sick, sick, sick. That story about walking around Hillsborough at four o'clock in the morning waiting for Trimble. I was walking around at four in the morning because I was pissed off with life. The Special Branch men asked me what I was doing. I said "looking at the birds nesting in the trees". That was Holy Thursday. But anyway, that was a great occasion.'

He has no hesitation when asked about his greatest disappointment.

'When I went to the European Council meeting as Finance Minister on that morning in early December '94, and all the headlines were about who would I have in my Cabinet and that I was going to be Taoiseach. And by the time I went to bed that night I was no longer going to be Taoiseach.

'I'll always remember *Prime Time* that night. It was all about "would Bruton be gone by Wednesday or Thursday". Bertie Ahern was going to be Taoiseach and that was just by the way.

'I got up the following morning and Geraldine (Kennedy) wrote that article and I was gone by the night.'

He pauses briefly before getting philosophical about it.

'That's life, and in actual fact, it didn't do me a damn bit of harm.'

One often wonders if the sheer gravity of the position ever overwhelms the Taoiseach of the day. Apparently not.

'You understand the responsibility of it. I don't think I wake up too much in the middle of the night. But you're conscious of it. There are calls you have to make and there are things you have to do, and you have to make changes in government and switch things around. They're all hard and you have to plan things out. There are tough things. Because eventually they'll all come down to you. Whether it's the finalisation of the National Development Plan or the next moves in the North, they all come back to you.'

His air of can-do cheeriness gives way to a rush of frustration and a touch of self-pity when he considers our astounding ingratitude for some of his most demanding work.

'It does bug me that nobody in this country, unlike all the other countries, takes any notice of the international work that a Taoiseach does. Nobody cares.'

When we're not ignoring it he says, 'we are making it the subject of ridicule. What was I doing in the jet? What hotel did I stay in? Had I got a big Jacuzzi in my room? Was there champagne?

'You bust your gut on these things. Most of the other Prime Ministers don't do Question Times – I spend more hours in the Dáil than any of them do – and still you have to go out there and present yourself and the country, and nobody in the national media at any level could care two damns. It's very demanding, but it's thankless. So as far as having airs and graces about that, I have none because nobody cares if I meet anyone or not. But maybe if I took a year where I met nobody then they might slag me for that.'

How does he deal with the stress?

'I love running and jogging. And when I'm in good humour I like having a pint. When I'm in bad humour, I don't. If I was under pressure I would not drink. It's just the way I am.

'I never considered walking away from it. I would consider when to walk away from it. You run the course as long as you can and then you get out of it. I don't think you should stay too long.

'You have to watch the public too. It's not just the party. You have to watch when there comes a time when people say they want a change. I think that happens in politics and you just have to make that judgment whenever it is. Hopefully it's not too soon.'

Albert Reynolds didn't see it coming. His government career was destined to end in traumatic circumstances. He remains bemused by the sudden collapse of his coalition arrangement with Dick Spring's Labour Party in 1994.

'It surprised me. We got on well. We'd done a deal,' he says now.

He has his own private theories about Spring's motivation for pulling out. He won't share them. But, like a melodramatic death scene in a classic Italian opera, Reynolds' political demise was a long drawn-out affair, which would end three years later in a multiple back-stabbing in the Fianna Fáil parliamentary party chambers in Leinster House.

He had spent £10,000 of his own money on an independent poll which showed he could expect to get forty-five per cent of the first preference vote in the 1997 presidential election. In the event, his party nominated Mary McAleese. He recalls that he was sitting beside the Munster MEP Brian Crowley when Bertie Ahern showed him his ballot paper to indicate that he had voted for him. As in Premiership football, as soon as the chairman expresses his undying support, you know the game is up.

'When Bertie showed me the bit of paper, Crowley said: "you're fucked".

'I knew it. I walked straight over to him after they went out to count the votes and said before the result of the second count "whatever the result of this is, I won't be the candidate".'

He admits that he still feels 'very disappointed, badly let down.' And he says the worst part of it was that it was so unnecessary.

'If I had been looking for the nomination I would have said, "well, that's my fault. I read it wrong". But I'd been asked twice to go. Bertie didn't want to take anybody out of the Cabinet at the time and he wanted to win it back for Fianna Fáil. That's what made me feel bad. Badly let down.'

But then Reynolds always conducted his politics along business lines. And he knows there is no point in dwelling on a deal that's gone sour.

You almost believe him when he concludes with a shrug: ' 'Tis over and gone and I'm probably the better for it, so good luck.'

Back in 1986 Garret FitzGerald was forced to consider his options.

'I made the decision on the basis that in five years I would have been sixty-six and I would have been too old to go back into government again.'

In fact, the next election came three years later in 1989. 'If I had known that I might have made a different decision. I probably would have stayed on.'

Or perhaps not.

'I was exhausted anyway. The portrait in the Dáil shows that. My daughter is going to do another portrait. You can see how drained I was. It was a disastrous time to do a portrait. Mary O'Rourke once said to me "you look exhausted and bland and Haughey looks like he's swallowed his false teeth".'

There was one final ignominy for the former Taoiseach.

'I used to go into the Dáil and use the library a lot. One day a librarian saw me leaving with some volumes and she said "ex-TDs can't take books out".'

'Funny, wasn't it?' he says, clearly not thinking it funny at all, before concluding with a sigh, 'so that was the end of that.'

Index